D0850610

Rochester's Poetry

A STUDY OF
ROCHESTER'S POETRY

DAVID FARLEY-HILLS

Rochester's Poetry

ROWMAN AND LITTLEFIELD
TOTOWA, NEW JERSEY

•

BELL & HYMAN
LONDON

First published in England in 1978 by
BELL & HYMAN LIMITED
37–39 Queen Elizabeth Street,
London SE1 2QB

ISBN 0 7135 0096 4

First published in the United States 1978
by Rowman and Littlefield, Totowa, N.J.

ISBN 0 8476 6078 8

Set by Gloucester Typesetting Ltd
and printed in Great Britain by
Ebenezer Baylis & Son Ltd
Worcester

Contents

1 Introduction   1

2 Seventeenth-century love lyrics   10

3 Heaven in Hell's despair—the anatomy of love in Rochester's lyric poetry   36

4 Hell in Heaven's despite—burlesque and lampoon   89

5 Satire in the seventeenth century   132

6 Upon Nothing: Rochester's satire   169

Notes   213

Index   223

OPHELIA I think nothing, my lord.

HAMLET That's a fair thought to lie between maids' legs.

OPHELIA What is, my lord?

HAMLET Nothing.

OPHELIA You are merry, my lord.

HAMLET Who, I?

OPHELIA Ay, my lord.

HAMLET O, your only jig-maker. What should a man do but be merry?

Note:
Hamlet's 'nothing', a reflection of Ophelia's earlier use of the word, is unquestionably yonic symbolism, a shape metaphor intended to call to mind the naught or O, which is elsewhere in Shakespearean, if not modern, 'bawdy' a symbol of *pudendum muliebre.*
(Thomas Pyles, 'Ophelia's Nothing', *Modern Language Notes,* 64 (1949) p. 322)

Textual Note and Acknowledgements

The problem of choosing a text of Rochester's poems from which to quote has proved a vexed one and I have ended by adopting what some, no doubt, will object to as a confusing compromise. The standard modern edition, David Vieth's *Complete Poems*, is unsatisfactory in a number of ways. Firstly in modernising spelling and punctuation so completely that the original emphasis and sometimes even meaning is lost. I note a number of instances in the course of my critical discussion. Secondly, and even more disturbingly, the attempt to place the poems in order of composition, though immensely useful in some instances, is very misleading in others. Of necessity this ordering is often based on guesswork and the suggestion of a firm ordering that the edition gives turns out to be spurious. Indeed it is occasionally contradictory: the *Dialogue between Alexis and Strephon,* for instance, is dated as 'possibly 1674' and yet is placed in a category headed 'Prentice Work, 1665-1671'. Pinto's older edition, while textually preferable in many instances, still leaves much to be desired and leaves out many important poems for prudish reasons. I have therefore been forced to go back, where possible, to early editions, and chose the Scolar facsimile reprint of the *Poems on Several Occasions*, 1680 as my copy text for those poems found in the collection. The particular copy from which the facsimile is made is in the British Museum Library and though full of printing errors seems to be generally textually reliable. Its convenience as a reference text and its probable closeness textually to Rochester's intentions were the main reasons for my choice. For poems of Rochester not in that collection I used the copy of Rymer's edition of 1691 in the Bodleian Library, Oxford, and checked Rymer's well edited (and bowdlerised) edition with the earlier volume for those poems printed in both. Separate (broadside) editions of Rochester's poems, published during his lifetime and versions of poems printed in contemporary anthologies were also consulted. Finally, I used Pinto's edition, *Poems by John*

Wilmot Earl of Rochester, second edition, 1964, and to a lesser extent, Vieth's, for those poems not in any of the seventeenth-century volumes. Where no reference is given in the notes the quotation will have been taken from the 1680 text. One looks forward to the promised edition of Dr Wilders. Where no place of publication is mentioned in the notes London can be assumed.

My acknowledgements are to the ladies who have helped me in so many ways and to whom the volume is dedicated: to my wife, to Barbara Manning for her patience in keeping me, as far as was possible, on the French and Italian rails, to Clare Jolley for handling the 'foul papers' (the term does not exaggerate) and to Miss P. Katt for her invaluable help and advice. Part of the book was written at the Folger Shakespeare Library in Washington and I am grateful to all the staff of the library for their help and especially to the Registrar, Mrs Cynthia Cocke, also to the British Academy and the English Speaking Union for helping to finance my trip to Washington. I am especially grateful to my home University, the Queen's University of Belfast, for consistently generous financial aid in helping me to get to libraries 'over the water' and to Professor Braidwood and the University Authorities for granting me study leave to allow me to finish the book on time.

ONE

Introduction

Rochester was a poet of many contradictions. Born into a world of contradictions, he was a rebel whose pranks in defiance of conventional morality and manners have been chronicled almost to the obliteration of both man and poet: he was also very much an aristocrat, a man of immense social privileges, and these could only be upheld by an insistence on the traditional forms and ceremonies which articulated a complex and age-old social hierarchy. Rochester's poetry expresses both the rebelliousness and the sense of form and it will be the purpose of this book to show how the poetry stems from a tension between these two contradictory attitudes. The rebelliousness is obvious enough. It is explicit in much of his poetry, and Rochester seems often to have prided himself on his open defiance of conventions. There is surely as much boastfulness in the notorious *Lines to a Postboy* as genuine penitence:

> Son of a Whore God damn thee, canst thou Tell[1]
> A Peerless Peer the readiest Way to Hell?
> I've outswill'd Bacchus, Sworn of my own Make
> Oaths, Frighted Furyes, and made Pluto quake:
> Swived Whore more ways than ever Sodoms Walls
> Knew, or the Colledge of the Cardinals,
> Witness Heroic Scars and Wounds: Ne're go!
> Sear Cloths and Ulcers from the Top to th' Toe.
> Frighted at my own Mischief's I am fled,
> And basely left my Life's Defender Dead.
> Broke houses to break chastity, and dyed
> That floor with murder which my lust denied.
> But hang't, why do I speak of these poor Things?

I have blasphemed God, and libell'd Kings!
The readiest way to Hell, Boy; Quick (Boy) Ne're Stir.
The readiest way, my Lord's by Rochester!

Frequently this rebelliousness is expressed in attacks on conventional morality, most obviously in the use of the four letter words that are not infrequent in his pages, but more seriously in his frank exploration (unique in his day) of the values and disappointments of sexual experience. This subject was not arbitrarily chosen, but central to his existential belief that only the experience of love and love-making can provide the brief moment of truth that 'heaven allows' as a compensation for the torment of being alive. For Rochester is no pornographer. The pornographer uses writing as sexual substitute; Rochester's poetry is an exploration of sexual experience that asks us to face up to all the facts, from the sublimest to the most ridiculous. In this he defies the taboos not only of his own society (which in some aristocratic circles at least was rather less prudish than ours) but of subsequent ages; for it seems harder for men to be honest about their bodily functions and the emotions they arouse than about almost anything else. Rochester's honesty has been the cause of his neglect as a major poet over the centuries. It is only because our own age is readier to be frank on sexual matters that it is now possible to attempt a serious assessment of Rochester's poetry for the first time.

It was not only in sexual matters, of course, that Rochester expressed his hostility to convention. His attacks on Charles II (inconsistently enough made on the King's sexual depravity) were attacks on the idea of authority itself, for Charles was still, in many people's theory if in few people's fact, the representative of God's order and power on earth, or at least the little piece of earth he presided over. Even to the sophisticated and subtle-minded Andrew Marvell, Charles had something of a divine status, as the lines towards the end of the *Last Instructions to a Painter* demonstrate:

> Bold and accursed are they that all this while
> Have strove to isle our Monarch from his isle . . .
> But Ceres Corn and Flora is the spring,
> Bacchus is wine, the country is the King.

No-one represents better the contradictions of his age than this lewd sun-king. Like Rochester, whose friend he remained even under dire provocation, Charles was himself a rebel against the morality of which he was the figurehead. Though a libertine, he was also probably a deist, if we are to believe the Earl of Mulgrave's account of the king.[2] Like his noble friend Rochester he was inspired with a death-bed conversion to Christianity. For many years, too, Charles had been a political rebel in the topsy-turvy world where God's anointed king, Charles's father, had been beheaded and the new authority had sought for the son's life.

Charles had no more wish than any of his aristocratic subjects to go on his travels again. Once in power he was determined to stay in power, and he was surprisingly competent at doing this. It was strongly in Charles's interest to restore and respect the outward forms of traditional authority, whatever his inward opinions. But it is quite likely that he believed as sincerely in the social proprieties as he believed in his right to flout them. Certainly Rochester's respect for form and convention is not mere lip-service. It is as important to understand Rochester's deep sense of conventional orderliness as to respond to his rebelliousness and originality in considering his poetry; just as important, but, for the modern reader, more difficult, because the old order which Charles represented has long since faded and needs to be reconstructed before we can have any idea how vital a part it plays in giving Rochester's poetry coherence. This book cannot attempt a reconstruction of the whole literary milieu in which Rochester worked, which is the work of the social historian, but it can and will attempt to describe those literary conventions that arose out of that milieu. For Rochester relies heavily on traditional poetic convention to establish communication with his reader through the appeal to shared assumptions, to impose a conventional order where no absolute order exists and to provide a point of reference for his iconoclasm. Unless we understand something of those conventions and the importance of the orderliness of the world to Rochester's readers we shall have no chance of assessing Rochester's peculiar and original contribution to poetry. Not to understand what Rochester borrowed from the past is not to understand what he contributed of his own. It is for this reason that I shall be endeavouring to present a picture of the more important literary conventions that are relevant to Rochester's work before each major chapter. So I have provided separate chapters on lyric poetry and satire in the seventeenth century and a separate section on the conventions of burlesque poetry as an introduction to a discussion of Rochester's lyric, satire and burlesque respectively. The purpose of these sections is to show what Rochester borrowed from his immediate predecessors, what conventions operated and how they had come to be used. This book is dedicated to the proposition that you can know nothing of a poet if you know nothing of the poet's literary background. It also accepts Northrop Frye's dictum, that poems are made (at least primarily) out of other poems. Rochester's poetry exemplifies this proposition to a remarkable degree. Like Charles, Rochester was both preoccupied with the disorderliness that had sent the King on his travels and which had effectively put paid to the old myths of a divinely ordained harmony, and concerned to assert the forms of orderliness which would, he hoped, prevent the travels from recommencing. Rochester's poetry is written out of the tension between a disbelief in any metaphysical sanction for orderliness and the social need for an aristocrat to insist on the inherited conventions that guaranteed his position and defined him as a social being. The conventional element, whether it is the conventional attitudes of the love poet or satirist or the conventional forms of verse he adopts, is therefore not there by accident, but represents a preoccupation with imposed orderliness in a world where all coherence is gone in a far more radical sense than Donne intended. In the background of all Rochester's poetry is that fearful picture of a universe without meaning that he describes (characteristically enough in borrowing from another poet) in the adaptation of a speech from Seneca's *Troades* he sent to his deist friend Charles Blount early in 1680. Occasionally this sense of the total futility of life leads Rochester to adopt methods that reproduce the anarchy, as for instance in his use of the Hudibrastic verse form for the *Ramble in St. James's Park*. But more often he adopts a stance of mock-heroic defiance, like the hero of his poem the *Maim'd Debauchee*:

> Thus Statesman-like, I'll saucily impose,
>   And safe from Danger, valiantly advise,
> Shelter'd in impotence, urge you to Blows,
>   And being good for nothing else, be wise.

And just as the ancient debauchee turns his syphilitic impotence to heroic defiance (as Rochester himself does in asking us to witness his 'heroic scars and wounds' in his *Lines to a Postboy*), so Rochester, the poet, 'saucily imposes' his orderly verbal patterns on the nasty business of living, on the rag-and-bone shop of the heart:

> Those masterful images became complete
> Grew in pure mind, but out of what began?
> A mound of refuse or the sweepings of a street,
> Old kettles, old bottles, and a broken can,
> Old iron, old bones, old rags, that raving slut
> That keeps the till. Now that my ladder's gone
> I must lie down where all the ladders start,
> In the foul rag-and-bone shop of the heart.

Rochester never became as conscious of his problem or so miraculously articulate as Yeats, but the problem was essentially the same.

The central preoccupation of Rochester's poetry is how to achieve order in a world that is essentially disorderly. His solution is arbitrarily and 'saucily' to impose the conventions that had been handed down from earlier generations. He had the advantage over his modern counterparts who have tried to do something similar (Eliot in the *The Waste Land*, Joyce in *Ulysses*, Beckett's use of the *Inferno* in *Watt*, for instance) since literary traditions in the 1660s when he began to write poetry, were much stronger and more clearly defined than those of our own times. In love poetry, as we shall see, the conventions were as much of attitudes as of forms. Seventeenth-century love poets inherited both matter and manner from their petrarchist predecessors, and the petrarchist tradition had itself been modified and was being modified throughout the century under the influence of classical love poetry. It was only right at the end of the seventeenth century that the petrarchist attitude came to be seriously challenged. Pope's friend, William Walsh, is inadvertently witnessing to the longevity of the petrarchist tradition when he writes in his *Preface* to the *Letters and Poems* (1692):

> I confess I can hardly forbear laughing when Petrarch tells us, he could live without any other sustenance than his Mistress's looks. . . . I have chosen to mention Petrach as being by much the most famous of all the Moderns who have written love

verses, and it is indeed the great reputation he has gotten that has given encouragement to the false sort of wit in the World.

Walsh need not have worried; by the 1690s the tradition was moribund, if not quite dead (for Pope was to make scintillating use of the petrarchist language of love for comic effect in the *Rape of the Lock*). Walsh's reference to the 'false sort of wit' is to the fondness of the petrarchists for witty conceits. The witty, paradoxical style and the rough, complex rhythms which frequently went with the petrarchist attitudes, however, proved less hardy than the attitudes themselves and generally gave way after Cleveland and Cowley, in the face of Augustan insistence on clarity and decorum, to a lucid style that valued mellifluousness and 'easiness'. Rochester's style is several times complimented as 'easy' by his contemporaries.[3] In this, like his Cavalier predecessors, he preferred the elegant clarity that derived from the sons of Ben to the gnarled complexity of the so-called metaphysicals. Rochester, however, retains the fondness for paradox of the metaphysicals.

From the late petrarchists, the witty, conceited 'school' of John Donne, Rochester derives the range of the attitudes towards love that is shown in his love lyrics. His scattered lyrics, written on and off throughout his poetic career, form as much an 'anatomy' of love as the *Songs and Sonets* of Donne (first published in 1633) or the *Mistress* (first published 1647) of Abraham Cowley, whom Rochester admired most 'among the English'.[4] All three poets cast themselves (or the 'speakers' of their poetry) in the three basic roles of the petrarchist lover: the platonic lover, the antiplatonic lover and the libertine sensualist; these roles, of course, are mutually inconsistent, but the function of the petrarchist love poet was not to express his own views and feelings so much as to explore the whole range of love attitudes opened to the lover by the conventions. As Cowley explained in his Preface to the 1656 edition of his poems:

> Poets are scarce thought *Freemen* of this *Company*, without paying some duties, and obliging themselves to be true to *Love*. Sooner or later they must all pass through that *Tryall*, like some *Mohammedan Monks*, that are bound by their Order, once at least, in their life, to make a *Pilgrimage to Meca* . . . But we must not always make a judgment of their [poets'] *manners* from their *writings* of this kind . . . It is not in this sense that Poesie is said,

to be a kind of *Painting*; it is not the *Picture* of the *Poet*, but of *things* and *persons* imagin'd by him. He may be in his own practice and disposition a *Philosopher*, nay a *Stoick*, and yet speak sometimes with the softness of an amorous Sappho.[5]

It is perhaps unkind to add that, unlike Donne's and Rochester's love poems, Cowley's give the impression that they were written by someone who had never been in love. The art consisted in making these conventional attitudes come alive for the reader. Rochester's lyrics express the whole range of the petrachist attitudes, though he takes the frankness of anatomical reference in his anti-platonic poems even further than Donne and much further than the chaste Cowley.

Formally, too, Rochester's lyrics make use of traditional patterns. Almost all the lyrics are written as songs, though not necessarily actually to be sung. Accordingly the favourite forms are those with fairly simple stanza patterns that are repeated stanza by stanza. A favourite form is the four line stanza which alternates iambic tetrameter with iambic trimeter:

> Such perfect Bliss, fair Cloris, we
> In our Enjoyment prove:
> 'Tis pity restless Jealousie
> Should mingle with our Love.

This stanza had been used by countless earlier poets including such Cavalier favourites as Suckling and Lovelace (as in the famous *To Lucasta, Going to the Wars*). The other most common stanza form in Rochester's lyrics is the four line iambic tetrameter stanza with alternate lines rhyming.

His satires are equally conventional though more complex in origin than the lyric and even more original, for it should not be thought that a conventional poet need not also be original. Indeed poetic originality is impossible without convention, for it is only in terms of deviation from normal expectation that originality can be judged. A totally unconventional poem is a contradiction in terms, for poetry is a conventional medium. The traditions which account for the content of Rochester's satires are too complex to be touched on here and must be left to the detailed discussion of

satire in the last two chapters. Formally Rochester follows his
Elizabethan predecessors in satire and such later verse satirists as
Cleveland, Cowley and Marvell in preferring the heroic couplet
above all other metres. The rhymed iambic pentameter couplet
was finally to sweep the board in the late seventeenth century as
the most 'symphonicall' of cadences, as Puttenham had earlier
expressed it. It is true that by the standards of the eighteenth
century Rochester's use of the heroic couplet seems rather casual
and undisciplined. Pope can characterise Rochester as a 'holiday
writer' and complain that he has 'very bad versification sometimes',
instancing (according to Spence) the *Allusion to Horace* as an
example; on another occasion, however, Pope contrasts Rochester
with Oldham in having 'much more delicacy'.[6] We might, however, point out (as I shall later in more detail) that traditionally
satire was thought to require a rough metre in Rochester's day.
We might also (rather more maliciously) point out that Rochester
was never held up for disapproval by the Romantics for being too
'mechanical' in his use of metre as was Pope, and never characterised as a classic of our prose.[7] To be fair, it must be assumed that
Rochester's exclusion from Arnold's backhanded compliment was
a result of Arnold's refusal to consider such a wicked and frivolous
man as Rochester as a poet at all; Rochester was rarely wholly
serious. Such past bickerings, however, need not concern us. We
must concern ourselves, not with any absolute standards of
metrical correctness, but with the appropriateness of Rochester's
use of the heroic metre for the job in hand. In historical perspective, as we shall see, Rochester's handling of the iambic pentameter rhymed couplet for satire marks a decisive step towards
Augustan orderliness compared to his predecessors. It is the stress
on formal orderliness that strikes us when we compare his satire
with immediate predecessors like Cleveland and even Andrew
Marvell. The fact that Dryden and then Pope adopted a still more
orderly medium for satire *after* Rochester has obscured the extraordinary stress on formal regularity represented by Rochester's
use of heroic couplets.

Rochester's experiments in the disorderly world of burlesque
are spasmodic and of less importance than either his lyric or
satire. One major poem, the morose *Ramble in St. James's Park*,
outvies even Butler in its use of Hudibrastic verse for destructive
purposes. But Rochester tends to shun the deriding negativity

that is a feature of earlier burlesque poetry, such as James Smith's and John Mennis' contribution to the drolleries and the burlesque poetry of Charles Cotton and Samuel Butler. Rochester's rebelliousness is more often expressed in a lighter vein, as in *Signior Dildo* and the *Imperfect Enjoyment*. Chaos was too dangerous and omnipresent to be furthered by the poet's art; the poet, like the lover, had to use his art to celebrate that short moment of meaningfulness before he too became the 'Lumber of the world'.

TWO

Seventeenth-century love lyrics

Modern readers might jib at Northrop Frye's dictum quoted in the first chapter that 'poems are made out of other poems' because many of us inherit the Romantic belief in poetry as personal statement.[1] To most seventeenth-century poets and readers Frye's comment would seem a truism. A poet's task was to say 'What oft was thought', but to say it in a way that made it come alive again for his contemporaries. Pope summarises a long tradition in his famous lines:

> True wit is Nature to advantage dressed
> What oft was thought, but ne'er so well expressed.

Quite literally poems were made out of other poems. Just as Wyatt and Sidney imitated Petrarch by using a Petrarch sonnet as a basis for their own meditation on Petrarchan themes, so Rochester's contemporaries would use a classical text or a contemporary text as a point of reference for their own works. Dryden would thus make extensive use of Milton's *Paradise Lost* in *Absalom and Achitophel*, of Cowley and Virgil (among other poets) in *Mac Flecknoe*, or when he wanted to be closer to his original would paraphrase Chaucer or Juvenal, recreating them to suit his own times.[2] Rochester frequently 'imitates' in a variety of ways. The so-called *Allusion to Horace* is the best known example, where Rochester keeps fairly close to his original, the tenth satire of Horace's second book of *Satires*, but there are plenty of other examples of various degrees of closeness. The imitation of Boileau in *Timon* is fairly close to the French poet's *Repas Ridicule* (Satire III), the *Satyr against Mankind* borrows occasionally from Boileau's eighth Satire. Some of Rochester's poems are line-by-line parodies of entire poems: Scroope's 'I cannot love as others do' opens in

Rochester's version as 'I cannot fuck as others do', and Quarles's religious poem beginning 'Why doest thou shade thy lovely face' (*Emblems* III 7, 12) by a few deft changes of words and a reordering of stanzas becomes in Rochester (if it is Rochester's) a love poem to his mistress.

Sometimes it is merely a matter of letting the opening line of an earlier poet get him started, at other times a question of using the whole of someone else's poem as a point of reference throughout. All this is not only common in Renaissance poetry, it was considered a necessary way of the poet's linking his work to the needs of his society. As in more primitive societies, one of the poet's roles in the seventeenth century was gatherer of the wisdom of his people and that meant using not only the wisdom of the past but often the words in which that wisdom was stored. Of course, in such an individualistic poet as Rochester, Rochester's own emphases are constantly appearing as he reorganises the traditional material. To many of his contemporaries no doubt it would appear as if he were wilfully perverting the wisdom of his tribe. For the modern reader, however, judgment of this sort is impossible until we understand the literary context, the literary climate, out of which Rochester's poetry grew. As Josephine Miles has well said:

> Whether one is interested in the personal achievement of the individual, the persistence of convention, the social matrix, or the sheer quality of the work of art as it embodies and transforms all these, it is necessary to distinguish between them, not to attribute to conventional demand the free choices of the artist, nor to the artist the full power of the medium itself.[3]

Hence the need for an account of the prevailing poetic climate when Rochester wrote and of those poets whom Rochester seemed to have found most important and imitable. We are not looking for sources, but describing a tradition.

The bulk of Rochester's poetry was written between 1665 and 1675, that is, when he was between the ages of 17 and 27, and if we ask ourselves what would be important to Rochester as an influence on his poetry in those years a very different picture emerges from our own assessment of the major literary influences of this period. In 1665 Milton would be considered by most readers a major political figure and an unfashionable, if not minor, poet. The first edition of *Paradise Lost* appeared in 1667, but, if Rochester read it, it is not likely to have influenced him: both the religious subject matter and the baroque style would have little interest for Rochester. Marvell too would probably be unknown to Rochester as a lyric poet, though he would undoubtedly have read the *Last Instructions to a Painter* soon after it was written in 1667, and would have read the few published poems, the satirical *Character of Holland* and the panegyrics on Blake and Cromwell. That Rochester read Marvell's satire is clear from the reference to the prose *Rehearsall Transpros'd* (1672) in Rochester's *Tunbridge Wells*, and of course Marvell returned the compliment, noting, according to Aubrey, that Rochester was the finest satirist among his contemporaries.[4] The two major poets of the Commonwealth period, in twentieth-century opinion, would therefore have been largely unregarded by Rochester, as by most of the readers of the day. The other major figure, John Dryden, was in 1665 the author of some impressive panegyric and two rather undistinguished plays. Rochester would never know the John Dryden who dominates the period in our estimation, the Dryden of the satire, the later occasional verse and the translations. The full bulk of Dryden's greatness (I think 'bulk' is the right word) appeared after Rochester's death in 1680.

We have two ways of assessing what Rochester would have regarded as important in the literary traditions he inherited: the direct evidence of his reading and the inferences that can be drawn from those writers who were most popular, or considered most important, over those years. We know from Rochester's use of other poets that he read most of the poets his own generation would regard as important. He quotes or alludes to Waller Suckling, Cowley, Lovelace, Jonson, Donne and makes extensive, use in the satires of his slightly older French contemporary Boileau.[5] In the *Allusion to Horace*, written about 1674, he makes knowledgable judgments on most of the contemporary literary figures: Dryden, Wycherley, Etherege, Shadwell, Otway, Lee and personal friends like Sedley and Lord Dorset as well as earlier writers—Jonson, Fletcher, Shakespeare. His adaptation of Fletcher's tragedy *Valentinian* shows not only a special interest in this fashionable Jacobean playwright, but, according to J. H. Wilson, shows that he had read Durfé's prose romance *Astrée*. His knowledge of Shakespeare is not only evinced by his interesting reference to Shakespeare's satirical genius in the *Allusion to Horace* but by the use of the name Timon as the raging satirist in the satire of that name. His satirical techniques—as I shall later argue—are partly derived from Elizabethan and Jacobean formal satire.

His reading of French literature has already been touched on. He read Boileau at a time when the French poet was only just beginning to establish himself in his own country. The two satires he uses are early works, written in the 1660s, and suggest that Rochester was more than ordinarily aware of what was being written on the other side of the Channel. There is other evidence for his quite wide reading in French. D. H. Griffin claims there is evidence (from the ending of *Timon*) of Rochester's reading of the early seventeenth-century satirist Mathurin Régnier,[6] while J. H. Wilson suggests the influence of Malherbe in the *Lines written in a Lady's Prayerbook*. That he read Montaigne and Rochefoucauld has been argued at some length.[7] His reading in Latin is shown from his adaptations of texts from Seneca, Lucretius, Petronius, Ovid and Horace. We also know from his paraphrase of a passage of *Leviathan* in the poem *Love and Life* that he had read at least a part of that great work, and that he is familiar with Hobbes is clear from his use of Hobbes' ideas in the *Satyr against Mankind*.[8] The influence of Samuel Butler was also, I think, important in helping him to formulate both his view of the world and his poetic techniques.[9]

None of this necessarily implies an exceptionally wide reading. The Latin texts he would largely have met at school and at Oxford; the Cavalier and Jacobean poets were the casual reading of most gentlemen. His knowledge of French is rather more than we might expect and, I think, more than he has yet been credited with. He seems to me to show an awareness of the French libertine poets, and Théophile de Viau in particular, and of French speculative writing.[10] He almost certainly had some knowledge of Italian, having travelled in Italy from 1662 to 1664 where he may have met Salvator Rosa, whose satires, Pinto believes, were familiar to him,[11] and I think he almost certainly had read the work of the greatest seventeenth-century Italian poet Gianbattista Marino. The comment of Robert Parsons, the Wilmot family chaplain, in his funeral sermon, that Rochester was 'thoroughly acquainted with all Classick Authors, both Greek and Latin; a thing very

rare, if not peculiar to him, amongst those of his quality',[12] probably means that he was well read as Restoration rakes go, which
may not get us very far. We have some evidence from contemporaries or near-contemporaries of Rochester's literary prefer-
ences: Gilbert Burnet records that he admired most 'Boileau
among the French and Cowley among the English', while John
Dennis, a major critic of the next generation, identifies Etherege's
Dorimant with Rochester partly because both were so keen on
quoting Waller: 'for whom that noble lord had a very particular
esteem'. In the *Allusion to Horace* Rochester gets as close to un-
equivocal praise of Waller as of anyone in that censorious poem.

Waller and Cowley were the two major poets of the 1660s in the
estimation of their contemporaries, and their influence must have
been well-nigh inescapable. If we add to their names those of
Suckling, Lovelace and Cleveland of the previous generation I
believe the most important English influences on Rochester will
have been mentioned. None of these poets would perhaps be
regarded as very important today, though that is as much our
ignorance as a just estimate of their value. Waller is a poet of great
subtlety and charm at his best, who should be better known,
while Cowley, having made an undistinguished start in the
petrarchist style of the *Mistress*, is, in the Pindaric Odes and in
some of the *Miscellaneous Poems*, a poet of great power, unjustly
neglected by the modern reader. Suckling is the kind of fashionable poet whose popularity in his time is easily comprehensible but
whose poetic merits were clearly over-valued because of the con-
geniality of his sentiments and his techniques. Cleveland is a more
difficult poet to estimate because of his fondness for obscurity and
the occasional nature and topicality of so much of his work. That
he was a poet of great intelligence and verve is clear to the atten-
tive reader; that he had anything of importance to say is not
clearly apparent. Butler's influence was strong, I believe, for a
short period of Rochester's poetic career when his mood most
nearly approximated the misanthropy of that most morose of
comic poets.

In this chapter, however, we must narrow down our concern to
the lyrical poetry of the period, and to the love lyric in particular,
in asking what were the traditions that helped to form Rochester's
lyrics. The seventeenth century inherited traditions of bewildering
variety from both a long tradition of medieval verse-making,

represented above all in the sonnets and *canzoni* of Petrarch and the conventions that stem from them, and also from the love poetry of Latin and Greek classical poets. The Restoration was the last period in England of the long petrarchist tradition of versifying which commences with the poetry of Sir Thomas Wyatt, and Rochester is the last of the major petrarchist poets. To explain in detail what this means is clearly beyond the scope of this book and the reader must be referred to such excellent expositions of the tradition as Donald Guss's book on Donne, *John Donne, Petrarchist*. By the mid-seventeenth century, however, the petrarchist tradition had bequeathed to its followers two things: a range of attitudes to heterosexual love and a style. The range of attitudes is best exemplified in Donne's *Songs and Sonets*, the high point of the tradition in English, and in Cowley's *The Mistress*, which unsuccessfully attempts to follow Donne. As we shall see in the next chapter the attitudes towards love displayed in these collections are closely reflected in Rochester's love lyrics.

Briefly there are three basic attitudes towards love developed by the tradition. Firstly, there is the highly respectful attitude to love, that has its origin in medieval courtly love, in Petrarch himself, and in the neo-platonic writers of the late fifteenth century and sixteenth century in Italy. Its most notable proponent in verse is that Pietro Bembo who figures largely as an advocate of courtly love in Castiglione's *Courtier*. It is from the neo-platonic writers and not from Plato that his high-minded attitude gets the name 'platonic' by which it is principally known in the seventeenth century. Secondly, there is the contrary view of the anti-platonic, whose main function it is to deride the tenets of platonic love for comic purposes and suggest that love is essentially an animal desire that prompts mostly animal behaviour. The term anti-platonic was not used much, if at all, before the early seventeenth century but the attitude it stands for appears long before. Traditions as precious and high-minded as those of courtly love inevitably provoke a complementary debunking attitude. This attitude is already well rooted in medieval verse, but it finds an especially vigorous advocate in Francesco Berni in Italy and in the pornographic sonnets of Pietro Aretino, and in the French poets of the late sixteenth century and the turn of the seventeenth century who follow the *style bernique*, such as Sigogne and Maynard. In England these debunking attitudes appear already in Wyatt's love verse (or, if earlier examples are wanted, in Chaucer) and in Gascoigne. A recent book on Shakespeare's sonnets somewhat unconvincingly claims the bulk of his sonneteering for this line of anti-platonic parody.[13] Increasingly, too, classical attitudes to love-making, and especially Ovid's cynical and explicit male chauvinism, came to reinforce those debunking attitudes. Thirdly, the libertine viewpoint occurs quite distinct from the anti-platonic view, and, though showing its belief in the physical basis of sexual love, combines this with the belief that physical sexuality offers a rich spiritual experience.

Platonic Love Lyrics

Donne evinces each of these three attitudes in the *Songs and Sonets*. The platonic viewpoint, for instance, is represented in *Twicknam Garden*, in the magnificent *Valediction forbidding Mourning*, which celebrates the triumph of love over physical separation, and in the ambiguous *Relique*. The flippant, anti-platonic viewpoint is represented by *The Indifferent*, the song *Go and Catch a falling Star* and the cynical *Farewell to Love*, among others. The libertine attitude is represented by such fine poems as *The Sun Rising, Break of Day, The Good Morrow* and the ambiguous *The Extasie*, which celebrates the spiritual refreshment of successful physical union between lovers. Some of these poems evince an ambiguity that ingeniously allows alternative readings, a feature of the petrarchist tradition that we shall find exemplified in Rochester's lyrics. Cowley offers a similar range of attitudes in *The Mistress*. The platonic mood is represented in such poems as *My Diet, The Despair, The Thief, Love and Life* (a title shared with one of Rochester's lyrics), *The Long Life, Counsel, The Discovery* (also a Rochester title), *Against Fruition* (a favourite subject in the seventeenth century, arguing that abstention is more enjoyable than consummation), *Love Undiscovered* and *The Soul*. Anti-platonic poems would include *Inconstancy, Not Fair, Platonick Love, The Resolution, The Welcome, Women's Superstition*. Libertine poems might include *Clad all in White, Answer to the Platonicks, Wisdom, The Wish, Then Like Some Wealthy Island, Maidenhead, The Gazers, The Innocent Ill, Dialogue, Bathing in the River*. Needless to say the line between one attitude and another is not always easy to draw. A poem may start in one mood and end in another or (as is frequent) a deliberate ambiguity will be made to run through a whole poem, and no doubt some readers might dispute my allotment of particular poems to the categories. There is no doubt, however, about the distinction between the categories themselves. Indeed controlled ambiguity is impossible without a clear differentiation of categories.

A good example of Cowley in his most platonic mood is *The Discovery*, which epitomises the platonic attitude. It is possibly this poem that Rochester had in mind in writing his one lyric in the Cowley manner, the song 'Twas a dispute 'twixt heaven and earth'. The lover of Cowley's poem humbly offers himself, asking only that she should deign to acknowledge his existence:

> Compar'd with her all things so worthless prove,
>   That nought on earth can tow'rds her move,
>   Till't be *exalted* by her *Love*.
>   Equal to her, alas, there's none;
>   She like a *Deity* is grown,
> That must *Create,* or else must be alone.

Even here there is some ambiguity, for it is not impossible that the 'creation' the lover is seeking might be a result of their carnal union. The tone of the poem is nonetheless highminded. Such effusions are apt to be dismissed by the modern reader as totally beyond human credibility, though readers whose memories go back to the days of the glossy Hollywood films of the 1940s will remember a not dissimilar cult of earth-goddesses in them. In the nineteenth century such views of womanhood were assumed to be the only ones possible for a civilised society as Bowdler's rather uncritical views of Shakespeare's attitudes evinces:

The gentler sex should be always grateful to the memory of our great Shakespeare, for his genius did sweet homage to their character. He invests his female creations with all that is most pure and generous in humanity, picturing them indeed as beautiful to the eye, but a thousand times more acceptable to the heart. There is a moral dignity about his women, a holy strength of affection which neither suffering nor death can pervert, that elevates them above the sterner nature of man, placing them on an equality with angels.

One would add now that most of them seem to have a taste for bawdy conversation. Shakespeare would certainly not have recognised himself here, but each generation uses the literature of the past as a looking glass. However unfashionable now (we live in an age more readily sympathetic to libertine and anti-platonic ideas) such woman-worship is a symptom of a recurrent male syndrome, which causes him to seek an object of worship in the opposite sex. The love poetry of the Renaissance is almost entirely written by men and not surprisingly, therefore, expresses principally, though not exclusively, the male viewpoint. Platonic poetry expresses one side of man's needs in relation to women and is obviously a legitimate subject for poetic expression. The fact that Cowley expresses the mood lamely should not lead the reader into forgetting that Donne can achieve great things in this vein and that much Elizabethan sonneteering handles such themes well and convincingly.

Platonic love does not necessarily rule out the possibility of sexual union: indeed in Spenser's *Epithalamion*, sexual union in marriage is seen as the culmination of the platonic relationship described in the *Amoretti*. If we are to believe Isaac Walton, Donne's *Valediction forbidding Mourning* was written for his wife. The platonic love poet always, however, insists on the superiority of the spiritual over the physical in the love experience. This is well conveyed in a poem called *Platonic Love* by the early seventeenth-century poet Edward Herbert, the brother of the more poetically famous George. Lord Herbert's poems, although written mostly in the second and third decades of the century, were not published until 1665 and would therefore be new reading for the young Rochester, recently returned from France and Italy. In this poem, beginning 'Madam, believ't, love is not such a toy', Herbert contrasts the sexual promptings of youthful love with the true spiritual love that 'checks' the appetite and only reaches its final growth in eternity:

> And thus a love, made from a worthy choice,
> Will to that union come, as but one voice
>   Shall speak, one thought, but think the other's will,
>   And while, but frailty, they can know no ill,
> Their souls more than their bodies must rejoice.
>
>   In which estate nothing can so fulfil
>   Those heights of pleasure, which their souls instill

Into each other, but that love thence draws
New Arguments of joy, while the same cause
That makes them happy, makes them greater still.

So that, however multiplied and vast
Their love increases, they will not think it past
    The bounds of growth, till their exalted fire
    B'ing equally inlarg'd with their desire,
Transform and fix them to one Starr at last.

Or when that otherwise they were inclin'd
Unto those publick joys which are assign'd
    To blessed souls when they depart from hence
    They would, besides what Heaven doth dispense,
Have their contents they in each other find.[14]

These noble lines are not dismissive of the sexual relationship, but
see it, in neo-platonic fashion, as part of a greater spiritual experience that transcends the physical. Platonic love poems continue to
be written to the end of the seventeenth century. They were
particularly favoured in the court of Charles I, where Henrietta
Maria encouraged a cult of high-minded courtly love with affinities
with the *précieux* movement across the Channel. The reality was
not always so high-minded. Court dramatists like Suckling and
Ludovick Carlell obliged by presenting suitably platonic dramas
and, though the Civil War hardly favoured such idealism, we shall
find Rochester after it expressing himself in this vein. Whether he
actually held the views expressed in such poems at any time we
can never know, but this is beside the point. It was the poet's
function to express Society's attitudes at least as much, and usually
more than, his own. In so doing he re-asserted the common
values that bound the men of rank, the leaders of the tribe, we
might say, together.

Anti-Platonic Poetry

Anti-platonic verse is as important in the period as the love verse
it sought to deride. Indeed it is both complementary and complimentary to it. By offering parody of the courtly attitudes it heads
off more destructive criticism and provides a release from the

strain of high ideals fostered by the verse to which it bears something of a parasitic relationship. So in anti-platonic love poetry the values of platonic love are inverted: inconstancy, not constancy, becomes a virtue, physical satisfaction, not spiritual, becomes the primary purpose of love making. The two attitudes could, of course, exist in the same poem, either in the form of paradox or in some sort of dialogue in which different speakers represent different points of view. An age that increasingly saw contradiction as a fundamental fact of man's existence not surprisingly fostered the sense of contradiction between these two attitudes to love. We shall find Rochester frequently juxtaposing such opposite viewpoints in the same poem. Simple illustrations of the anti-platonic attitude, however, are not hard to come by in the seventeenth century. Suckling, though, like any other good poet of the time, he could turn his hand to the opposite viewpoint when it suited, was the poet most clearly at home in this debunking poetry. For it he tends to adopt a style that is suitably pared of all fanciful impediments on the Jonsonian principle that a plain style befits a plain attitude.[15] We shall reserve the discussion of Suckling, however, until we turn to the problem of style. A plain style was not an essential part of the anti-platonic poems of Cowley and Cleveland. Cowley's *Platonick Love*,[16] one of the happier efforts of the *Mistress*, is couched in the paradoxical, witty style of the petrarchist tradition, but its theme (in spite of its title) is the anti-platonic theme that true love needs to be expressed in physical terms:

> In thy immortal part
> *Man*, as well as I, thou art.
> But something 'tis that differs *Thee* and *Me*;
> And we must *one* even in that *difference* be.
> I Thee, both as a *man*, and *woman* prize;
> For a perfect Love implies
> Love in *all Capacities*.

The theme that love is equally spiritual and physical is strictly a libertine rather than an anti-platonic one, but the title, suggesting that the poem sets out to show the deficiencies of platonic love, and the flippancy of tone justify including it as anti-platonic. The anti-platonic attitudes are nearly always couched in comic terms, while the libertine are primarily sensuous and even erotic. Here Cowley's fondness for witty paradox, such as the assertion that the

difference between men and women should be the means of unit-
ing them, or that spiritual love is homosexual, and the comparative easiness of the rhythmic groupings (Cowley is rarely smooth
and easy, but this gets as near as he ever is) suggests a not-too-
serious contradiction of the platonic rather than a serious assertion
of the spiritual values of carnal love. One of Cowley's main weak-
nesses in *The Mistress*, however, is his uncertain command of tone,
which makes it difficult to assess how seriously we are to take the
assertions.

If there is some libertine element in Cowley's anti-platonic
poem, there is none at all in Cleveland's poem the *Anti-Platonick*.
This debunking subject entirely suits Cleveland's delight in verbal
gymnastics:

> For shame, thou everlasting Woer,
> Still saying grace, and never falling to her!
> Love that's in contemplation plac't,
> Is *Venus* drawn but to the wast.
> Unless your Flame confesse its gender,
> And your Parley cause Surrender,
> Y'are Salamanders of a cold desire,
> That live untoucht amid the hottest fire.

There is no eroticism here, the poet is not himself concerned with
sexual feelings, but with exhorting someone else to indulge in
them. The voyeurism suggests a detached cynicism that gets its
energy from the desire to deride, to contradict the elaborate ceremonies of the courtly love dance. So Cleveland adopts a derisively
unmusical rhythm, jerking out his couplets without any thought
of organic unity; indeed he deliberately seeks to avoid any suggestion of unity. This is a poetry of disintegration related to that
fashion for burlesque and parody in this period, which we shall
need to discuss in a later chapter. The very waywardness of the
imagery suggests a topsy-turvy world—the platonic lover saying
a perpetual grace and never getting down to his food, the pun on
'drawn' ('depicted' and 'naked', by analogy with 'drawn sword')
suggesting that the lover's interests are aesthetic where they ought
to be sartorial (or anti-sartorial), the phallic pun on 'flame', the
outlandish references to the mythical Salamander. Cleveland sees
no positive virtues in physical sexuality. He sees it simply as the
negative of courtliness, and writing his poem gives him an

opportunity to undermine those courtly virtues which the very act of deriding helps paradoxically to reassert. For the attempt at destruction is not serious either; this kind of debunking can only exist on the assumption that what it is deriding is indestructible—much as Shaw's plays assume that the British Empire will go on for ever.

One more example of the anti-platonic mood helps relate it even more clearly to its platonic models. Cartwright's *No Platonique Love* opens with that favourite opening gambit 'Tell me no more' which Rochester also uses in his anti-platonic poem 'Tell me no more of constancy'.[17] In the second stanza Cartwright gives an excellent description of that platonic love she (the lover) is now rejecting:

> I was that silly thing that once was wrought
>   To practice this thin Love;
> I clim'd from Sex to Soul, from Soul to Thought,
>   But thinking there to move,
> Headlong, I rush'd from Thought to Soul, and then
>   From Soul I lighted at the Sex agen.[18]

(It is just possible, I think, that these lines were in Rochester's mind as he turned Boileau's line 'Voltige incessament de pensée en pensée' into English in the *Satyr against Mankind* as 'Stumbling from thought to thought, falls headlong down'). Cartwright in this stanza describes the neo-platonic *scala*, the ladder that leads from carnal to spiritual desire, only to present it, not in the metaphysical terms of the neo-platonists, but as an example of the lover's psychological restlessness. As in Rochester's great satire, Cartwright sees the aspiration to spirituality as simply one of many psychological drives which his sexual drive succeeds as readily as *it* has succeeded the sexual. The poem shows the characteristic tendency of seventeenth-century lyric to concern itself increasingly with the psychology of the lover as the century advanced,[19] even before Hobbes had written on the subject of psychological imperatives. Cartwright is not, of course, seriously concerned to provide an alternative view to the idealising love of the platonist. This is a light-hearted poem, if not quite as frivolous as Cleveland's, more out to titillate its readers than to upset their notions of things. But it shows how the anti-platonic tradition helped to suggest an alternative viewpoint that would ultimately force a poet like Rochester into a relativism in which he no longer feels able to make any absolute assertions about true love, or true life come to that.

Libertine Poetry

Libertinism in the seventeenth century is largely an uncharted territory. The attitudes it fostered towards love and sexuality, which is what concerns us here, partake something of both the platonic and the anti-platonic viewpoints. Libertinism was essentially a naturalistic doctrine arguing that the closer man got to his animal nature the happier he was likely to be. To avoid the rather lurid modern overtones of the word libertinism a term like 'sexual naturalism' might be more appropriate. Such naturalism shared with the anti-platonic attitudes its rejection of the idea that love was exclusively, or primarily, a spiritual experience. But, unlike the anti-platonic viewpoint, its attitudes towards sexuality are celebratory rather than derisory. It does not indulge in anti-feminism, tending to treat the sexual partners as equals, and assuming, usually without sneering, that women are as interested in sexual enjoyment as men. It shares with the platonic love cult the idea that sexual love transcends the physical, but places more emphasis on the centrality of physical climax, the orgasm, as spiritual experience. Modern readers tend to be sympathetic to poems of this viewpoint because it is echoed in modern cults of sexual naturalism like those of D. H. Lawrence and Wilhelm Reich. There is always a danger here for the critic that libertine poems will be over-valued.

Donne is the first English poet to show an interest in libertinism, and several of his poems (some of which I discuss in the next chapter) show a more than superficial knowledge of libertine doctrine. Sexual naturalism, of course, can be found much earlier, in Wyatt, in Chaucer and, perhaps unexpectedly, in a delightful passage in praise of 'loyal' sexual experience in a fourteenth century homily, Purity[20] Donne's libertinism, however, reveals some of the attitudes that became especially characteristic of seventeenth century libertine thinking: the idea of sexual freedom as recovering a pre-lapsarian happiness, of man's need to assert this connection with the animal world, its suspicion of abstraction and rationality, especially abstractions like honour, its praise of spontaneous feeling and of promiscuity. Donne, too, is able to cultivate the sensuous, erotic tone that is the distinguishing voice of much libertine poetry. The famous nineteenth elegy *Going to Bed* is sufficient illustration.

Cowley, though, unlike Donne and Rochester, he generally gives the impression that love is for him a duty rather than a pleasure, nevertheless writes in a libertine vein in a number of the poems of *The Mistress*. Such poems as *Inconstancy* and *Called Inconstant* hover between an anti-platonic and a libertine stance (the distinguishing lines are easily blurred) but in poems like *Maidenhead*, *The Gazers*, *Bathing in the River*, *Then like some wealthy island* or the Dialogue *What have we done?* the libertine voice is distinct. In *Bathing in the River* Cowley manages to resist following his *fata morgana*, the witty paradox, sufficiently to imbue his poem with a convincing sensuousness:

> The *fish* around her crowded, as they do
>   To the fake light that treach'rous Fishers shew,
> And all with as much ease might taken be,
>   As she at first took me
>   For ne're did *Light* so clear
>   Among the *waves* appear,
>   Though ev'ry night the *Sun* himself set there.[21]

The poem is a version of the *carpe diem* theme so favoured by seventeenth-century poets and only just satisfies the promise to eschew the 'unpardonable vices' of 'obscenity and prophaneness' Cowley makes in his 1656 *Preface*. This he does by promising the lady marriage in the last stanza.

Few libertine poems are as concerned with moral respectability, though the veiled eroticism of Cowley's poem is favoured among poets who incline to preciosity, of whom Waller is the most distinguished. Waller's libertinism is nothing if not discreet. His version of *The Fall*, for instance (which I discuss at some length in the next chapter as a starting point of Rochester's lyric of the same title), at least ostensibly, concerns itself only with a lady's happening to trip and fall to the ground. The erotic element in *To a fair Lady, Playing with a Snake* is even more elusive—though all the more effective for being so. In this poem the poet-lover complains that the snake provides yet another protection of the lady's chastity in addition to her 'coldness'; but it is quite clear, too, that the snake is a rival to his love, as well (paradoxically enough) as love's (and even perhaps the lover's) ambassador:

> Thrice happy snake! that in her sleeve
> May boldly creep; we dare not give
> Our thought so unconfined a leave.
>
> Contented in that nest of snow
> He lies, as he his bliss did know,
> And to the wood no more would go.
>
> Take heed, fair Eve! you do not make
> Another tempter of this snake;
> A marble one so warmed would speak.[22]

As often with Waller it is difficult to know how far one should go in turning the concrete (or in this case marble) object into symbol. Clearly Waller is asking the reader to make what associations he dare and leaving it to the reader to decide how firmly the associations need to be controlled. Waller's elusive and subtle handling of metaphor is a trait he may have developed from French example. A poem playing on the same erotic associations by the French poet Tristan l'Hermite (*c.* 1601–1655), for instance, called interestingly enough *Fantasy*, describes a serpent who finds his way into Cupid's quiver:

> Un jour Amour sur la verdure
> Reposoit à l'ombre d'un Bois;
> Lors qu'un Serpent par avanture
> Se glissa dedans son Carquois.
>
> Diane le vint relever;
> Mais soudain l'animal se jette,
> Et diligent à se sauver,
> Se lance comme une sajette.
>
> Voyez un peu quelle merveille
> Dit elle, les sens estonnez:
> Soit qu'il veille, soit qu'il sommeille,
> Il a des traits empoisonnez.[23]

[Love, one day, was lying on the grass in the shade of a wood;

3

when, by chance, a snake slid into his quiver. Diana came to take
it away, but suddenly the animal reared up and hurled itself like
an arrow trying to escape. Just see, she says, in astonishment, how
marvellous it is: whether awake or asleep it has poisonous
qualities.]

Rochester's libertinism is a good deal more robust than Waller's
and wherever Rochester appears to be alluding to Waller or using
Waller's poetry as a point of departure it is to reject the equivoca-
tions in favour of direct statement. Rochester would have found
plenty of models for a more direct approach in the work of earlier
poets. Carew's *The Rapture* provides the most famous (or, according to taste, infamous) example. A poet who is perhaps closest to
Rochester in this vein and whose poetry Rochester sometimes
echoes is Richard Lovelace. Vieth,[24] for example, suggests that
the lines from the song, 'How happy, Chloris, were they free':

> For did you love your pleasure less,
> You were not fit for me.

may be an echo of Lovelace's famous lines to Lucasta:

> I could not love thee, dear, so much
> Loved I not Honour more.

The song itself is on the same libertine subject (the pleasures of
love and alcohol) as Lovelace's *Loose Saraband*. Lovelace's lines
express a recurring libertine sentiment deploring abstract notions
such as honour as a hindrance to nature:

> Now, is there such a Trifle
> As Honour, the fool's Gyant?
> What is there left to rifle
> When Wine makes all parts plyant?[25]

In the song 'What cruel pains Corinna takes' Rochester makes a
similar, but more explicit connection between the rejection of
thought abstractions and the natural:

> Poor feeble *Tyrant*, who in vain
> Would proudly take upon her,
> Against kind *Nature*, to maintain
> Affected rules of *Honour*

These ideas, it should be noted, are in direct opposition to the conclusion of Rochester's poem *The Fall* where the lover argues that all he has to offer is abstraction: but then it is part of Rochester's implied philosophy, as well as the petrarchist tradition we are discussing, that there are many and often contradictory ways of looking at the same phenomenon. Rochester's song differs somewhat in tone from Lovelace's and is closer perhaps to the platonic than the libertine mood, though Lovelace's poem deftly hovers between the sensuous and the ludicrous:

> Nay, prithee Dear, draw nigher,
>   Yet closer, nigher yet;
> Here is a double Fire,
>   A dry one and a wet:
> True lasting Heavenly Fuel
> Puts out the Vestal jewel,
> When once we twining marry
> Mad Love with Wild Canary.[26]

Lovelace's poem *Love Made in the first Age* also has affinities with Rochester's love lyrics. Its subject is related to that of Rochester's *Fall* in that it describes the sexual freedom of pre-lapsarian man:

> 'When cursed "No" stain'd no maid's lips'

Like Rochester's poem, where Adam and Eve are described as 'naked beneath cool shades', and are as innocent as they are nude, Lovelace's pre-lapsarian lovers are 'Naked as their own innocence,/ And unembroider'd from offence' and, like Rochester's poem, the argument turns suddenly at the end to express a contrast between the fortunate past and the unfortunate present. Rochester's ending of 'Then, Chloris, while I duty pay' seems to echo Lovelace's

> Now, Chloris! miserably crave
> The offer'd bliss you would not have.

But there are important differences: Lovelace spends much more time describing the libertine delights of pre-lapsarian man and the tone is far more sensuous than that of *The Fall*, for Rochester's poem is not a libertine poem at all; it ends by proclaiming platonic necessities. Lovelace's poem on the other hand is couched in the form of an erotic dream vision—a sub-genre Rochester explores with great originality in 'Fair Chloris in a pigsty lay'. Like most examples of this sub-genre, including Rochester's, Lovelace's poem is given an unashamedly orgasmic ending:

> Now, Chloris! miserably crave,
> The offer'd blisse you would not have;
>   Which evermore I must deny,
> Whilst ravish'd with these Noble Dreams
> And crowned with mine own soft Beams,
>   Enjoying of myself I lie.[27]

This is not quite as explicit as the ending of Rochester's dream poem or as a closely similar dream poem by the notorious contemporary French poet Saint Pavin (1595–1670) who writes in a sonnet:

> Ma vie est plus réformée,
> Qu'elle n'etait cy devant,
> Alidor est à l'armee
> Et Philis dans un couvent.
>
> Ma main est là bien aymée
> Qui me sert le plus souvent,
> Le soir, ma porte fermée,
> Seul, je n'en joue en revant.
>
> Ne croy pas que je me pasme
> Que souvenir d'une dame,
> Ou quelque beau garçon.
>
> A moy seul je n'abandonne
> Et je conserve le nom
> Que tout le monde me donne.[28]

[My life is more reformed than it has been hitherto, Alidor is in the army and Phyllis in a convent. My hand, which most often comes to my aid, is there well beloved; in the evening when my door is closed and I am alone, I play with myself (punning on: I enjoy myself) and dream. Do not imagine that I faint away at the memory of a lady or some handsome boy, I give myself up to myself alone and so keep the name that everyone gives me.]

Lovelace, like Rochester, was a great reader of French, and several of his poems are translations from that language. There is one other point of resemblance between Lovelace's poem and a poem of Rochester. Lovelace ends his poem with a curse on the lady's frigidity, the poem is thus a threat poem like Donne's *Apparation* or like Rochester's song 'Phyllis, be gentler I advise'.

As we can see from these examples, libertine poems can be libertine in the more modern, perjorative sense of sexually promiscuous, sexually self-indulgent. This perjorative view of libertinism was already strong among the opponents of the cult in the seventeenth century, but the libertinism of the period is not necessarily morally unorthodox, as we have seen in the examples quoted from Cowley's *Mistress*. Rochester's libertine poems are far less outspoken than his anti-platonic and burlesque love poetry and several of them, including the song 'Give me leave to rail at you' may be addressed to his wife. There is an 'answer' to this poem in Lady Rochester's handwriting in the Portland MS. Generally Rochester's sexually outspoken poems are poems of rejection, and of disgust, while the libertine poems convince us of genuine feeling and are normally discreet in sexual reference. There is little that can be called erotic in his poetry, as a comparison between his *Imperfect Enjoyment* and the other poems in the mode will show.

Lovelace, though often as robust as Rochester, still retains some of the influence of French *préciosité*. A dialogue between Lucasta and Alexis shows both a willingness to be more explicit and straightforward than Waller and at the same time a similar ability to hover ambiguously between alternative meanings. The reader is never quite sure in this poem whether the situation is that of two lovers parting or whether they are talking of the separation after coitus. The point of the poem is to keep the reader guessing:

LUCASTA: Tell me Alexis what this parting is,
              That so like dying is, but is not it?
ALEXIS: It is a *swounding* for a while from blisse,
              Till kind '*How do you?*' calls us from the fit.
              If then the spirits only stray, let mine
              Fly to thy bosome.
LUCASTA: And my Soule to thine. . . .

The poem is especially interesting because it rehearses a favourite theme of Rochester's poetry: the transience of love. In Lovelace's poem a Chorus comments:

> Vaine dreams of Love! that only so much blisse
> Allow us, as to know our wretchednesse;
> And deale a larger increase in our Paine,
> By showing Joy, then hiding it againe.[29]

The poem ends, however, by asserting the transcendence of love over time and fate—an assertion that stresses the spiritual significance of sexual love. Lovelace shows here that traditional faith in transcendent values that Rochester, the sceptic, rarely attained in his poetry. As he said to Burnet: 'they are happy who believe, for it is not in every man's power'.

These comparisons between Rochester's poems and those of his predecessors show how much Rochester took from the past and help us to decide to what extent he contributed his own, individual voice.

It is not always easy to decide in which category any particular poem should be placed. Indeed one favourite device of Rochester's is to raise an expectation of a platonic type of poem and then surprise us by ending it on a libertine or anti-platonic note. The lyric 'Twas a dispute 'twixt heaven and earth' starts out as a highly orthodox, platonic, love poem and ends by insinuating libertine ideas. *The Fall*, perhaps the most original of all, starts out as a libertine poem and ends, surprisingly enough, as a poem advocating platonic attitudes. 'Fair Chloris in a pigsty lay' starts as anti-platonic and ends as libertine. Such surprising shifts were meant to cause admiration of the ingenuity of the poet and in none more so than Donne's lyrics. Donne is a master at raising our expectations in one direction and then taking them in another. *The Relic*, for instance, is a platonic love poem in the sense that it explicitly celebrates an asexual relationship between a man and a woman. But the way that asexuality is expressed—the lovers lying together in the grave, the devotional attitude expressed towards the lovers and strange ambiguities like calling the lady a Mary Magdalen and (even more) the lover's complaining of the 'late law' of chastity having 'injured' nature—suggests libertinism rather than platonic love. It was a central tenet of libertine thought that law had made us unnatural in sexual matters. Donne, of course, is playing a mannerist game of keeping us guessing *where* the emphasis is to fall. And both Donne and Rochester can suggest by this challenges to our ability to categorise, an idea Rochester

likes to exploit. No poem better illustrates Donne's ability to un-
settle his reader by keeping him hovering between one expectation
and another than *The Extasie*. In a sense this poem is about hovering, for it tells of two intertwined souls hovering above their
respective bodies, male and female. This suggests a platonic poem
on the transcendent power of love and until the end that is what
we think we have got. But Donne unexpectedly turns the argument to a libertine plea that the lovers may 'descend/T'affections,
and to faculties':

> To our bodies turn we then, that so
>   Weak men in love reveal'd may look;
> Love's mysteries in soules do grow,
>   But yet the body is book. . . .[30]

The poem ends, rather cheekily, by suggesting that the unity the
two souls have achieved in spirit can be observed in the flesh by
any onlooker: the lovers are presumably united in sexual intercourse. And having come to this conclusion we realise we have
been subtly prepared for a libertine ending by the imagery used
earlier in the poem. For the poet describes the two lovers lying
together in highly erotic terms. They lie on a 'pregnant' bank 'like
a pillow on a bed', their hands are cemented 'with a fast balme,
which did spring'—presumably they have the sweaty palms that
to the Elizabethans denoted sexual desire—their eyes meeting and
reflecting each other is described as 'propagation'. Donne has
managed subtly to intertwine platonic and libertine elements together so that until the end we cannot be sure at what kind of conclusion we shall arrive. And even at the end ambiguities remain: is
the poem about a ruse to get the girl to grant sexual intercourse?
Is it mocking the idea of a detached love or are we really to believe
the lovers only return to their bodies to enable *others* to admire
their love?

Style in the Love Lyrics

The methods Rochester uses are equally dependent on past example. His verse forms are usually the stanzaic forms of the song.
Like earlier Cavalier lyricists, Rochester chooses a language that is
clear and natural, a style associated principally with Jonson and
his 'sons'. In this he differs markedly from late petrarchist poets

such as Cowley and Cleveland whose dense style bears the hall-marks of that *difficoltà* that was one of the delights of Mannerism grafted on to the petrarchist tradition. An example of the contrast between the typical late petrarchist, witty style and the style of Jonsonian clarity can be found in a single poem by Sir John Suckling. In *Upon my Lady Carlisle's Walking in Hampton Court Garden* Suckling records a conversation between J S (himself) and T C (Thomas Carew) in which Suckling contrasts his own anti-platonic views in a plain straightforward style with T C's platonic attitudes expressed in the rather more complex rhythms and vocabulary of the late petrarchist poet:

> TC: Didst thou not find the placed inspir'd,
>   And flow'rs, as if they had desir'd
>   No other Sun, start from their beds,
>   And for a sight steal out their heads?
>   Heardst thou not musick when she talk't?
>   And didst not find that as she walk't
>   She threw rare perfumes all about
>   Such as bean-blossoms newly out,
>   Or chafed spices give?—
> JS: I must confess those perfumes (Tom)
>   I did not smell; nor found that from
>   Her passing by, ought sprung up new:
>   The flow'rs had all their birth from you;
>   For I pass'd o'er the selfsame walk,
>   And did not find one single stalk
>   Of anything that was to bring
>   This unknown after after-Spring.[31]

T C's language makes use of those witty, extravagant conceits that have their origin in the *dolce amara*, the bitter sweet, of the courtly lover's experience of love. The lady is the sun who brings out the flowers as she passes; music and perfumes accompany her. Carew's language too has something of the rhythmic complexity of the metaphysical style, with its on-running lines, though Suckling's usual fondness for end-stopped lines and simple rhythmic effects gradually gets the better of T C's style as the poem progresses. Suckling is sufficiently able to sustain the unaccus-tomed style, however, to provide an adequate contrast in the poem with his own drastically simplified use of language. This bare style with its strong, uncompromising, formal rhythms, achieved principally by strong end-stopping, is a suitable counterpart to the uncompromising materialism of JS's attitudes. The world about him is to be stripped of its magic as drastically as the lady is to be stripped of her clothes and the language of its embellishments. Imagination is to give way to fact, fantasy to common sense, sentiment to sensation:

> Alas! Tom I am flesh and blood,
> And was consulting how I could
> In spite of masks and hoods descry
> The parts deni'd unto the eye:
> I was undoing all she wore;
> And had she walk'd but one turn more,
> Eve in her first state had not been
> More naked, or more plainly seen.

This connection between the plain style and common sense realism, however, is not invariably maintained. Rochester tends to prefer this style whether he is expressing platonic, anti-platonic or libertine sentiments. The effect of using it for platonic poems, however, and even libertine poems, is sometimes to undercut the seriousness of what is said. For the effect of reducing everything to a question of material causes and effects is to bring everything to the same evaluative level and so it tends generally to devalue. Love is nothing more than bodily appetite; language is nothing more—in Spratt's words—than 'so many *things* almost in an equal number of words'.[32] Rochester's primary purpose in using such language, however, is, I think, to assert control over material that becomes more and more recalcitrant and uncertain as the conventions become less convincing. The Restoration was a period of uncertainty because the old order had so clearly failed and it was therefore all the more important to hang on to those conventions that remained. The complex, witty, petrarchist style, as used by John Donne or Cowley or Cleveland, was no longer safe: it suggested disruption and uncertainty, and if the substance of what was being said no longer provided its own sense of order all the more reason for imposing an orderly *form* on that substance. Much of Rochester's concern as a poet is to find an orderly way of asserting a metaphysic of disorder.

The witty style of the petrarchist tradition certainly survived

into the Restoration. Rochester rarely uses it but something of its
flexible rhythmic qualities can be found in the song 'Twas a dispute 'twixt heaven and earth'. The style can be found quaintly
surviving even perhaps into the early eighteenth century in the
excruciatingly unfunny wit of Wycherley's poetry. Cowley had
used the style not too successfully in the *Mistress* and it is characteristic of John Cleveland's verse. In Cleveland's love poetry the
desire for unusual comparison that is the essence of the witty conceit runs riot, and Cleveland is concerned more in surprising and
shocking us by his methods than in arousing our interest in his
subject. *To Julia, to expedite her promise* from the *Poems* (1653) shows
the extreme lengths to which Cleveland will go in his use of the
witty style. The poem plays a variation on the familiar *carpe diem*
theme, in which the lover urges his mistress not to delay her con-
sent to sexual consummation. Cleveland takes the theme as an
opportunity to search out metaphors that take him from the legal
world, to the animal, to duelling, the market place, the methods of
computing the date and to the world of sieges and trench warfare:

> Now since you bear a Date so short
>   Live double for't.
> How can thy Fortresse ever stand
>   If't be not man'd?
>
> The Siege so gaines upon the Place,
> Thou'lt find the Trenches in thy Face.
> Pitty thy self then, if not me,
> And hold not out, least (like Ostend) thou be
> Nothing but Rubbish at Deliverie.[33]

Whatever sexual excitement there was in the original theme has
been totally obliterated by the grotesque quality of the language.
For Cleveland is using the petrarchist, witty style here not to
express a theme but to exploit comic incongruity. The comedy is
based on the absurd picture that is conjured up from the results
of delay. Lover and mistress are imagined as delaying until age
makes their coupling ludicrous, 'the Anticks of benighted love',
or the 'withered' mates are compared to 'Hymens Monkeys' playing at 'Rebated Foynes' (swords blunted for duelling practice).
The comic disenchantment is also reflected in a considerable
simplification of rhythmic effect in Cleveland compared to earlier

petrarchists, Donne especially. Cleveland is not concerned with the validity of the ceremonies of love, but only with exploiting them. His poetic concern is not, therefore, to pattern his language to reflect the ceremonies so much as to parody them. The loss of belief in the traditional ceremonies is characteristic of Cavalier poetry. Rochester's refusal to have much truck with this debunking style is a measure of his concern to insist on shapeliness in a shapeless universe. No doubt Lisideus's outburst against Cleveland's clenches is the *Essay of Dramatick Poesie* helped to banish the petrarchist style, but Rochester's choice of Jonsonian perspicuity depended less on fashion than on the inner necessity of seeking a man-made order where the divine order had failed.

THREE

Heaven in Hell's despair – the anatomy of love in Rochester's lyric poetry

It is important to remember that Rochester was not only a rebel, he was also an aristocrat and a personal friend of the King. In his rebellious mood he could write in a *Satyr on Charles II*:

> I hate all Monarchs and the Thrones they sit on,
> From the Hector of *France* to the Cully of *Britain*.[1]

In the *Allusion to Horace* equally he can turn on *hoi polloi*:

> I loath the *Rabble*, 'tis enough for me,
> If *Sedley, Shadwell, Sheppard, Wicherley*
> *Godolphin, Butler, Buckhurst, Buckingham,*
> And some few more, whom I omit to name,
> Approve my sense,: I count their censure *Fame*.[2]

We should not be surprised, then, that his poetry evinces an odd combination of the conventional and the unconventional. As an aristocrat he was as concerned with traditional form and ceremonies as with maintaining as far as he could the ideas of order from which his social privileges derived. As someone who had lost his belief in a divine order and saw life as ultimately meaningless he could only view attempts at establishing order as arbitrary and unstable. The 'deserts of vast eternity' which are part of a seduction trope to the Anglican Andrew Marvell are an expression of the true state of things to Rochester:

> Dead, we become the *Lumber* of the *World*,
> And to that *Mass* of *Matter* shall be swept,
> Where things *destroy'd* with things *unborn* are kept.
>   Devouring Time swallows us whole,
> Impartial *Death* confounds *Body* and *Soul*:

For *Hell,* and the foul Fiend, that rules
God's everlasting fiery *Gaols,*
Devis'd by *Rogues,* dreaded by *Fools,*
With his grim, griezly *Dog,* that keeps the *Door,*
 Are senseless *Stories,* idle *Tales,*
Dreams, Whimsieys, and no more.

These lines, an adaptation of a choric speech from Seneca's
Troades were sent to his friend Charles Blount six months before
Rochester died; they sum up the view of a harsh universe and a
remote, uninterested God that is propounded at greater length in
Rochester's conversations with his biographer Gilbert Burnet and
which seem to have been a part of his thinking all his adult life.
They provide a backdrop against which all his poetry must be
brought into perspective.

 Rochester's view of life owed something perhaps to classical
Stoic and Epicurean philosophy: he translated two fragments of
that classic of ancient Epicureanism, Lucretius' *De Rerum Natura,*
as early as 1672–3, according to Vieth, the second of which he obviously found particularly meaningful, for he translates it closely:

The *Gods,* by right of Nature, must possess
An Everlasting Age of Perfect Peace:
Far off remov'd from us and our Affairs,
Neither approach'd by *Dangers,* or by *Cares;*
Rich in themselves, to whom we cannot add:
Not pleas'd by *Good* Deeds; nor provok'd by *Bad.*[3]

Man was very much on his own. He found himself without purpose in a hostile universe. It was a ridiculous position, and Rochester's response is frequently to laugh at mankind, including himself,
and the absurdity of the situation in which man finds himself. At
times the laughter becomes sardonic, close to despair, but equally
he could respond with a heroic defiance. Like his own Maim'd
Debauchee he could, as poet, urge others to blows in his impotence:

Thus States-man-like, I'le saucily impose
And safe from Danger, valiantly advise,
Shelter'd in impotence, urge you to Blows,
And being good for nothing else, be wise.

In the Sackville (Knole) MS 79 version the poem is headed: 'Lord
Rochester uppon himself'.

It was partly because the world about him was falling apart that traditional poetic forms and traditional ideas came to play so important a part in Rochester's poetry. Just as Charles II somewhat arbitrarily encouraged the unlikely application of the myth of the Sun King to himself in the hope that he could avoid having to recommence his travels by sufficiently bolstering up his subjects' respect for law and order, so Rochester grasps eagerly at traditional forms and ceremonies to give orderliness to ideas that were inherently disorderly. It is not so surprising, then, as it might at first seem, that much of his lyric poetry makes use of conventions of thought, feeling and form that had been handed down over the generations. Rochester's love verse explores the three areas of love we designated earlier as platonic, anti-platonic and libertine. In this he follows his admired Cowley in the *Mistress* and, indeed, Cowley's master, Donne. One could even extend the line further back to Sidney and to Wyatt and to countless European examples, for in subject matter Rochester's love lyrics exemplify that petrarchist tradition we discussed earlier. As a courtier poet, an amateur writing for amateurs, he not surprisingly adopts those conventions that had evolved as *courtly* love conventions. His career at court would not have been so very different from that of Chaucer's young squire three hundred years before:

> He koude songes make and wel endite
> Juste and eek daunce, and weel portraye and write,
> So hot he loved that by nightes tale,
> He slept no more than doth the nightingale . . .[4]

Of course, there had been some changes in attitude too. Rochester's own explanation of what he was up to in his love lyrics (if we can for the moment accept that Timon is speaking for his creator) is a good deal more forthright than most courtly poets would allow themselves to be:

> I Vow'd I was no more a *Wit* than he,
> Unpractis'd ,and unblest in *Poetry*;
> A *Song* to *Phyllis*, I perhaps might make,
> But never Rym'd but for my *Pintles* sake.

But the mocking mood in which this is written is as much part of the courtly tradition as the idealistic love verse that Rochester can equally well indulge in. Writing love songs to ladies with the names of *précieuses* shepherdesses—Chloris, Phyllis, Daphne, Corinna—was as much a fashion for the Restoration courtier as writing to Sacharissas and Lucastas had been in the court of Charles I, or as writing to Stellas and Delias in the court of Elizabeth I:

> Women that make men do all foolish things make 'em write songs too, Everybody does it. 'Tis as common with lovers as playing with fans; and you can no more help rhyming to your Phyllis, than drinking to your Phyllis . . .[5]

If the attitudes expressed in Rochester's love verse sometimes go back to medieval times, the style he employs derives from more recent example. Like Ben Jonson's 'sons'—Herrick, Suckling, Lovelace—Rochester adopts a suave, well-mannered language of love, an 'easiness' as his contemporaries termed it, expressed most frequently in melodious stanzaic forms that are models of orderliness. His overwhelming preference (as we have already seen) is for a song-like stanza that either alternates iambic tetrameter and trimeter lines, usually with alternate rhyming in four line stanzas, or adopts the even simpler form of a four line tetrameter stanza. As Dr Johnson put it: [Rochester's songs] 'have no particular character. They tell like other songs, in smooth and easy language of scorn and kindness, dismission and desertion, absense and inconstancy with the common places of artificial courtship. They are commonly smooth and easy, but have little nature and little sentiment.'[6] In implying that the songs have little originality Johnson is undoubtedly wrong. Once we have understood the conventions, I think we shall see that his handling of them is sometimes remarkably original. But Johnson is right to stress both the conventionality and Rochester's 'easiness'. Rochester had as much right to the epithet 'easy' as one of his models 'easy Suckling'—as a number of his eulogists noted.[7]

Like Cowley's *Mistress* and Donne's *Songs and Sonets*, Rochester's love lyrics form what can best be described as an 'anatomy' of love, a series of poems showing the lover in the three basic moods, but varying the moods, combining them, juxtaposing them in such a way as to give overall a picture of the love experience from cynicism to adoration, from despair to indifference. Samuel Butler's admirable description of Donne's poems exactly describes Rochester's:

Dr Don's writings are like Voluntary or Prelude in which a man is not ty'd to any particular Design of Air; but may change his key or moode at pleasure: So his compositions seeme to have been written without any particular scope.[8] [i.e. aim]

To search for the 'real' Donne or the 'real' Rochester in this is futile: no doubt both Donne and Rochester sometimes wrote for their pintles' sake; both were great visitors of ladies. Nor is it impossible for men to change rapidly in mood from devotion to hate and back again (sometimes with the same woman and within the same hour). If they are sometimes talking about themselves, therefore, sometimes they are definitely not; like Donne, Rochester has several poems where the 'speaker' is a woman (for instance, *The Song of a Young Lady to her Ancient Lover*, *The Platonic Lady* and, most notably, *Artemisia to Chloe*). On two occasions Rochester writes in the popular Cavalier form of the love dialogue. Once the lovers have become characters in particular poems they are all equally fictitious and it is as fictions we must understand them, not using the poems to psycho-analyse their authors, but trying to understand precisely how the fictions are being used. To do this we must understand the conventions of fiction that are being employed, so that we can measure the individual contribution to the tradition from an understanding of the tradition itself.

One important feature of the 'anatomy of love' in Donne and Cowley is that the poems are presented in a largely arbitrary order. There are exceptions to this arbitrariness: Cowley, for instance, finishes his sequence with a farewell-to-love poem (*Love Given Over*) and a similar poem is placed third from the end of the *Songs and Sonets* in the early editions. Cowley tends to show more evidence of orderliness, in general, than Donne. In the *Songs and Sonets* there is so little reason for the order we find in the early editions that the poems' most recent editor has printed them alphabetically.[9] The arbitrariness of the order is important, however, for it suggests the waywardness of love's moods and their unpredictability. Rochester's love lyrics were never collected separately. Most of them, like Donne's were published posthumously. It seems clear, however, even if Vieth's dating is generally (and perhaps inevitably) vague that Rochester wrote love lyrics through most of his poetic career and that the various moods are reflected on and off throughout. Even less than with Donne can one designate a platonic phase or a libertine phase to correspond to some supposed biographical crises. One can, I think, say that the earliest of Rochester's love poems tend to be the most closely tied to the conventions, though to some extent Vieth's placing of a poem early depends on whether he finds it conventional or not. The first poem in his edition, for instance, the song 'Twas a dispute 'twixt heav'n and earth' is placed under the general heading 'Prentice Work 1665–1671', though Vieth describes the dating as 'uncertain', and notes that it was only first published in 1934. In the notes Vieth admits there is no way of telling when Rochester wrote the poem (it exists in Rochester's autograph) and places it so early because its style seems 'old-fashioned'. I personally find nothing 'old-fashioned' in the style, though it is in a very unusually free stanza form for Rochester. A critical analysis of the poem (which I reserve until later) reveals good poetic reasons for the form, however, and the poem turns out to be an extremely original and surprising re-working of platonic love themes. If it is prentice work it is extraordinarily precocious, but I think it very unlikely that it is a particularly early poem.

The point of these observations here, however, is that the love lyrics as we have them are as arbitrarily arranged as Donne's and for the same reason: no clear order emerges from them. Both Donne and Rochester in writing love lyrics explore the whole gamut of the love experience as it was treated in the petrarchist tradition and the very arbitrariness of their order tells us something of the nature of that experience. This sense of arbitrariness is more explicit in Rochester than in Donne because, like everything else in an arbitrary world, love's moments cannot be predicted. The lover tries to capture the 'lucky minute', but it is as likely to end in the ribald disasters of the *Imperfect Enjoyment* as in the blissful consummation of the song 'As Chloris full of harmless thoughts' (though even this bliss is the result of violent rape). Love is nearly —but not quite—as uncertain as everything else in this uncertain world. In some ways it even highlights man's absurdity, for the 'heaven' of love, which promises 'everlasting rest' in the song 'Absent from thee I languish still' turns out to depend on an absurdly unpredictable part of the male anatomy in *The Fall*. This suggests to the lover in that poem that the lady should be encouraged to rely on the platonic 'tribute of his heart' rather than to

4

love him for his 'frailer part'. Yet in spite of this, love, as Rochester saw it, is one of the few experiences in life that can give heightened meaning to our existence. And this is true even though that meaning is glimpsed only momentarily, and, from the perspective of the chaos of eternity, is as meaningless as everything else:

> *Love* the most gen'rous Passion of the Mind,
> The softest Refuge Innocence can find,
> The safe Director of unguided *Youth*,
> Fraught with kind Wishes, and secur'd by Truth;
> That Cordial drop Heaven in our *Cup* has thrown,
> To make the nausious draught of Life go down,
> On which one only Blessing *God* might raise,
> In *Lands* of *Atheists, Subsidies* of praise;
> For none did e're so dull and stupid prove,
> But felt a *God* and Bles'd his Power in Love . . .

This is Artemisia talking, not Rochester (even here we must measure ironies); but only an insensitive ear, I think, can fail to pick up a special intensity, a special fluency in those words, that give the passage the backing of poetic approval. Here Rochester is expressing an idea that recurs in such lyrics as 'Absent from thee I languish still', 'An Age in her Embraces past', 'All my past life is mine no more', that love can provide moments of enrichment that snatch meaning out of meaninglessness.

The depiction of love in Rochester's lyrics, then, from platonic devotion to ribald sexuality, comes to stand as an analogy for man's relationship to life itself. The penis comes to stand for the man in more than just an anatomical sense. It is capable of generating ecstatic enjoyment, it is as frail as life itself; stimulated by beauty at the same time it finds itself 'Huddl'd in dirt' (as Rochester describes the mind in the *Satyr against Mankind*):

> Fair Nasty Nymph, be Clean and Kind,
>   And all my Joys restore;
> By using Paper still behind,
>   And Spunges for before[10]

Rochester was as concerned as Yeats with the irony that 'Love has pitched his mansion in/The place of excrement'. Irony in fact dominates Rochester's love poems and it is this that justifies our reading of them together as an anatomy of love. Each poem comments on the others by presenting another aspect of experience. Irony lies in love itself and in love's relation to eternity: it awaits us in the lady's lap and in the grave. For Rochester's method is always to see the contradictions inherent in human experience, to see things from a multiplicity of angles. Sometimes this irony only appears by setting one poem side by side with another, sometimes the irony comes from a juxtaposition of opposites within the same poem (as in the dialogues), sometimes, more subtly, as an unexpected revelation of implications we, the readers, have not foreseen or expected.

And another analogy is being suggested throughout these poems: that as the lover snatches his meaning in the 'lucky minute' of successful orgasm so the poet snatches his meaning, consummates a moment of truth, in the flux of time. Never does this analogy become fully explicit, though it comes nearest to full expression in the *Maim'd Debauchee* and in *Artemisia to Chloe*. In the latter poem Artemisia is both advocate of love and poet, a role that Rochester himself plays in lyrics like the *Mistress* ('An Age in her Embraces past'). The act of ordering words, giving them harmony, creates something out of nothing, much as the young girl Chloris, as she lies dreaming in her pigsty, creates a magic world of 'snowy arms', 'ivory pails' and 'love-convicted swains', masturbating in her sleep. Indeed Artemisia thinks of her poetry as analogous to sexual indulgence:

> That *Whore* is scarce a more Reproachful Name
> Than *Poetess* . . .

In the *Epistolary Essay from M.G. to O.B.* Rochester extends the analogy of writing to evacuation (in this case anal):

> What tho' the Excrements of my dull Brain
> Flow in a harsher and insipid strain,
> Whilst your rich Head eases itself of Wit,
> Must none but Civet-Cat have leave to shit?

Good and bad poets alike 'ease' their brain of poetry as their bodies of excrement—or the clammy joys of the sexual encounter. Poetry, defecation, ejaculation are compulsive acts easing us of tensions that accumulate in head and body and make us feel that much readier to cope with the world about us. This negative view of poetry and sex as a release of tensions has as its positive counterpart an implied analogy between the making of meaning in sexual love and in writing poetry. In both cases the emphasis is on poetry as a psychological phenomenon. Poetry is conceived as a subjective imposition of order on disorderly material. The shapes emanate not from the reflection of a living order, or any order outside ourselves, but from the patterns our mental constructs impose. Poetry is not about truth, but about the ordering of feeling. These ideas of the subjective nature of our view of the world are met with frequently in the French satire which we shall need to discuss in a later chapter as an influence on Rochester's poetry.

Poetry, however, is also a social activity and the patterns the poet imposes on his chaotic material derive not simply from within himself, but from the stock of patterns that are available to him at any given time and place. Rochester's poetic patterns, both verbal and intellectual, are largely borrowed patterns. They articulate not just the feelings of an individual, but of a society. It is in this that Rochester is most like his contemporaries and least like us. For the seventeenth-century poet inherited an array of traditional patterns of thought and word that has been largely lost for modern poets. It is partly to reconstruct this language that I have concerned myself with sketching in the nature of the traditions within which Rochester worked. Let us look more closely to see how Rochester uses some of them.

Platonic Verse

The ceremonies of courtly love were evolved in the Middle Ages to give social expression to a view of heterosexual love that saw it primarily as a spiritual and only secondarily as a physical experience. It was from this that the cult of platonic love developed in Italy. Inspired by Petrarch's example Italian sonneteers of the sixteenth century evolved an extreme statement of the superiority of spiritual love over carnal, sometimes to the exclusion of the sexual. This cult exalted women as virtually untouchable goddesses and their suitors were conceived of as servants or humble priests devoting their energies to the praise of the mistress' virtues. The cult of platonic love persisted into the seventeenth century and indeed was received with special favour in England during the reign of Charles I. Charles' Queen, Henrietta Maria, encour-

aged poets and playwrights to adopt the conventions of the platonic code and most love poets of the period (as we have seen)
exercised themselves from time to time in the conventions. Needless to say, the attitude to women expressed in this literature was
rarely reflected in actual behaviour, and many courtier poets make
it clear that they are indulging in a polite game rather than in a
serious exploration of feeling. None the less the conventions express a perennial and recurring attitude in men's attitude to women.

Rochester's least original use of the platonic cult is, perhaps not
surprisingly, in his early poetry. A poem called the *Discovery*, published in 1672 in Hobart Kemp's *Collection of Poems Written upon
Several Occasions*, though not written in lyric form, provides an
extreme example of Rochester exercising himself in the platonic
mode. Indeed the poem can be taken as a model of the type for it
is furnished with all the defining appurtenances: faithful servant
lover; cold, disdainful lady; willing chains, fruitless sighs, un-
pitied pain of the humble lover; killing eyes, scorn, anger of the
frigid lady. Petrarchist paradox is developed in the conceit of the
lover who glories in his captivity and his humiliation and whose
only fear in dying for love is that it will release him from his servi-
tude. Even Rochester is unable to enliven such a catalogue of
platonic cliché, the tone of which can be gauged by a short extract:

> For I am one, born only to admire,
> Too humble e'er to hope, scarce to desire,
> A thing, whose bliss depends upon your will;
> Who cou'd be proud, you'd deign to use him ill.[11]

It would improve the poem immensely if the reader could gloss
such words as 'Thing' and 'Will' with the help of Partridge's
Shakespeare's Bawdy, but alas, no sexual *doubles entendres* are intended; the poem is unambiguous and very boring. Even at this
early stage, however, it is interesting to note that the poem was
accompanied in Kemp's collection by another of Rochester's
poems called the *Advice*, a rather better poem, which puts forward
the anti-platonic viewpoint. We may, therefore, have a contrasting
pair in these poems in which opposing viewpoints are deliberately
being juxtaposed. This kind of juxtaposition is met with as early
as Wyatt (for example, the three poems in Egerton MS 2711, 'Lo
what it is to love', 'Leve thus to slander love' and 'Who most
doeth slaunder love').[12] If they are to be taken as a contrasting

pair it would show Rochester already engaged in his favourite
device of demonstrating the relativity of values. Rochester delights in showing the contradictoriness of human attitudes,
though he is to develop far more subtle techniques for doing so.

Rochester's interest in platonic love is not confined to his early
poetry. The date of the song 'While on those lovely looks I gaze'
is not so easy to determine. It was first published in a volume of
1676, *New Songs*, and Vieth places it comparatively early. It is a
much better poem than the *Discovery* because, apart from its deft
mellifluousness, it manages a neat play on ambiguities that ingeniously lead the poet to the surprising conclusion that a platonic and
a libertine response on the part of the lady will come to the same
thing:

> The *Victor* lives with empty pride,
> The *Vanquisht* Dye with pleasure.

This is capable of a perfectly straightforward, platonic interpretation. The poet has been expressing his complete enslavement to
the lady and his willingness to die 'wishing and admiring'.
Rochester makes use of the traditional petrarchist conceit that he
sees himself reflected in his lady's eyes, so captivated is he in gaz-
ing on her 'lovely looks'. In the second stanza he humbly pleads
with the lady to forego his murder, 'Your *Slave* from Death
removing', either by learning to love him in return or by teaching
him her art of charming. So far the poem has been impeccably
platonic. In the last four lines of the poem, however, Rochester
insinuates a clever paradox:

> But whether Life or Death betide,
> In Love, 'tis equal measure,
> The *Victor* lives with empty pride,
> The *Vanquisht* Dye with pleasure.

In a platonic sense this could mean that the lover (who dies) and
the beloved (who lives) are equal in the end because equally deprived of what gives them their being *as* lover and beloved—the
lady lives but has merely empty Pride with no one to exercise it on,
the lover loses his life, but does so willingly. But a completely
different interpretation is possible, and here sexual innuendo is
brought deliberately into play. For these lines could be envisaging
the result of the lady's alternative responses: if she gives life to the

lover (by saying 'yes') then the lover (the victor) will have the pride of conquest and the emptiness of the *post coitum* melancholy (described vividly in Donne's *Farewell to Love*). The lady (the vanquish'd) on the other hand will 'die' (achieve orgasm) with pleasure. Alternatively if the lady says 'no' ('Death betide') we are back to the platonic interpretation. The pleasure of finding a platonic poem revealing libertine ambiguities is just that pleasure of surprise or 'admiration' that was sought after in the petrarchist, 'witty' tradition, as I argued in the previous chapter in discussing Donne's *Extasie*. The implication in terms of the ceremonies of love is that the lover is artfully concealing his real sexual motivation beneath the cult of platonic spirituality.

It is not always easy to categorise the lyrics. *Woman's Honour* employs some of the conventional ideas of the platonic love poem: it describes a cold, unresponsive lady and an importunate lover, but the lover's attitude is far from being as subservient as the mode usually expects. For the lover complains that the lady's concept of honour is to blame for her coldness, with the implication that she should forget about it. This complaint that the abstract concept of honour destroys natural inclination is a commonplace of the libertine literature of the seventeenth century. Rochester himself in the Song 'What Cruel Pains Corinna takes' makes an explicit connection between honour and the destruction of impulse, complaining of Corinna:

> Poor feeble *Tyrant,* who in vain
> Who'd proudly take upon her
> Against kind *Nature,* to maintain
> Affected Rules of *Honour.*

'The Giant Honor that keeps cowards out' as Carew calls it in his libertine poem the *Rapture,* and Donne asks his mistress in the *Damp* to 'let the enchantress Honour next be slain'. Mathurin Régnier, whose satires we shall discuss in a later chapter, devotes his sixth satire to an attack on 'cursed honour'. Rochester here then is using a libertine idea, but the tone of the poem is not libertine, rather he is using the idea as part of a traditional platonic complaint against the hard heartedness of his mistress.

By far the most original of Rochester's platonic poems, the *Fall*, is a poem that Vieth places fairly late in the canon, though there is no clear evidence as to its date. Here again Rochester makes use of libertine ideas and in this case the poem has every appearance, at least until the third stanza, that it will come to libertine conclusions. In the opening two stanzas Rochester contrasts the unhappiness of post-lapsarian man with mankind before the fall from Paradise, and he describes the situation in Paradise in libertine terms:

> Naked beneath cool Shades they lay,
>   Enjoyment waited on desire,
> Each *Member* did their Wills obey,
>   Nor cou'd a wish set pleasure higher.

The tone here is complex. On the one hand there is no doubt that we are meant to feel the attractions of the sensual situation. The tone is libertine, even erotic; for just as the fall of the title refers not only to the expulsion from the garden but the detumescence of the uncompliant penis, so the sexual reference to 'members' obeying the wishes of pre-lapsarian man and their achievement of maximum pleasure (maximum tumescence) is fairly obvious. There may even be a Shakespearean pun on 'will', which Eric Partridge claims means 'now the male, now the female sexual organ' in two of Shakespeare's sonnets and there is no doubt that in Elizabethan drama the word was used in this way.[13] Rochester's third line then may mean 'each penis obeyed its (corresponding) cunt' as well as the more modest meaning that pre-lapsarian man (and woman) were simply able to do whatever their limbs were asked to do. The fact, however, that these erotic allusions come in the form of sexual puns modifies the erotic tone. The element of the comic, the ludicrous, becomes as important as the erotic, even though it tends to work in the opposite direction. There is very little erotica in Rochester's poetry, the sexual act is nearly always seen with as much amusement (or sometimes anger) as with uncontaminated pleasure. Indeed it is a condition of our fallen state that this should be so.

Rochester's mood, therefore, is very complex in this poem. It is a tragedy that we are not able to live as our pre-lapsarian ancestors in a libertine state of nature, where behaviour was spontaneous, like that of the other animals. But it is also a comedy that man is constantly trying to live spontaneously and failing, and that his efforts depend on such a frail and unpredictable instrument as the penis. In libertine poems it is argued or taken for granted that a return to nature is possible. Waller's poem the *Fall*, which would seem to be the poem that Rochester's fall poem answers, rather daringly suggests that the fall itself gave man the *opportunity* to return to nature. The poem tells how a young woman accidentally falls to the ground while out walking with a young man:

> Here *Venus* smil'd to see blinde Chance
> It self, before her son advance
> And a fair image to present
> Of what the Boy so long had meant:
> 'Twas such a chance as this made all
> The World into this order fall:
> Thus the first lovers, on the clay
> Of which they were composed lay;
> So in their prime with equal grace
> Met the first patterns of our race . . .

This is a dazzling display of libertine ideas, using those elusive metaphors that make Waller's subtleties so hard to detect for a modern reader. The literal fall of the young lady suggests the metaphorical level of 'falling' in love, Venus uses the girl's fall to present an image, a metaphor, of the psychological process of falling in love (symbolised as blind chance by the blind Cupid, her son). The result of this accident is not chaos but order, the ordering process that love brings into the world. So far this could be a Christian platonic concept that is being presented, for the neo-platonist held that the love that emanated from God was the principal ordering power in the universe. Waller, however, gives his version a libertine twist by associating the impulse to love with the sexual freedom enjoyed by the first lovers, Adam and Eve. It is not entirely clear whether the reference to the 'first patterns' of humanity reiterates the reference to Adam and Eve or represents the libertine idea that all early man had sexual freedom—an idea that Donne assumes in *Elegy xvii* and in *The Progress of the Soule* (191 ff):

> In this world's youth wise nature did make haste,
> Things ripened sooner, and did longer last;
> Already this hot cocke, in bush and tree,
> In field and tent, ore flutters his next hen . . .
> Men, till they took laws which made freedom less

> Their daughters, and their sisters did ingresse;
> Till now unlawful, therefore ill, 'twas not . . .

The ending of Waller's poem, however, with the young man having tripped up on top of his girlfriend, unmistakeably associates the natural order, in which love reigns supreme, with post-lapsarian sexuality. The suggestion is that of the libertine, that paradise can be restored in sexual enjoyment:

> If ought by him amiss were done
> 'Twas that he let you rise so soon,

Waller's libertinism is characteristically reticent, unlike Carew's in the *Rapture* where his mistress is invited to a sexual enjoyment that knows nothing of abstract law and is pure nature:

> No wedlock bonds unwreathe our twisted loves;
> We seek no midnight arbour, no dark groves
> To hide our kisses: there the hated name
> Of husband, wife, lust, modest, chaste or shame,
> Are vain and empty words, whose very sound
> Was never heard in the Elysian ground.
> All things are lawful there that may delight
> Nature or unrestrained appetite;
> Like and enjoy, to will and act is one:
> We only sin when Love's rites are not done.

This is a description of the libertine, natural world where man becomes, like the other animals, able to act spontaneously without constructing a system of abstract laws to inhibit him. It is a world without guilt, a world of sensual innocence, a world before a dissociation of sensibility set in.

Rochester's view of man can never be as uncomplicated as this. He writes of post-lapsarian man and of a world of dissociated sensibility. So his libertine vision of the garden of Eden is a vision of what has been, or what might have been, for it is unlikely that he believed the Genesis story literally. Man's actual situation now is quite different. Whether man likes it or not he is a thinking animal, an animal that *must* project his thoughts into the future and think of consequences and possibilities. His capacity for abstract thought is as much part of him as his animal feelings. It is, therefore, impossible to return to Paradise, the poem asserts:

> But we poor *Slaves,* to hope and fear,
>   Are never of our Joys secure;
> They lessen still as they draw near
>   And none but dull delights endure.
>
> Then *Chloris,* while I duty pay,
>   The *Nobler Tribute* of my *Heart,*
> Be not you so severe to say
>   You love me for a frailer part.

In the third stanza the language begins to deal in abstracts because in this fallen world experience comes though a filter of abstract concepts. The 'cool shades' become 'dull delights', the lover's 'members' give way to 'duty'. The lover, therefore, ironically comes to the conclusion that what is natural is no longer available and all he can offer his girlfriend is his abstract 'duty', the 'nobler tribute of his heart'. This is, of course, what the platonic lover traditionally offers; Rochester's lover has come to a platonic conclusion by means of libertine premises. The irony of the word 'nobler' in the last stanza rests on the contrast between the conventional, platonic assumption that spiritual love is superior to sexual love and the lover's miserable offer of his duty as the best he can do. His 'frailer part', inhibited by hopes and fears, has failed to rise to the occasion. The situation is ribald and ludicrous. Man is made to look a fool standing there with his fool's bauble. But the poet (and we, too, the readers) can laugh. The reassuring pattern of the stanzas has given a shape to shapelessness, articulated the inarticulate. This is one of the best examples of the way Rochester manipulates conventional material in a totally original way and where the originality is not meretricious, but a reflection of a deep conviction of the absurdity of the human situation.

The Dialogues

The *Fall* achieves its success through the juxtaposition of libertine and platonic ideas. In the two pastoral dialogues between Alexis and Strephon and the *Dialogue between Strephon and Daphne* Rochester adopts a simpler method of juxtaposing viewpoints. *A Pastoral Dialogue between Alexis and Strephon* contrasts the platonic viewpoint of Strephon with the anti-platonic viewpoint of Alexis. Vieth rather contradictorily dates the poem as 'possibly 1674', but puts it in a group with the general heading 'Prentice Work, 1665–1671'. His reason for placing the poem early, he explains in a note, is that it is of a 'conventional character'. But it would be difficult to find any poems of Rochester that are not conventional and there seems to me no good reason for ignoring the broadside heading that the lines were written 'At the Bath, 1674'. The dialogue is a discussion of two opposing views of love. Alexis, disillusioned by the unresponsiveness of Corinna, takes the anti-platonic view that he can get his revenge by transferring his attentions elsewhere. The platonic view of the faithful lover is replaced here by the anti-platonic view that the only mistresses worth having are compliant. Strephon, representing the platonic viewpoint, says that life would be meaningless were it not for love and that he will keep faith whether his suit prospers or not:

> Bless'd in whose Arms I will expire,[14]
> Or at her Feet despair.

The debate here is between a realistic, rational view of sexual relations and an idealistic, romantic view (like that between J S and T C in Suckling's poem). If courtship is merely the method by which the male achieves sexual satisfaction then Alexis is right to move on to the next girl. But if Strephon is right and love is an act of faith that gives meaning to life then to renounce his love is to make life meaningless.

Rochester leaves the question unresolved. The dialogue, therefore, takes that sceptical form of airing different sides to a given problem that became fashionable in the Restoration as an intellectual exercise. Dryden's *Essay of Dramatic Poesie* (1666) is perhaps the most famous prose example of the period. That the form suited Rochester's sceptical and unbelieving nature can well be imagined though generally Rochester prefers to reveal contradiction as an inevitable concomitant of the limitations of human reason: this is the 'hidden' subject of both the *Satyr against Mankind* and of *Upon Nothing*, and it plays an important part in the structure of *Artemisia*. It is worth noticing, however, that in this dialogue there are some hints in favour of Strephon's point of view. Strephon not only gets the last word, but the poem's ceremonial language and rhythms seem to reinforce his argument. One should note, too, that Strephon was popularly adopted as Rochester's soubriquet by his contemporaries (several of the commemoratory poems at his death refer to him as Strephon). The element of identification with the platonic viewpoint, though not what one would expect from the traditional account of Rochester, is not so surprising when we consider that the importance of love as an enriching experience is a recurring theme of his poetry. There is, of course, the possibility that here Rochester ironically identifies himself as Strephon.

Anti-Platonic Verse

The other dialogue, the *Dialogue between Strephon and Daphne,* brings us to the subject of Rochester's anti-platonic verse. I suggested earlier that the verse dialogue in which differing points of view are juxtaposed was part of a fashion for sceptical writing at this period, but the verse dialogue as such originates from a much earlier period. J. B. Leishman, in discussing Marvell's use of the pastoral dialogue, argues that it is of native growth, developing from the earlier, classically inspired, pastoral dialogues of the Elizabethans.[15] But one suspects at least some foreign influence in the suave, sophisticated tone of Cavalier pastoral of which there are numerous examples: Lovelace, Suckling, Marvell, for instance, use the form on a number of occasions. An instructive parallel can be drawn between Rochester's poem and a longer pastoral dialogue from Giambattista Marino's *La Sampogna* (1620). Such a comparison shows the same petrarchist use of a witty, paradoxical style, the same flippant, cynical attitude on the part of the lovers, the same narrative strategy whereby the 'shepherdess' overturns the expectations of the 'shepherd' lover (and also the expectations of the reader). There is no direct evidence that Rochester had read Marino. It would be difficult to believe, however, that with his wide, if desultory, reading he had not become familiar with the most famous Italian poet of the seventeenth century during his Italian tour, if not before. Certainly Marino's poetry was well-known in England, having been translated and imitated by Crashaw (who was in many ways a disciple of Marino) and Marvell, among other poets. At any rate the dialogue between Fileno and Filaura called *La Ninfa Avara* (the greedy nymph) has much in it to suggest a relationship with Rochester's dialogues. Like *Alexis and Strephon,* Marino's poem consists of an argument between a platonic and an anti-platonic point of view. Like *Strephon*

and Daphne, the participants are male and female. The 'shepherd'
Fileno takes a high-minded platonic point of view, expressed in
the best petrarchist manner:

> Amor, fiamma gentile,
> desta a nobil' imprese anima vile;
> anzi, foco fecondo,
> è sostegno de l'alma, alma del mondo.

[Love, the noble flame, arouses the base mind to noble under-
takings, thus its fruitful flame is the support of the soul, the soul of
the world]

Filaura, the 'shepherdess', at first appears to take notice, but then
adopts a very different attitude:

> Fileno, il tuo discorso
> è vago e dotto invero,
> ma si trito e commune,
> e già si antico ormai, che sa di vieto.

[Fileno, your words are indeed graceful and learned, but so trite
and commonplace and already so out of date now, that they smack
of obsolescence.]

She goes on to deride the whole business of courtly sentiment and
platonic cliché:

> Tiento pur il tuo core, io cor non curo.
> Non sono augel grifagno,
> che di cori mi pasca;
> né voglio esser un mostro
> con due cori nel petto.

[Just keep your heart! I don't care for hearts. I am not a bird of
prey who feeds on hearts, nor do I wish to be some monster with
two hearts in one breast.]

Here, with anti-platonic scorn, Filaura derides two related and
recurring petratchist conceits: that the lover gives his heart to his
lady and that she possesses it together with her own heart in her
breast. Instead Filaura wants a man who can give her money, and
plenty of it—'un cumolo d'oro'.

 I am not, of course, arguing that Rochester was imitating
Marino directly in either of his dialogues, but clearly Filaura is a

close relative of Daphne in Rochestre's poem. Daphne remains demure enough while Strephon gives her all the fashionable, anti-platonic sentiments in favour of inconstancy—a favourite theme of anti-platonic poetry as we have seen. Characteristically, however, Rochester gives us a surprise ending, for instead of disagreeing with him Daphne outbids Strephon in cynicism and triumphantly turns the tables on him:

> Silly *Swain*, I'll have you know,
> 'Twas my practice long ago:
> Whilst you Vainly thought me true,
> I was false in scorn of you.
> By my Tears, my Heart's Disguise,
> I thy Love and thee despise.
> Womankind more Joy discovers
> Making Fools, than keeping Lovers.[16]

This is an excellent example of the detached, flippant, comic note characteristic of anti-platonic poetry. Rochester has frequently been accused of anti-feminism in his poetry. If anything the opposite is true. He frequently (as I have mentioned) writes poems from the woman's point of view. *Artemisia* is a poem totally dominated by the feminine voice and in the account of the sex war that is given by the fine lady (firstly in relation to herself and secondly in the narrative of Corinna and her booby) it is the male who finally succumbs. There also exists a fragment of a satire against men in which a lady complains that the age of chivalry is no more and that men are now allowed too much sexual liberty:

> What vaine unnecessary things are men
> How well we doe without em, tell me then
> Whence comes that meane submissiveness wee finde
> This ill bred age has wrought on womankinde . . .[17]

It is true that Rochester can write (as we shall see) with considerable animus on the predatory nature of women and their insatiable sexual demands, though the most anti-feminine diatribes associated with Rochester are in fact spurious. But there are equally poems of great tenderness which we shall discuss as examples of libertine verse, and the letters both to his wife and his mistress, Elizabeth Barry, show anything but hostility. Again, we are forced to the conclusion that it is not possible to detach Rochester's own

views from the conventions he adopts in his poetry and he is capable of adopting traditional, 'anti-feminist' attitudes as well as
attitudes of tenderness and admiration for the opposite sex. In the
dialogue between Strephon and Daphne, Daphne is given the last
word and the triumph. The purpose of the poem, I think, is not
seriously to express views on the relationship of the sexes, but to
surprise and delight the reader by the sudden and unexpected
reversal of fortunes at the end of the poem (a favourite device in
Donne's love poetry). The paradoxical element (tears as a sign of
strength and lack of feeling, for instance), the aphoristic ending,
the argumentative tone are common in the petrarchist tradition.
This is the anti (or 'antic') masque of the courtly dance; the negative, comic counterpart to the platonic idealising of women, exist-
ing primarily, not in its own right as a serious view of sexual relations, but as a foil to the platonic ceremoniousness. As such it
helps to maintain the tradition much as the anti-masque aided by
contrast the solemnity of the masque proper or the feast of fools
helped to emphasise the real authority of Church and State. The
platonic tradition could not have survived as long as it did had it
not been for the ability of the courtly poet to laugh at himself.

Rochester, however, is capable of using the anti-platonic conventions with as much originality as we have seen him using the
platonic conventions. The dialogue between Strephon and
Daphne is typical of the rather playful use of the conventions that
we find in earlier examples of the mode, in Donne, Cowley and
Suckling, for instance. But Rochester is also capable of using the
conventions with considerably more satiric bite than his predecessors to express that real male fear of feminine sexuality which
the flippant, comic tone of earlier anti-platonic poetry manages
fairly successfully to conceal. It is to the credit of Rochester's
honesty as man and poet that he has extended the range of the
anti-platonic conventions to reveal more clearly the genuine hostility between the sexes that provides the psychological basis for
taking anti-platonic verse seriously. Men do not like to admit
their fear of the weaker sex and so hen-pecked husbands, cuckolds,
impotence, female domination in general are frequently presented
through comedy, that is, as something abnormal, incongruous, not
what we normally expect. The comic presentation is, therefore,
often a kind of defensive posture in which the male tries to reassure himself that the norm is one of male dominance and that

feminine triumphs are aberrations. Rochester was never one to kid himself about anything and his treatment of anti-platonic themes is an excellent example of this. He is not merely willing to play the game of supposing that women are a threat, he reveals the genuine feelings that underlie this fear. It is this honest attempt to face up to the reality of feminine sexuality, the threats that it poses or seems to pose for men and the unpleasant side of sexuality (both psychological and physical) and his honesty in revealing male psychological and physical vulnerability in this relationship that accounts for much of Rochester's willingness to indulge in what is sometimes called pornography. If pornography means relishing sexual detail for its own sake, however, Rochester's poetry is scarcely pornographic at all. If pornography means being frank about the facts of human sexual behaviour then he stands convicted (as in other matters) of speaking the truth plainly as he saw it.

The assumption behind anti-platonic verse is that women are as much creatures of physical passion as men and are equally (if not sometimes more) eager to satisfy their sexual appetites, whatever convetional gestures are required by society to hide their feelings. This is, of course, one of the major themes of Restoration comedy, and Etherege in particular exploits its comic potential in his two brilliant plays *She Would if She Could* and *The Man of Mode*. Like the libertine mode, the anti-platonic is naturalistic in its assumptions, but whereas libertine poetry celebrates and rejoices in the mutual pleasures of heterosexual love, anti-platonic verse derides sexuality, and feminine sexuality in particular. Written almost invariably from a male point of view (partly because it was mostly men who wrote the poetry, but also—dare one say—because men are more likely to need to seek release of sexual tensions than women) anti-platonic poetry presents feminine sexuality as a joke and, therefore, as a way of releasing the tensions caused by the assumptions of the platonic tradition that women are mysteriously different from men, either in not having sexual passions at all, or —unlike men—in having them firmly under control. The anti-platonic tradition, therefore, is to be seen as an appendage to the main platonic tradition of courtly love, dependent on it and only able to survive with it. Like platonic poetry it is frequently expressed in the *précieux* pastoral idiom.

As in his platonic love poems Rochester rings the changes with

5

a good deal of ingenuity in his excursions into anti-platonic poetry.
A poem addressed *To Corinna* beginning 'What cruel pains Corinna
takes' suggests all the conventional scorn and frowning that
Corinna indulges in is quite useless because she is at least as
anxious to have sexual intercourse with her lover as he is with her.
Here the platonic assumptions are being challenged directly:

> Poor feeble *Tyrant*, who in vain
>   Would proudly take upon her,
> Against kind *Nature*, to maintain
>   Affected Rules of *Honour*.
>
> The Scorn she bears so helpless proves,
>   When I plead passion to her,
> That much she fears, but more she loves
>   Her *Vassal* shou'd undo her.

We are still in the world of mistress-tyrants and lover-vassals, the
world of courtly love, but now all the values are reversed, the
proud lady is only too anxious not to have her 'honour' respected;
the vassal 'pleads passion' on the assumtpion that the whole
courtly game is merely a prelude to fornication. Rochester is
particularly successful at this kind of lyric because his unerring
sense of melody can provide exactly that formal, conventional surface that acts both as a metaphor for the lady's cosmetic indifference and as a perfect foil for the actualities of lust that the poem
assumes. The conflict between the suave, singing style and the
sweatiness of the real subject create a similar tension to that of
mock heroic. The formal antithetic balance between the two half-
lines in 'That much she fears, but more she loves' is nicely contradicted by the use of syntactical climax in the 'much', 'more'; the
balance is in fact spurious. Rochester enacts the game of hypocrisy
that Etherege exploits so well in his plays.

Even closer to Etherege is another anti-platonic poem, a song
beginning 'As Cloris full of harmless thoughts', which actually gets
a mention in Act V of *Man of Mode*. The theme here is the favourite
anti-platonic theme of the disdainful lady overcome by her own
sexual feelings when she is brought to face up to them. What
many modern readers will find the characteristic male chauvinism
of this tradition is especially evident in this poem because it describes in the suavest and best mannered verse what begins as a rape:

> She blush'd to be encountere'd so,
>   And chid the Amorous Swain;
> But as she strove to rise and go,
>   He pull'd her down again.

Clearly the harmonious concern of the poet is tacit approval of his violent 'shepherd', an approval that is apparently justified by the subsequent revelation that the 'shepherdess' enjoyed the sexual encounter as much as the shepherd. It would be naive, however, to condemn the poem on moral grounds. Poetry does not advocate, it reveals states of mind. The purpose of this kind of poetry (so frequently met with that an important psychological function must be presumed for it) is surely to reassure men that women are not so very different from themselves after all. There is certainly an element of sadism in the way the rape is condoned, but the laughter that results from the revelation of woman's sexual nature is not primarily malicious here. It is the benevolent laughter that comes from being reassured. These are, of course, no more Rochester's views necessarily than the platonic views we have already encountered or the libertine views we shall encounter. Like many Renaissance poets before him Rochester is exploring all the ways of love in his verse.

Because anti-platonic love poetry is the mirror image of platonic love poetry it delights to invert the expectations of its idealistic complement. Whereas platonic poetry is usually non-comic in tone, anti-platonic poetry is usually comic; whereas the idealising poet writes songs in praise of his mistress, the realistic poet of anti-platonic poetry writes in dispraise; whereas platonic poetry is written to defend constancy and faithfulness, anti-platonic poetry is written in defence of inconstancy and unfaithfulness; whereas the lovers in platonic poetry are equally young and (we are to assume) equally fair, anti-platonic poetry likes to present love matches between old women and young men, young women and old men, black women and white men (and *vice versa*). One of Rochester's most original anti-platonic poems is a very ingenious version of the theme of a young lady making love to an old man. The origin of these contrast poems seems to have been in school exercises in rhetoric. In an earlier book on seventeenth-century poetry, I listed a number of examples of the sub-genre.[18] Sometimes, as in Thomas Flatman's *Advice to an old*

Man about to marry a young Woman, the poet is concerned to warn of the absurdity and dangers of the situation. Perhaps Horace's Ode *Audivere Lyce* (Book IV, 13) was an important model here. Usually, as in the example I cited from Henry King's poetry, 'Paradox: that it is best for a Young Maid to Marry an old Man', the poet is primarily concerned to see what ingenious arguments can be presented in defence of the indefensible (a game that Donne plays in his prose *Paradoxes and Problems* as well as in some of the *Songs and Sonets*). In the *Song of a Young Lady to her Ancient Lover* Rochester is characteristically concerned more with the feelings of the girl and less with the display of contradiction for its own sake. The poem is ingeniously conceived as a kind of lullaby in which the young girl murmurs reassurances to her ancient lover. By engaging our emotion Rochester changes the source of the incongruity from the straightforward contrast between youth and age, to a contrast between the sympathetic feelings of the young girl and the absurd and rather repulsive situation. This sets up a very strange ambiguity that runs throughout the poem, between the basic incongruity of the situation, which repels us, and the sympathetic kindness of the young girl, to which we are attracted. Rochester centres his paradox not so much in the ideas presented as in the feelings they arouse (he does this more elaborately in the *Maim'd Debauchee* and in the *Satyr against Mankind*). The song is not a deeply serious poem, but it does raise the uncomfortable problem of the relativity of feeling as well as of our intellectual judgments. Which is the proper response to such a poem, revulsion or sympathy? At what point does loving kindness become perversion? At what point does naivety become sophistication?

> Ancient Person, for whom I,
> All the flatt'ring Youth defy;
> Long be it e'er thou grow Old,
> Aking, shaking, Crazy Cold.
> But still continue as thou art,
> *Ancient Person of My Heart.*[19]

The absurdity of the idea of the 'aking, shaking' old man being loved by a young girl who defies the youth of her own age in preference to him is unnervingly challenged by the undoubted kindness and sympathy which the young lady shows and evokes.

Ought we then to be revolted? Shouldn't we, too, be sorry for the old man and welcome his being comforted? The dilemma is increased by the lilting tone, with its curiously ambiguous refrain,
'Ancient Person of my Heart'
which reveals schizophrenic discrepancy between the frigidity of 'Person' and the warmth of the lady's heart. The second verse continuous the same knife-edge balancing act between sympathy and repulsion:

> On thy withered Lips and dry,
> Which like barren Furrows lye;
> Brooding Kisses I will poor,
> Shall thy youthful Heart restore . . .

These ambivalences are made even more complex in the last stanza when the sexual aspect of the relationship is made explicit. We have been led gradually to accept the possibility of the girl's genuine concern for the old man, especially by the second stanza, which seems to tip the balance slightly towards our sympathy. But in the last stanza we are asked to accept the full sexual implications and the balance is uncomfortably restored:

> Thy Nobler part, which but to name,
> In our Sex wou'd be counted shame,
> By Ages frozen grasp possest,
> From their Ice shall be releast:
> And, sooth'd by my reviving hand,
> In former Warmth and Vigor stand . . .

Added to the incongruity of age and youth, attraction and repulsion, is now a further uncertainty, this time about the girl's attitude. Her refusal to name the gentleman's private parts suggests the modesty of platonic love verse and her willingness to hold them (or it) suggests anti-platonic boldness. The victim of this ambivalence is the reader, who finds it impossible to settle into any consistent way of treating the poem. We are being asked to respond to the poem as both anti-platonic and libertine, even platonic at the same time. It is a perfect example of that balanced comedy where the incongruities refuse to resolve themselves. Like so much of Rochester's work they suggest the limitations of human responses, the ultimate failure of the human mind to make things add up. The game of paradox is being played at more than the level of game and at the reader's expense. Anti-platonic debunking has come here to be more unsettling than just to our ideals of womanhood.

Rochester has two lyrics on the well-worn anti-platonic subject of the defence of inconstancy, though both give the theme original treatment. Donne had exercised himself on this subject in the *Songs and Sonets* (in the *Inconstant*) and in the prose paradoxes where one of the subjects is *A Defense of Women's Inconstancy*. There are poems in defence of inconstancy, by, among many others, Sir John Suckling ('Out upon it! I have lov'd/Three whole days together'), Cowley (*Inconstancy*) and Lovelace (the *Scrutiny*), not to mention the famous special version of the theme in *To Lucasta, going to the Wars*. In his poem *Upon his leaving his Mistress*, Rochester finds an ingenious new twist for his poem surprising at this date in the development of petrarchist themes. It would be a scandal, argues the lover, to confine his mistress to one man because she is capable of satisfying mankind in general:

> See the kind Seed-receiving Earth,
> To ev'ry Grain affords a Birth:
> On her no Show'rs unwelcome fall,
> Her willing Womb retains 'em all.
> And shall my *Celia* be confin'd?
> No, live up to thy mighty Mind;
> And be the Mistress of Mankind.[20]

Anti-platonic playfulness has perhaps (as it sometimes does) tipped over into satire here. The grotesqueness of a lady with a universal sexual capacity suggests a nightmare version of the myth of the *Magna Mater*, the earth-mother from whose capacious womb all life springs. This earth-mother is rather more menacing, however, for she 'retains' the showers that fall on her (the earth's own processes as understood in Rochester's time are modified to accommodate the analogy) and the analogy with the earth receiving grain will not quite hold, after all the lady can scarcely afford a birth for all the seed she receives; so should we perhaps understand 'berth' as more appropriate? The syntax helps the shift from the Earth to the girl by making it possible for the 'womb' to apply equally (not simply by analogy) to the girl and the earth. Like the earth, too, the girl is frighteningly impersonal about who does the impregnation:

While, mov'd by an impartial Sense,
Favours, like Nature, you dispence,
With Universal Influence.

It is notable that the suave, melodious language characteristic of
the lyric poetry is here modified by a slight element of irregularity
(in the use of an unusual seven-line stanza and the use of weakly
stressed syllables in strong stress positions), suggesting some disruption and unbalance. Again the game of anti-platonic parody
has taken on a slight air of menace. This time not from our uncertainty of the way we are to respond, but because it presents men
with the daunting task of satisfying a limitless appetite. There is
one further touch of the grotesque. The 'mighty mind' that the
lady, in mock heroic fashion, is asked to live up to, we might think
resides elsewhere than in her head. Yet the title of the poem *Upon
his leaving his mistress* is the right one: the poem is an anti-platonic
defence of male inconsistency in spite of its macabre argument.

The song 'Tell me no more of constancy' is a rather more regu-
larly patterned poem, but opens in an even more biting, satirical
tone. For constancy here is scorned not simply because inconstancy is preferable, but because it is a hypocritical virtue only
cultivated by those who are too old or weak to be inconstant. The
poem reminds us of the *Maim'd Debauchee* in its triumphant assertion, at the end, of the heroic values of promiscuity:

Then bring my bath, and strew my bed,
    As each kind night returnes;
I'le change a Mistress till I'm dead,—
    And fate change me to worms.[21]

The Don Juan-like assertion, of course, is to be regarded as much
as a fiction as all the other *personae* we have seen Rochester adopt.
It is what Cowley calls 'a picture of the person imagined by the
poet' and what was technically called a *prosopopoeia*, that is, a
dramatic impersonation of a character. Alexander Brome, in his
poems of 1661, is at pains to reassure his readers that 'those Odes
that may seem wild and extravagant [are] not . . . ideas of my own
Mind, but characters of divers humours, set out in their own persons. And what reflected on the Times, to be but expressions of
what was thought and designed by the persons represented.' That
Rochester is doing something similar in this poem is indicated by
the echo in the opening line of a whole series of poems which

begin 'Tell me no more' and which suggest we are to see the poem in the context of its literary forebears. The series perhaps begins with Carew's splendid 'Ask me no more where Jove bestows/ When June is past, the fading rose'. It remains attached to platonic themes through Henry King's 'Tell me no more how fair she is', but becomes increasingly the vehicle for mockery via Thomas Weever and such Drollery examples as that in the Mennis and Smith collection *Wit Restor'd* (1658) which quotes Carew's poem and then parodies it in such mock verses as:

> Ile tell you true whither are blowne
> The airy wheels of Thistle down,
> They fly into your mind, whose care
> Is to be light as thistles are.

In *Merry Drollery Complete* (1661) the parody takes a political turn in a poem called *Pim's Anarchy* (presumably dating from the early 1640s) and Etherege continues the series with two examples. It may be, as Treglown suggests, that Rochester's poem involves the most complete inversion of the original sentiments, but it clearly has many competitors for this honour.

The element of parody is likely to be strong in anti-platonic verse because it tends, as I have said, to be a parasitic form. It arose as a literary game of inverting the sentiments of platonic love poetry. A few of Rochester's lyrics are direct parodies of other poets' work. The best example of this can be found in the parody of a platonic lyric probably by Sir Carr Scroope beginning:

> I Cannot change as others do,
>   Though you unjustly scorn,
> Since that poor *Swain,* that sighs for you,
>   For you alone was born.
> No, *Phyllis*, no your Heart to move,
>   A surer way I'll try,
> And to revenge my slighted Love,
>   Will still Love on, will still Love on, and Die.

The lover goes on to say that when he dies of love the lady will be smitten with remorse. Rochester's anti-platonic reply is very bawdy and quite funny. It is a good example of his use of dramatic impersonation, for he turns the poem into a dialogue between the lover and his mistress (the silent, scornful, platonic lady becoming the articulate and scurrilous anti-platonic). It illustrates, too, both the literary nature of Rochester's inspiration and his unerring ear for rhythmic effect. One of the best things about his version is the way he has picked up and slightly modified the idiosyncrasies of Scroope's rhythmic patterns. Here is Rochester's version of the opening stanza:

> I swive as well as others do;
>   I'm Young, not yet Deform'd,
> My tender Heart, sincere and true,
>   Deserves not to be Scorn'd.
> Why *Phyllis* then, why will you Swive
>   With *Forty Lovers* more?
> Can I (said she) with *Nature* strive,
>   Alas I am, alas I am a *Whore*.

Enough of the language of platonic love survives to make the contrast between the polite language and the harmonious sounds and the fleshy purposes of the lovers effectively funny. Rochester's precise rhythmic sense, too, can be seen especially in the effective modification of the hesitant rhythms of the last line of Scroope's stanza. There are plenty of examples of this kind of parody in Restoration verse collections: a whole volume largely devoted to them appeared in 1671 entitled *Mock Songs and Joking Poems*. Few, if any, manage to be either as deft or as funny as this.

A more complicated example of anti-platonic parody can be found in the song 'Fair Chloris in a pigsty lay'. This is not, as far as I know, a parody of any particular poem. Behind it lies, perhaps, the passage in Ovid's *Fasti* (II 195f.) where the poet describes the rape of the earth nymph, Chloris, by the divine wind, Zephyrus, which transforms her into the spring goddess, Flora. Certainly, even in parody, a good deal of the spring myth, the myth of fertility, survives in Rochester's poem. As in an earlier poem we discussed where classical myth is used, *Upon his leaving his Mistress*, the mythic element is given primarily psychological import in this poem. The psychological interest in this case is in the way the young girl, Chloris, creates a dream world of myth under the strong compulsions of her sexual drives. As Vieth remarks with deliberate anachronism, there is a strong Freudian element in the poem. The poem itself is an example of the erotic dream poem the seventeenth century was so fond of; we have already met an example in Lovelace's poem *Love Made in the First Age*, a poem also inscribed 'to Chloris'. Richmond deals with the classical origins of these poems and their diffusion in the sixteenth and seventeenth centuries.[22] The usual purpose of these poems, as in the song 'She lay all naked in her bed' of *Merry Drollery Complete* (1661) and Suckling's *His Dream*, is to give the reader erotic excitement: they are, if you like, mildly pornographic. It is characteristic of Rochester that he changes an erotic kind of verse into something else. For though a poem could hardly be more sexually outspoken the tone is both comic and serious. It is certainly not pornographic.

The poem tells how Chloris falls asleep in the heat of the day while she is minding her pigs. She dreams that as she is employed feeding her charges: 'Her snowy arms employed/In Ivory pails', a handsome, but rejected, suitor comes to tell her that one of her pigs is caught up in a 'gate' leading into a cave—Flora's cave, no less. The swain says he would have rescued the pig himself:

> But I am so abhorr'd by thee,
> That ev'n the Darling's Life from me
> I know thou wou'dst refuse.

The nymph dashes off to save her pig. The swain follows her to the cave where he rapes her. The whole story has been made up to persuade her to open the gate of her cave:

> This Plot, it seems the Lustful Slave
> Had laid against her Honor,
> Which not one God took care to save,
> For he pursues her to the Cave,
> And throws himself upon her.

As she feels herself violated and hears the 'panting lover's fainting moan' in 'the happy minute' of orgasm she wakes in a fright 'and waking frigs' (that is, has an orgasm) to discover it is the pigs murmuring and that her thumb is the intruding member—her rape has been a dream and she wakes to find herself 'innocent and pleased'.

The Ovidian myth here has been internalised to explain psychological compulsion. Flora's cave is the girl's own vagina and the gate her hymen. The use of the term 'gate' for the hymen or the entrance to the vagina is familiar from Elizabethan and later examples. Eric Partridge in his *Shakespeare's Bawdy*, under 'gate' (which he glosses 'vulva') quotes *Winter's Tale* I, ii, 196–198. He might also have quoted the Clown in *All's Well* (IV, v, 52) 'I am for the house with the narrow gate' and, even more clearly, the bawdy song of Feste at the end of *Twelfth Night* (which Partridge in a note to the 1968 edition rightly says 'has little meaning unless it be taken to summarize his [Feste's] lifetime's sexual experience'[23]). Feste, it will be remembered, complains that once his foolish 'thing' had ceased to become merely a 'toy' men refused him and others like him access to their women:

'Gainst knaves and thieves men shut the gate'

Perhaps the clearest early reference is in Nashe's *Unfortunate Traveller* where a rape is described in some detail: 'On the hard boards he threw her, and used his knee as an iron ram to beat ope the two-leaved gate of her chastity.'[24] Spenser describes the entrance to the vagina allegorically as an 'iron gate' in *Faerie Queene* III, 12 (in the House of Busirane) and in III, 6, 31 the entrance to life of the Garden of Adonis (among other things signifying the womb) is described as an iron gate attended by 'A thousand, thousand naked babes' waiting to be given their clothes of flesh.[25] The most famous seventeenth century use of 'gates' to mean vagina (again the reference is to 'iron gates') is, of course, at the end of Marvell's *To his Coy Mistress* (the fact that Marvell's prudish modern editor is sceptical of this reading merely emphasises how reluctant people are to recognise the obvious when sexual matters are discussed, as if the sexual organs will go away by not being referred to.)[26]

There is not much doubt, then, what Rochester's 'gate' stands for or why it is at Flora's cave. Clearly it is no ordinary gate (an unusual thing to have at the entrance to a cave) for the swain is not permitted to enter (to rescue the pig) until he follows her in. As in *The Rape of the Lock* where it is only when Belinda allows the Beau to enter her heart that the Sylph is distracted and the rape occurs, so here it is only when Cloris' own impulses free the gate that the swain can take advantage of the situation. The pig is removed (her prudish association of sex and dirt) and so the fear that has kept her 'platonically' chaste is removed. The platonic language—the snowy arms, the ivory pail, the suitor as 'swain' and 'slave'—contrast incongruously with the earthiness of the setting, just as the girl's prudish fears contrast with her natural desires.

Platonic reticence is set against libertine impulse. The resulting incongruity might seem to be at the girl's expense. The poem might be illustrating, in characteristic, anti-platonic fashion, that women like their sex as much as men. But the poem is more complex in tone than this. It *is* a funny poem, of course, because the conventions are used so cleverly and so surprisingly and the critic must beware in reading the poem not to sound too solemn, not to over-read. But clearly the poem is not simply laughing at women's sexual hypocrisy or the discrepancy between their desires and their prudery.

Chloris' sexual compulsions are not so much being laughed at as being asserted. The anti-platonic theme that women are after all as compelled by their sexual desires as are men is here taken as a fact of nature; it is as much a part of nature that Chloris shall become sexually awakened as that the earth nymph Chloris should become Flora, that the spring should follow the winter. No-one triumphs in this situation, there is no lustful male to satisfy, except in the girl's dream, only that the girl discovers a potential in herself that it has taken the dream to realise. If anything Chloris has discovered that the enrichment of experience that comes with realising sexual potential is not dependent on a man wakening her—no modern feminist could object to that idea. She awakes to a brave new, libertine, world 'innocent and pleased'. Chloris' experience then is not just that of a young girl finding her sexual appetite but that of the libertine, male or female, discovering a new world magically enriched by a new dimension of sensation, like the lovers waking from their seven sleepers' sleep in Donne's *Good Morrow*. Rochester is here adumbrating the theme that recurs in his verse: the ability of human beings to impose significant meaning on a world that is frightening and sordid. As the dream-man (the girl's own sexual drives) goes to rape her the poet reveals that 'not one god took care to save' the girl's 'honour'. It is not the gods who achieve anything in this poem, they are as remote and indifferent as ever, it is the girl herself. The abstractions like 'honour' and 'the gods', that inhibit our real natures, having here lost their power in sleep, allow the girl to discover within herself a capacity for creating meaning. Through anti-platonic parody Rochester has been able to assert the libertine truth that meaning lies in being true to our natural selves, a brilliant example of the manipulation of the conventions.

'Fair Chloris in a pigsty lay', though a funny poem, mockingly pointing up the frail foundations that our hopes of bliss rest on (in this case a thumb), is also a poem asserting the libertine pleasures and the possibility of happiness. Several of Rochester's anti-platonic poems, however, veer towards satire against feminine sexuality as a threat or as aesthetically distasteful. Again, whether these express certain moods of the poet himself or whether they are a further example of Rochester relentlessly exploring all facets of the love experience, there is no way of deciding. As he was a man, he no doubt had moods approximating to the fear and hatred of women that few men (if they are honest with themselves) fail to experience at some time or other. In any case what is valuable about these poems (however unpleasant some may find them) is their being willing to look on sexuality in some of its most repellant aspects. It is Rochester's willingness to use the anti-platonic tradition in this honest way that distinguishes his poems of the mode from the countless anti-platonic play poems that abounded in the seventeenth century. The lyric 'Love a woman, you're an ass' begins in a purely conventional anti-platonic manner like Suckling's 'Why so pale and wan fond lover' or the same poet's 'There never yet was woman made,/Nor shall, but to be curs'd'. But usually such poems retain their flippant, devil-may-care mood to show that the lover is not greatly concerned with the problem anyway. This is Rochester's conclusion too, for in the third stanza he decides that he will leave womankind to others while he tipples with his (presumably male) friend—a common conclusion to Cavalier drinking lyrics. There are two things, however, that make this different from the conventional poem on the rejection of women: stanzas two and four. Stanza two aristocratically recommends the satisfaction of female lust to the lower orders with considerable animus:

> Let the Porter and the Groom,
>   Things design'd for Dirty Slaves,
> Drudge in Fair *Aurelia*'s Womb,
>   To get Supplies for Age and Graves.

The sardonic and thoroughly characteristic suggestion in the last line that the whole business of copulation is part of a meaningless cycle of birth and death expresses a metaphysic of rejection far stronger than the conventional rejection of women for wine.

Drinking is more likely to be an anodyne than a pleasure in such a world, a desperate remedy in an attempt to retain some hold on some meaning:

> With my Lewd Well-natur'd Friend,
> Drinking, to engender Wit.

Here the theme of the poet, heroically struggling to force out a meaning, becomes unusually explicit. The fourth stanza (omitted in Pinto's edition) continues the defiance and increases the anti-feminist malevolence:

> Then give me health, wealth, mirth, and wine,
> And if busie Love intrenches,
> There's a sweet soft Page of mine,
> Do's the Trick worth Forty Wenches.

An even less genial version of the theme of love versus wine is provided in the lyric *To a lady in a letter*, a version of which exists in Rochester's autograph in the Portland MS. The earlier version (from the autograph MS) as printed by Pinto in the notes of his edition (pp. 167–8) has an interesting last stanza that neither version as printed by Vieth retains:

> For wine (whose power alone can raise
> Our thoughts soe farr above)
> Affords Idea's fitt to praise.
> What wee think fitt to Love.

The idea of wine as a stimulus for poetic composition is taken a step further to the suggestion that the ideas themselves are the result of alcoholic stimulation. Throughout the poem the sexual 'juices' that Chloris enjoys indiscriminately from the men she fornicates with are compared to the wine that the lover tipples (she is allowed her juices, if he is allowed his); we can see that a comparison is implied in this final stanza between sexual and poetic activity—a comparison we have already noted in other poems by Rochester. Fornication and writing love poetry are analogous responses, both are stimulated by wine and women. In the later versions of the poem, however, this idea gives place to the anti-feminist theme of the insatiableness of woman's sexual appetite, which is already present in the earlier version. The lady's cunt is seen as a mouth tippling seminal fluid:

> Since you have that, for all your haste
>   (At which I'll ne'er repine),
> Will take its liquor off as fast
>   As I can take off mine.

The nightmare vision of women as of infinite sexual capacity is increased by the impersonality of Chloris' sexual responses. This is a theme that becomes prominent in Rochester's burlesque nightmare *The Ramble in St James's Park*. For both Corinna in that poem and Chloris in this are so unconcerned about the personalities of the men they use that they actually prefer fools so long as they have sexual stamina:

> Nor do you think it worth your care
>   How empty and how dull
> The heads of your admirers are,
>   So that their cods be full.

In this poem it is not clear whether the 'lover' is drinking in order to avoid feminine sexual rapacity or so that he can face up to it. Perhaps this uncertainty is intended, for the force of the poem lies in the frightening picture it gives of female sexuality. There is certainly an element of bravado in the penultimate verse:

> All this you freely may confess,
>   Yet we ne'er disagree,
> For did you love your pleasure less,
>   You were no match for me.

Vieth suggest a possible echo of Lovelace's famous lines from *To Lucasta going to the Wars* in these lines:

> I could not love thee dear, so much
>   Loved I not Honour more.

Such a reminiscence would point up the irony of the whole poem, for the lover's preference for an honour that heightens love in Lovelace's poem would be echoed in the lover's preference for wine that heightens love in Rochester. Another Lovelace poem that seems comparable is *A Loose Saraband* beginning 'Nay, prithee dear, draw nigher'. In this Lovelace describes the aphrodisiac powers of Sherry in making his mistress pliant:

> Now tell me, thou fair cripple
> That dumb canst scarcely see
> The almightiness of tipple
> And th'odds 'twixt thee and thee . . .

Lovelace's poem, however, has more of farce in it and less of nightmare. These denigratory love poems bring us to the verge of the vision of chaos of the burlesque *Ramble*. Because Rochester saw love as one of the few possibilities of escaping from the universal chaos (drink and poetry were the two others) the failure of love or the revelation that it, too, was ultimately without meaning is treated with particular force in Rochester's poetry. The failure of love and the poet's triumph over that failure is the subject of Rochester's finest poem *Artemisia to Chloe*.

The nightmare of love's failure is frequently in the lyrics treated as an essentially absurd business, another example of the ludicrousness of man's general situation:

> By all *Love*'s soft, yet mighty *Pow'rs*
> It is a thing unfit,
> That *Men* shou'd Fuck in time of *Flow'rs*,
> Ot when the *Smock's* beshit.

> Fair nasty *Nymph*, be Clean and Kind,
> And all my Joys restore;
> By using Paper still behind,
> And Spunges for before.

> My Spotless *Flames* can ne're decay,
> If after ev'ry close
> My smoking *Prick* escape the *Fray*
> Without a Bloody *Nose*.

> If thou wou'dst have me true be kind,
> And take to Cleanly Sinning;
> None but fresh *Lover*'s *Pricks* can rise,
> At *Phillis* in Foul Linnen.

Such scatological verse differs from Swift's in being less concerned with morality and more with the comedy of the situation. Rochester even here is not writing a dissuasion to love in the vein of Ovid's *Remedia Amoris*, he is advising women how they may get the best out their men. He is more concerned with the aesthetics of the situation than with the morality. It is the sheer incongruity of seeking pleasure in such odd circumstances, and stylistically of mixing the *précieux* delicacies of language with the four lettered words that create the amusement. This is not so much satire against women as a reminder of just how absurd the whole business of sex is, with men equally implicated because however messy it is men cannot leave it alone. It is right to leave Rochester's anti-platonic verse by stressing its comicality, for just as sexuality brings us closest to the gods so its constant failure illustrates our vulnerability and the ludicrousness of our situation. In the libertine verse we can see Rochester emphasising its possibilities. We can move from the ridiculous to the sublime.

Libertine Verse

Platonic love verse enacts the ceremonies of spiritual love and anti-platonic the 'antic' parody of those ceremonies; libertine verse enacts the ceremonies of physical love. It is, therefore, in a celebratory vein, like platonic love verse; but like anti-platonic centres on the sexual experience. For the libertine lover the moment of truth is the sexual orgasm, the 'lucky minute' of Rochester's poem 'As Chloris full of harmless thoughts'. But to the libertine the orgasm is not merely a pleasurable release of tension, it provides a moment of heightened awareness; it links man to that pre-lapsarian world of fulfilment that mankind lost when he took the apple of the tree of knowledge and started to think in abstractions. From that moment he ceased to be like the other animals living the life of nature, but could catch a glimpse of that world through the uninhibited exercise of his natural impulses and, in particular, his sexual impulses. There is a strong theriophilic element in libertine poetry which sees in animals the blissful condition to which man should aspire. We have already met this idea in Donne's poetry. That Rochester was interested in the theriophilic tradition is clear from the ending of *Tunbridge Wells* and in the extensive use of theriophilic ideas in the *Satyr against Mankind*. The lyric poetry, however, contains comparatively little that can be related precisely to this tradition of theriophily. Where it expresses libertine sentiments it does so in simple terms of sexual enjoyment or in statements of the supreme value of sexual

6

experience. In using the term 'libertine' of Rochester's love poetry, I am using it, not in a strict philosophical sense, but in a rather general way of those poems where physical sexuality is being presented as spiritual experience, a theme that was of special importance to Rochester.

As in the other categories I have adopted, there are some poems that do not fit too easily. This is true of the song 'Twas a dispute 'twixt heaven and Earth' that I mentioned earlier. At first sight this might seem to be a typical platonic love poem. It combines several conventional petrarchist ideas that recur in platonic poems: the dispute between rival beauties resolved by the appearance of the transcendent beauty of the lover's mistress, the description of the dazzling effect of the lady's eyes upon the lover, the adoption by the lover of a priestly role in his worship of his mistress' divinity. Similar ideas occur in a multiplicity of combinations in earlier courtly love poetry and it would be too laborious a task to attempt to trace them all. Indeed several volumes of historical criticism would be needed to trace them through the labyrinthine ways of the petrarchist tradition in all the languages of Western Europe over the three centuries from Petrarch's time. However, a few comparisons will help point up the tradition in which Rochester is working. The devastating effects of the lady's eyes on her lover is a commonplace of the courtly love tradition. The seventh sonnet of Sidney's *Astrophil and Stella*, for instance, combines the theme of the dazzling effect of the lady's eyes with the need that the lover should be protected from such brilliance. Did nature give Stella dark eyes, asks Astrophil, to protect ordinary mortals:

> Lest if no veil these brave gleams did disguise,
> They sun-like should more dazzle than delight.

Behind this idea lies the neo-platonic belief that only the initiate in the divine mysteries can bear to look on truth unprotected. William Cartwright refers to this idea in his poem *On a Gentlewoman's Silk Hood*, where he compares the lady's head covering to the veil hiding truth:

> So Truth lay under Fables, that the Eye
> Might Reverence the Mystery, not descry . . .

Cartwright also makes ingenious use of the idea that the lady's eyes have the power of the sun's rays in a poem called the *Gnat* where the gnat is said to have got into the lady's eye by mistaking it for the sun, 'wont in the Sun-Beams so to play'. In the song *Murd'ring Beauty* Carew plays with the idea of the 'killing' eyes of his mistress bringing death whether she smiles or frowns (an idea Pope can still make great fun with in the battle between the beaux and the belles in Canto V of the *Rape of the Lock*). In another poem, *A Divine Mistress*, Carew plays with the idea that his mistress is the perfection of beauty and that this makes her more than mortal:

> but my fair love
> Was form'd by hands far more divine
> For she hath every beauteous line.

Rochester's poem, like these two poems of Carew, is intended as part of the liturgy of the rites of courtly love. Both poets are participating in a ceremony which not only defines an attitude of lover to mistress, but also of poet to audience. The proprieties whereby men, the dominant sex, assume an attitude of humility, are not simply a reflection of attitudes of love, but a gesture of submission to the complex rules that give meaning to society itself. In both Carew's and Rochester's poems the ceremonial has become more important than what it stands for, or, rather, there is a gap between the formal niceties and the underlying sexual realities. In both poets the exaggeration, the hyperbole of adoration, is shown to be such by the suavity of the tone in which the ideas are presented. No-one really believes, these poems seem to assert, that women are in fact goddesses or men the inferior creature, whatever the literal meaning says. Yet these are not mock poems, not in the anti-platonic mode. For the poems are also asserting that, whatever the reality of the situation, society is held together in civilised concourse by our *pretending* that these conventions reflect the truth. The poems assent to an order they are themselves helping to establish. So the lady in Rochester's poem becomes mythologised into a successful rival of Diana and the lover becomes a votary of the god of love. Yet even while the game is being played Rochester is reminding us that it *is* only a game and that the underlying purpose of the game is sexual enjoyment. It is this that qualifies the poem for its inclusion as a libertine rather than a platonic love lyric. The second stanza of the poem is not entirely clear, but the lady (the goddess) has, it seems,

veiled her beauty in some way to allow the lover to perform his
intimate rites protected from exposure to her burning rays:

> I must have perrish in that first surprize,
> > Had I beheld your Eyes.
> Love, like Appollo when he would inspire
> > Some holy brest, laide all his gloryes by.
> Els the God, cloath'd in his heavenly fire,
> Would have possessed too powerfully,
> And making of his Priest a sacrifize
> Had soe return'd unhallow'd to the Skyes.

Presumably the lover has been allowed to 'possess' his lady in a
manner befitting mortals, and a less arduous kind of love's sacrifice (a frequent euphemism for sexual intercourse) has allowed the
lady to return to the skies 'hallowed' by her lover's sexual tribute.
Formally, too, the poem suggests something different from the
harmonious, song-like regularity of the platonic and anti-platonic
conventions. It recalls the disturbed, exploratory irregularity of
Cowley rather than such predecessors as Carew. The second
stanza does not attempt to repeat the pattern of the first. Rochester
twice breaks the thought sequence, at the end of the first stanza,
where the poem changes focus from the lady to the lover, and at
the beginning of line 11 (the third line of the second stanza above),
where the power of love becomes the subject. These discon-
tinuities and irregularities suggest the breakdown of cremony and
the change of focus from the social to the private act of love, from
the mythological to the psychological, with the abrupt opening of
the second stanza 'I must have perrish . . .'. The reader is reminded that the ceremony of love gets its ultimate sanction, not
from its forms, but from the usefulness of those forms for specific
purposes. Here Rochester is converting platonic language to libertine use. The actual ceremony being celebrated is not that of
platonic woman-worship but the ceremonies of sex play. The
social forms have been made to serve personal needs. The physical
consummation gives meaning and substance to the formal ceremonies. Rochester is turning a platonic game to serious personal
assertion.

Another poem of considerable, but controlled, ambiguity which
I think should be included as a libertine poem in spite of its title is a
poem called *The Platonic Lady*. This is an adaptation of a Petronius

fragment on a theme that became a favourite in seventeenth-century collections: that there is greater pleasure to be had in avoiding orgasm in sex play than in reaching it. Both Suckling and Cowley, for instance, wrote poems *Against Fruition*. Such poems are usually platonic, arguing for restraint in love making. Rochester's poem, however, rather infuriatingly has the lady, who is the speaker, conjure up all or most at least of the erotic pleasures of love, only to warn her lover that if he tries to go too far she won't allow him to go anywhere:

> I love a youth will give me leave
> His body in my arms to wreathe;
> To press him gently, and to kiss;
> To sigh, and look with eyes that wish
> For what, if I could once obtain,
> I would neglect with flat disdain.[27]

This is undoubtedly libertine in tone, but it is libertinism put perversely at the service of platonic ideas:

> I'd give him liberty to toy
> And play with me, and count it joy.
> Our freedom should be full complete,
> And nothing wanting but the feat.
> Let's practice, then, and we shall prove
> These are the only sweets of love.

This is taking perversity to the point of perversion and perhaps the echo of Marlowe at the end that Vieth notes would allow us to consider the poem as a woman's revenge on the kind of male exclusiveness that Marlowe was associated with. This is hardly, in any case, typical libertine poetry, though it would be hard to put it in either of the other categories.

Libertine poetry asserts the personal over the social, and one of the great gifts of the petrarchist tradition from Wyatt onwards is to provide a vehicle of expression for the increasing, modern concern with private sensation. For Rochester private sensation was all we ultimately know. I feel, therefore I (momentarily) am. Hence the stress on the importance of physical love and the strength of the disappointment when it fails. Rochester's awareness of the frailty of sexual happiness means that he rarely writes libertine poetry that is not to some extent undercut by irony. As I have said there is little erotic poetry in the Rochester canon. Perhaps the nearest he gets to a simple celebration of sexual pleasure is in the song 'My dear Mistress has a heart'—a poem Vieth places early in the canon, but without, it seems, much in the way of good authority for his placing. Here is the second (and last) stanza:

> Melting Joys about her move,
>   Killing Pleasures, wounding Blisses;
> She can dress her Eyes in love,
>   And her Lips can arm with Kisses.
> Angels listen when she speaks,
>   She's my delight, all Mankinds' wonder
> But my jealous Heart would break,
>   Should we live one day asunder.

Even this poem, however, is partly about the fears of the lover that his mistress might prove unfaithful:

> But her Constancy's so weak,
>   She's so wild, and apt to wander;
> That my jealous Heart wou'd break,
>   Should we live one day asunder.[28]

Apparently her very wildness and unpredictability makes her sexually desirable even while it is a source of torment to the lover —emotions rarely come singly in Rochester's world. Nonetheless this is as pure a celebration of the sensual pleasures of sexual love as Rochester attains.

Rochester's sense of the ironies of life, the inability to forget the backdrop of inanity against which even the happiest moments of life are experienced perhaps accounts for his unwillingness to celebrate sexual pleasure without irony or some sense of comic bathos. Where he does attempt it he fails because the literary conventions he is using—the suave, melodious language, the literary echoes, the paradoxes—suggest some degree of detachment so that direct involvement looks insincere or gawky. This I think explains the comparative failure of the libertine poem 'Absent from thee I languish still'—a poem much praised for its 'sincerity' by those who (like Pinto) see Rochester as a romantic before his time, but which I find rather embarrassingly lacking in control. Ezra Pound praises Rochester 'because he is used to singing',[29] but here one feels the intrusion of the singer to the detriment of the song:

Absent from thee I languish still,
  Then ask me not, when I return?
The straying Fool 'twill plainly kill,
  To wish all Day, all Night to Mourn.

Dear; from thine Arms then let me flie,
  That my Fantastick mind may prove
The Torments it deserves to try,
  That tears my fixt Heart from my Love.

When wearied with a world of Woe
  To thy safe Bosom I retire,
Where Love and Peace and Truth does flow,
  May I contented there expire.

Lest once more wand'ring from that Heav'n
  I fall on some base heart unblest;
Faithless to thee, False, unforgiv'n,
  And lose my Everlasting rest.[30]

It is perfectly legitimate to point to parallels in the letters to Rochester's wife, as Pinto does, or, like Griffin, to show that the quest for security and stability is a recurring theme not only in the poems but in the conversations with Burnet.[31] We need to understand both the full autobiographical and historical context of the ideas from which the poetry stems in order to understand those ideas properly. But the critic's task is different: it is to ask, how are these ideas being used in the poetry? Rochester is using the traditional language of love here without much irony, that is, much less obliquely than is usual within the traditions we have been discussing. Such directness is not without earlier parallels, we find it sometimes in Sir Thomas Wyatt's poetry, for instance, and there is nothing wrong with being direct. There are, in any case, some traditional elements in Rochester's poem; it is not simply personal effusion. The use of religious imagery in love poetry is very much part of the petrarchist tradition. But the feel of the poem is unconventional, towards a simple expression of feeling that consorts badly with the conventional elements. The formal and the personal are imperfectly related. The first two stanzas with their witty, paradoxical suggestion that the lover's torments are the result not of the lady's disdain (as in the traditional courtly situation), but of the lover's mercurial fancy, are poised and detached in the best tradition of petrarchist wit. We are asked to accept the irony of a situation in which the courtly lover *asks* to be allowed to leave a mistress who is proving unconventionally kind. This is a nice, witty combination of the platonic theme of the tormented lover and the anti-platonic theme of the need for inconstancy. But the third and fourth stanzas are an odd and unexpected collapse into a different mode. The 'fantastic mind' that has created the poised irony of the opening stanzas gives way to a mood of devotional attachment that purports to describe a future situation—'when wearied'—but ends by seemingly asserting a present state as a kind of eternity. Are we, at the end then, meant to take seriously the traditional hyperbole that the lady's bosom is 'everlasting rest'? The tone of the stanza seems to suggest so. The traditional ironic context which allows the hyperbole, with the suggestion that both the lover and the lady know that they are indulging in a polite ritual game, is lost here in the overwhelming feeling that the lover really *does* think he has found everlasting rest and the fount of love, peace and honour. And what are we to make of that word 'expire' in stanza three? Is the poet using the word with the anti-platonic, sexual, orgasmic meaning that it often has, or are we to take the word at a psychological level to mean that the lover has found a passive role in the Elysium of the lady's lap? Has he become a lap dog? Usually we can be certain what puns and ambiguities are intended in Rochester's poems because the tone guides us to interpret the possible range of meaning. Here the tone is uncertain because the poet seems to be wallowing in feeling. Only a momentary loss of control, or emotions too strong for the formal niceties of the medium could explain what is certainly the worst line in Rochester (he writes remarkably few bad lines)

'when wearied with a world of woe . . .'

This is more like emotional indulgence than emotional expression. It is not surprising that with such uncertainty of tone critics like Griffin are tempted to move from criticism to psycho-analysis. We shall resist the temptation.

If this is one of the least satisfactory of Rochester's love poems, the libertine mode also must be credited with Rochester's finest lyric *Love and Life*. The subject of the poem is perhaps not libertine at all and this may, therefore, be cited as yet another example of a poem where Rochester surprises us by reversing our expectations. The subject is that favourite anti-platonic theme, the plea for inconstancy that we discussed in the previous chapter. But the tone of the poem is certainly far from the flippancy of the anti-platonic. With great ingenuity the poem combines the conventional male plea for inconstancy with the libertine theme common to the *carpe diem* poems of the period that one should make the most of fleeting time. Unlike the *carpe diem* poems, however, the lover is not here concerned with seducing the lady, she is already obviously won over, he is using the theme of the fleetingness of time to explain why he cannot vouch for his future behaviour:

> All my past Life is mine no more,
>   The flying hours are gone:
> Like transitory Dreams giv'n o're,
>   Whose Images are kept in store,
>   By Memory alone.
>
> The Time that is to come is not,
>   How can it then be mine?
> The present Moment's all my Lot,
>   And that, as fast as it is got,
>   *Phyllis,* is only thine.
>
> Then talk not of Inconstancy,
>   False Hearts and broken Vows;
> If I, by Miracle can be
>   This live-long Minute true to thee
>   'Tis all that Heav'n allows.[32]

I think this *is* a libertine poem because Rochester manages to convey a sense of deep sincerity in the lover's attitude to his mistress. His offer of 'all my Lot' we accept not, I think, as a ruse, but as the best he can do in the tragi-comic circumstances of man's predicament. For what dominates this poem is the shadow of time and the bleakness of the poem's metaphysic. In this, comparison with Marvell's poem *To his Coy Mistress* is inevitable.

As in Rochester's poem Marvell sets human love against an awesome metaphysical background which seems to envisage a meaningless universe. Marvell's poem, however, is essentially an exercise in paradox (it is unlikely that Marvell ever personally believed anything other than the Christian view of the cosmos). The paradox arises from a juxtaposition of sensual and eschatological values. For, unlike Rochester's poem, *To his Coy Mistress* is a seduction poem in which an eschatological argument is used as part of the seduction device. In Marvell's poem physical and metaphysical are juxtaposed so successfully together that we are confused to know whether we are being asked to celebrate sexual opportunism or indirectly being warned of the dangers of fleshly lust by the frightening picture of the deserts of eternity against which the lover's pleas are being made. It is this complete and unfathomable ambiguity that has led to such varied interpretations of the poem—as a representation of sexual orgasm at one extreme or as a Christian warning of the perils of sexuality at the other. The ambiguity is embedded in the poem. The two aspects of love as experiential enrichment, an oasis of truth in the desert or as a futile vanity in the context of eternity, are left in nice juxtaposition, unresolved and unresolvable. Images of sex and death are so cleverly intertwined that we are at a loss whether to warm to the sensuality or be repelled by the charnel images:

> But at my back I alwaies hear
> Times winged Chariot hurrying near:
> And yonder all before us lye
> Deserts of vast Eternity.
> Thy Beauty shall no more be found,
> Nor, in thy marble Vault, shall sound
> My echoing Song: then Worms shall try
> That long preserv'd Virginity:
> And your quaint Honour turn to dust;
> And into ashes all my Lust.
> The Grave's a fine and private place,
> But none I think do there embrace.

Even if we accept Elizabeth Donno's scepticism of interpreting 'Quaint' as a pun on 'queint' (cunt) here, the lines abound in sexual innuendo: the 'worms' attacking the lady's virginity, which cannot fail to conjure up the snake in the grass that is usually blamed for such violation, the lust of the lover, the 'private place' which lovers usually seek in their embraces, not to mention later references to rolling sweetness into one ball (puns of ball/balls meaning scrotum or testicles, as in modern slang, are common in Elizabethan drama[33]) and the *double entendre* on 'gate' already discussed. The subject, too, demands this level of interpretation. The lover is pleading with his lady to come to bed with him and the sexual excitement of the last lines could only be ignored by someone who did not know what sexual excitement was:

> And while thy willing Soul transpires
> At every pore with instant Fires,
> Now let us sport us while we may,
> And now like am'rous birds of prey,
> Rather at once our Time devour,
> Than languish in his slow-chapt pow'r.
> Let us roll all our Strength, and all
> Our sweetness, up into one Ball:
> And tear our Pleasures with rough strife,
> Thorough the Iron gate of Life.
> Thus, 'though we cannot make our sun
> Stand still, yet we will make him run.

The sexual excitement, however, is always being checked and contradicted by the equally intrusive reminders of death and decay in the poem. If the worms can stand for the penis, none the less they are literally worms eating into the girl's dead body. The second section of the poem (the passage I quoted first) starts with that immensely evocative reference to the inevitable onrush of time and the deserts of eternity. The quaint honour (sexual pun or not) turns to dust, lust to ashes and the private place is literally the grave where the lovers do *not* embrace. In all this, that association of sexuality and death, which is frequently present in the sexual use of 'die' in seventeenth-century love poetry, and, of course, is embedded in the psychological association of sexual detumescence with death (again Spenser uses the idea in the Garden of Adonis sequence in book III of the *Faerie Queene*), is part of the paradox that what gives life, gives death, what gives pleasure, gives pain. But Marvell does not so much develop these paradoxes as use them to develop two alternative systems of value which he allows to remain in juxtaposition. The poem is contradictorily *both* about sexual enjoyment and the vanity of earthly lust. Like the sheen of shot silk it depends on which way you look at it. It is an example of the Mannerist delight in *trompe l'œil* adapted for the medium of poetry. Elizabeth Donno's assumption that one critic's (Margo-liouth's) interpretation of 'gates' to mean the mouth of the Danube and another's (Dennis Davison's) interpretation of it to mean the labia of the female genitalia must invalidate *both* inter-pretations, is unfounded.[34] On the contrary, it demonstrates the skill with which Marvell has combined two systems of alternative meaning in his poem. Multiplicity of meaning, when so brilliantly controlled, is not to be accounted for by the desperation of modern critics, but by the incredible virtuosity of the poet; a virtuosity that is even carried into the structure of the poem, which both enacts sexual climax and presents an example of the three-fold division of the syllogism—a favourite device in dis-putation of the medieval metaphysical speculators.

Rochester's poem *Love and Life* is, in contrast, not a virtuoso poem, but a picture of human love as something snatched out of a momentary freedom from emptiness. Rochester's vision of death is not the charnel house vision of the worms eating into the dead body, but of a frightening abstraction of life, a world from which life is excluded:

> All my past Life is mine no more,
>   The flying hours are gone
> Like transitory Dreams giv'n o're,
>   Whose Images are kept in store,
>   By Memory alone.
>
> The Time that is to come is not,
>   How can it then be mine?
> The present Moment's all my Lot,
>   And that, as fast as it is got,
>   Phyllis, is only thine.

This is the 'existential' view of a world in which only the here and now can be said to exist. In other poems, notably *Upon Nothing* and the adaptation of the lines from the *Troades*, Rochester gives the picture of a chaotic, meaningless universe to which man returns after death:

> But Turn-Coat *Time* assists the Foe [i.e. being] in vain,
> And, Brib'd by thee [Nothing] destroys their short-liv'd Reign
> And to the hungry *Womb* drives back thy Slaves again.

Against such a background the love of the two lovers becomes, not a trivial interlude, nor a moment of erotic excitement, but an heroic defiance of an indifferent universe. It has been pointed out that the first two stanzas of *Love and Life* virtually paraphrase a passage of Hobbes' *Leviathan* which reads:[35]

> The present only has a being in nature; things past have a being in Memory only, but things to come have no being at all. . . . *Leviathan* I, iii)

As often with Rochester's borrowings, however, it is the differences that prove more significant than the similarities. For Hobbes is here primarily interested in the relation of human thinking to time and there is no attempt to extend the psychological observation into a metaphysical statement, except that at the end of the paragraph from which this quotation is taken Hobbes goes on to envisage the possibility of foreseeing the future by divine aid. Rochester's rigid logic draws the metaphysical conclusion,

> 'The present Moment's all my Lot'

a sentiment to which Hobbes certainly would not have acceded.

It is also characteristic of Rochester that the metaphysical condition in which man finds himself as a searcher for meaning in a universe that, as far as he is concerned, is meaningless and temporary, should be seen as absurd and ironic. So Rochester undercuts the solemnity of the metaphysical statement by using the argument as a conventional ruse in defence of inconstancy. The sublime is related to the ridiculous:

> Then talk not of Inconstancy
>   False Hearts and broken Vows;
> If I, by Miracle can be
>   This live-long Minute true to thee,
>   'Tis all that Heav'n allows.

Even the truth in this cruel universe is an expedient for furthering the sexual compulsions of the lover. But the poem also asserts the possibility of communicating meaning against this hostile background. The very harmony of the song form asserts the possibility of order in defiance of the metaphysical meaninglessness. Poet and lover are again analogues of one another. Man not only snatches his moments of sexual truth in a world where truth does not exist, he asserts the possibility of order where order does not exist. In this, perhaps the greatest of Rochester's lyrics, and one of the great poems of the century, Rochester asserts the central paradox of his poetry: that meaning and order are possible in a meaningless and disorderly universe. It is perhaps not in tone a libertine love poem but in its assertion of the value of love in life (love and life become virtually synonymous) it asserts the unique creative power of love.

One of the central paradoxes of petrarchist love verse is the idea that love is both intense pleasure and intense pain at the same time. This idea is congenial to Rochester because the sense of enhanced life that love gives also makes us aware more intensely of the meaninglessness of life without love. The contrast between the painful joys of the lover and the dull painlessness of the wise is the theme of *The Mistress*. Here Rochester argues that the torment of jealousy that only lovers can know is a proof of the intensity of their love. The poem opens with an eloquent libertine celebration of the intense joys of love and its power to transform experience:

> An age in her Embraces past,
>   Would seem a Winter's day;
> Where Life and Light, with envious hast,
>   Are torn and snatch'd away.
>
> But, oh how slowly Minutes rowl,
>   When absent from her Eyes,
> That feed my Love, which is my Soul;
>   It languishes and dies.
>
> For then no more a Soul but shade,
>   It mournfully does move;
> And haunts my Breast, by absence made
>   The living Tomb of Love.

Rochester is again on the subject of love as a moment of truth in a meaningless world, contrasting the brief experience of the life and light of his mistress' embrace with the death of the soul in her absence.

The poem first occurs in Rymer's edition of the poems in 1691 and the punctuation, which Pinto and to some extent Vieth follow,

is so chaotic that I have largely ignored it; this is especially true of
stanza four where the semi-colon after the third line (colon in
Vieth) makes nonsense of the verse. The difficulties over punctuation are, however, critically revealing. The syntax of each stanza
requires a good deal of on-running from line to line while the
regularity of the rhythms seem to suggest an orderly lyric form
that to some extent undercuts the complexity of the emotions
Rochester is seeking to describe. Rymer, Pinto and Vieth are so
convinced of the priority of the rhythmic regularity that they are
willing to make nonsense of the syntax by end-stopping where the
sense will not allow it (Pinto, following Rymer, does the same in
line two of stanza two by end-stopping with a semi-colon). But
the point of the tension between form and meaning is that
Rochester's vision of love forces a meaningful pattern on recalcitrant material. This is particularly clear in stanza four, a very 'free'
stanza syntactically with much over-running, because it describes
the tension between the 'mad' world of love and the sober (and
dead) world of the wiser sort who think love is madness:

> You wiser Men despise me not,
>   Whose Love-sick Fancy raves
> On 'Shades of Souls' and 'Heav'n knows what
>   Short Ages live in Graves'.[36]

Here he is reproducing the 'raving' of the previous stanzas that
concerned themselves with souls becoming 'shades' in parting and
the 'heaven knows what short ages', in which he is absent from
her, which get mixed up with the 'graves' he lives in when he is
absent from her. Here he is parodying and mixing up the conventional images to represent the wiser men's view of his love ravings.
It is they, the wise men, however, who provide the chaos, not his
love. If they were not dead essentially they would be as 'madly' in
love as he:

> When e'er those wounding Eyes, so full
>   Of Sweetness, you did see,
> Had you not been profoundly dull,
>   You had gone mad like me.

This is a characteristically witty and paradoxical re-statement of
the situation where it is not clear which is the wisdom and which
the madness and throws doubt on the standards that are to be

applied in judgment. The world of love is a world where different standards apply from those of the dead world of the wiser sort. Rochester picks up the contrast of life and death, meaning and unmeaning only to assert at the end that love is reality, in the further paradox that the fear of losing love confirms its reality:

> Alas! 'tis Sacred Jealousie,
>   Love rais'd to an Extream;
> The only Proof 'twixt her and me,
>   We love, and do not dream.

The fact that love gives them pain is the final proof that it is Wisdom that is the dream and love that is the reality. As in Donne's *The Good Morrow* love (and poetry) have wakened the lovers from the dream time of the ordinary world into a world of heightened meaning.

Rochester's libertine songs, then, are lyric vehicles for his existential notions of the importance of the heightened moment that only love can give. They assert the pleasure in the faith that the anti-platonic poetry derides, just as the platonic poems wittily present that flight into abstraction which is man's defence against too much reality. Each of these ideas we shall find present again in the satire. Rochester sees the world from a number of contradictory angles which the traditional approaches of petrarchist love verse help him to explore and juxtapose. The result is an exercise in doubting, in scepticism, which in the *Satyr against Mankind* comes to be seen as precluding man from ever finding an answer to the mystery of his existence. But as in the *Satyr* the doubt is passionately presented. If man's position is ludicrously uncertain it is also heroic because he can, in love and in poetry, defy the absurd conclusions of his own logic. The dominant mood of the lyrics, however, is one of gaiety, one of an enjoyment of the absurdity of man's predicament. In the next chapter we shall examine poetry that stems from Rochester's other characteristic mood: anger.

FOUR

Hell in Heaven's despite – burlesque and lampoon

Burlesque is not an easy concept to pin down in definitions. The word itself derives, via the French, from the Italian word *burlesco* meaning comic. Burlesque poetry is always comic, whereas satirical poems can be either comic or non-comic. But the term burlesque cannot be equated with comic poetry in general, it has come to have a more limited meaning. It is sometimes defined in terms of a discrepancy between style and subject matter. So R. P. Bond defines it in his book *English Burlesque Poetry 1700–1750*:

> Burlesque consists . . . in the use or imitation of serious matter or manner, made amusing by the creation of an incongruity between style and subject.[1]

This definition, however, is unsatisfactory for the most famous of all seventeenth-century burlesque poems, Butler's *Hudibras*. Bond himself is clearly unhappy with his own categorisation of *Hudibras* as 'low' burlesque, which places subject matter above style, for *Hudibras* certainly does not render 'heroic matter undignified';[2] its verse form reflects its undignified subject matter. There can be fewer less dignified encounters in literature, for instance, than the ludicrous fight between Hudibras and the termagent Trulla, not to mention that the hero spends a whole canto of Part 2 of the poem with his feet in the stocks. Bond argues that the poem is serious because its satire has a serious purpose. I have argued elsewhere that the poem cannot be considered primarily as satire at all.[3] But even if we allowed his point, it would hardly justify Bond's claim that the subject matter of the poem was 'heroic'. There are other difficulties in the way of Bond's definition of burlesque in terms of a discrepancy between style and subject. He naturally wishes to include the mock heroic verse written between 1700–1750, which is the principal comic verse genre in his period, but we do not normally think of poems like *The Dispensary* or the *Rape of the Lock* as burlesque poems. The *New English Dictionary* gives the meaning of burlesque (in the literary sense) as 'that species of literary composition . . . which aims at exciting laughter by caricature of the manner or spirit of serious works, or by ludicrous treatment of their subject'. This definition assumes an element of parody, which is certainly not a principal part of either the *Dispensary* or the *Rape of the Lock*. In the seventeenth century itself a clear distinction was made between burlesque and mock heroic. Dryden, for instance, in his essay the *Original and Progress of Satire* (1693) differentiates between his own *MacFlecknoe* as mock heroic and Butler's *Hudibras* as burlesque, principally on the grounds of style. He regards both as Varronian or mixed satire, but disapproves of Butler's burlesque style:

> It tickles awkwardly with a kind of pain, to the best sort of readers: we are pleased ungratefully, and, if I may say so, against our liking.[4]

Later he adds, rather caustically, 'a burlesque rhyme I have already concluded to be none'. Dryden makes the same distinction between Scarron's burlesque poetry and Boileau's mock heroic poem *Le Lutrin*. His distaste for burlesque is unmistakeable as he alludes to Boileau's attack on burlesque in the *Art Poétique*:

> He [Boileau] had read the burlesque poetry of Scarron, with some kind of indignation, as witty as it was, and found nothing in France that was worthy of his imitation.[5]

To Dryden, therefore, there was a fundamental distinction *between* burlesque and mock heroic; it was not, as Bond maintains, that mock heroic was a kind of burlesque. And surely we must side with Dryden (a reassuring ally), for a term that fails to distinguish fundamentally between Scarron's *Le Virgile Travesty* and Butler's *Hudibras* on the one hand and Dryden's *MacFlecknoe* and Pope's *Rape of the Lock* on the other, is hardly a term worth fostering.

Butler regarded *Hudibras* as burlesque, according to E. A. Richards,[6] and we can perhaps take that problematic poem as a touchstone in helping us towards a definition of the term. The other great pillar of burlesque poetry in the seventeenth century was Paul Scarron's *Virgile Travesty* (1648), a poem not only immensely popular in its own country, but, in a revamped version, even more popular in ours. For while Scarron's work had a brief if spectacular, vogue for about twenty years,[7] Charles Cotton's 'imitation' of it, *Scarronides or Virgil Travestie*, not only achieved immediate fame in 1664, when the first book was published, but went on being published until the early nineteenth century (the thirteenth edition is dated 1804). This popularity is unparalleled for any other Restoration poem, not even *Hudibras* being able to rival it. Cotton's poem and *Hudibras* are very different poems. *Scarronides* is a travesty poem guying books 1 and 4 of Virgil's *Aeneid* by presenting Dido and Aeneas as sex-craved fishwife and bumpkin respectively, whereas *Hudibras* has no close literary model, though (as Richards argues) it makes fun of romance literature generally. Both poems, however, are comic narrative poems and both are written in a 'low' style. More important still, although both poems are comic, on analysis they are seen to be inspired by essentially destructive impulses in the sense that neither presents a clear, positive alternative to the world it mocks. Butler's poem is the more bewildering of the two, the product of what Richards describes as a 'cold and scornful mind':

> There was an unchanging, frozen quality in the mind and temper of this artist-philosopher, a quality beyond restraint, that indeed would have made restraint meaningless—an unshakeable, inactive and scornful rationalism that discounted all claims of party, and that was incapable of lending itself with enthusiasm to any cause, or movement, or hope or prophecy.[8]

We shall have an opportunity of saying something more of *Hudibras* later, but Richards' picture is essentially right. Butler was a man with a profound distaste for his own species that expresses itself in all his work in spite (as I have argued elsewhere[9]) of a theoretically optimistic outlook. In *Hudibras* his dislike of people in general expresses itself in a mocking and destructive scorn for the hero. Hudibras, the hero of the poem, not only embodies (if that is the right word for so negative a concept) the ludicrous inadequacies of men as Butler sees them, but he also provides Butler with an opportunity for self-denigration. The author associates himself constantly with his hero by adopting a derisively disruptive style, which echoes and supports Hudibras' derisory clowning, and by frequently assuming the voice of his hero.

Cotton's poem is not as profoundly disorientating as this, indeed its rough humour sometimes has the energy of benevolent comedy, yet it is a parasitic poem whose main purpose is to rouse laughter by putting the dignified and meaningful in an unfavourable light. Nowhere does it attempt constructive criticism either of its original or of what its original stood for.

Both poems, therefore, share with satire the tendency to attack and destroy, but unlike satire proper no standards are suggested as an alternative to those under attack. In general we can say that burlesque is a mode of comic writing that has the negative aim of making fun of the material it describes without attempting to suggest anything better. Butler, it is true, implies by his scorn of fanaticism that reasonableness would be better, but he nowhere in his poem gives grounds for hope that such reasonableness can be expected, even from the author himself. *Absalom and Achitophel* and the *Dunciad* are unmerciful in their destruction of the disapproved, but we have no doubt that the voice of the poet, through his assertion of the supremacy of orderliness and form, is holding up to us the prospect of achieving a sanity which his satiric victims lack. Satire, however destructive, presupposes right standards, things are destroyed because they are seen to be bad. In burlesque things are destroyed for the fun of destruction, though, as there can be exuberance even in this, it is not impossible for burlesque to appear buoyant and cheerful. And because burlesque suggests no positive viewpoint it is essentially directionless and ambiguous in its effect. Butler and Cotton give us little but laughter, predominantly scornful in *Hudibras*, ribald in *Scarronides*. Burlesque is thus a comic form where laughter is used to destroy and without thought of what could replace what has been destroyed. In the travesty the object of destruction is literary, in *Hudibras* the object more profoundly is to destroy our confidence in man himself. One might call the former 'light' and the other 'heavy' burlesque.

Rochester's excursions into burlesque are not numerous and include few poems of outstanding importance. It will not, therefore, be necessary to give as much attention either to them or to their literary background as we have paid to the lyric or will pay to the satire proper. I shall assume that the basic distinction between burlesque and comic satire is, as I have argued, the difference between a primarily destructive and primarily constructive point of view. Along these lines of distinction we shall certainly place such poems as the *Ramble in St James's Park,* the *Imperfect Enjoyment, Signior Dildo* and—less securely—the *Maim'd Debauchee* among burlesque poems. In addition, in this chapter, we can consider Rochester's lampoons, those personal attacks on his enemies, which, though the subject matter is quite distinct from the general targets of burlesque, has a similar tendency to negation and repudiation. In practice it will be impossible to draw an exact line between Rochester's burlesque and his satire. The two modes clearly merge, differing often only in the degree to which they are concerned with stating an alternative and superior viewpoint to that under attack. The burlesque poetry, however, is much less concerned with formal regularity. Rochester almost invariably prefers the rhyming pentameter couplet for his satire proper. For the burlesque he uses a variety of metres: the rhymed pentameter couplet for the *Imperfect Enjoyment,* hudibrastic for *St James's Park* and stanzaic forms for *Signior Dildo* and the *Maim'd Debauchee.* There is also considerable difference in the subject matter, his burlesque poetry being mostly concerned with deriding sexual experience; his satires have a more general and philosophical concern. I am hesitant about placing the *Maim'd Debauchee* in the category of burlesque primarily because it does express alternative standards of judgment, but as neither viewpoint is clearly asserted the poem remains highly ambiguous and, therefore, does not provide us with criteria for making a choice between the approved and unapproved. Ambiguity of point of view, however, and the development of paradox is also a characteristic of some of the poems I am including under the category of satire. *Upon Nothing,* for instance, the *Satyr against Reason and Mankind* and the *Epistle from Artemisia in the Town to Chloe in the Country* each present us with alternative viewpoints; but I believe that in each case a preference is to be inferred, or at least a standpoint can be reached, which allows the reader to make a judgment that transcends the limitations of the argument. There is also a point where the anti-platonic poems I discussed in the previous chapter become indistinguishable from the burlesque mock songs and clearly anti-platonic poetry can well take the form of parody and burlesque. Nevertheless it seemed sensible to discuss anti-platonic lyric poetry along with the platonic poetry it mocks.

The Seventeenth-Century Fashion for Burlesque

The best way of refining on a definition of burlesque is by examin-
ing and describing some seventeenth-century examples. The word
itself was borrowed into English in the seventeenth century and
the periods of the Commonwealth and Restoration remain the era
of burlesque par excellence. Burlesque poems of course existed
earlier; they were simply called something else. George Kitchin
traces burlesque poetry from such medieval examples as Chaucer's
Rime of Sir Thopas and the *Nonnes Preestes Tale* to Elizabethan examples before moving on to our period.[10] There was something particularly congenial about burlesque to the people of the mid-
seventeenth century, to those readers at least who were anxious to
defy Puritan sobriety. It is sometimes asserted that the English
were simply following the lead given by French example, but
English burlesque was already flourishing before Scarron's poem
was written. Moreover a comparison of Scarron's *Virgile Travesty*
and Cotton's *Scarronides* is as revealing in the differences it un-
covers as in the similarities. Cotton's poem is far coarser, far less
well-mannered, rather less amusing than Scarron's, and it seems
likely that Cotton was at least as much following such coarse
homespun English examples of burlesque as can be found in the
Commonwealth drolleries as following his avowed French model.

An example of this English burlesque humour, which glances
back to an even earlier poem, is James Smith's *Innovation of Ulysses
and Penelope*. This was published in 1658 in a volume of largely
burlesque poems called *Wit Restor'd*, but it was certainly written
before 1640 because it is prefaced by a commendatory poem by
Philip Massinger, who died in that year. Antony Wood in his
Athenae Oxoniensis tells us that Smith matriculated at the age of
18 at Oxford in 1622/3 becoming a bachelor of divinity in 1633
and eventually doctor of divinity.[11] Wood described the *Innovation*
as it is described on the title page as 'a mock poem'. Massinger's
commendatory verses describe the poem as written 'in a new
strain', but Smith's own Preface seems to be asking us to compare
it with Marlowe's burlesque version of *Hero and Leander*:[12]

> This History deserves a grave translation,
> And if comparisons be free from slanders,
> I say as well as Hero and Leanders.[13]

This is a very interesting remark as it confirms those modern readings of Marlowe's poem that see it primarily as parody. Smith's poem is no more a 'translation' of a classical work than was Marlowe's; it is a travesty of the first of Ovid's *Heroides*, the epistle of Penelope to Ulysses. The travesty is not sustained very long, but a taste of Smith's boisterous and coarse method can be given in the following extract describing Ulysses' response to the letter he has received from Penelope imploring him to return home:

> When that Ulysses, all in grief enveloped,
> Had markt how right this Letter was Peneloped,
> Laid one hand on his heart, and said 't was guilty,
> Resting the other on his Dagger-hilty,
> Thus gan to speake: O thou that dost controule
> All beauties else, thou hast so bang'd my soule
> With this thy lamentation, that I sweare,
> I love thee strangely, without wit or fear;
> I could have wish'd (quoth he) myself the Paper,
> Inke, Standish, Sandbox or the burning Taper,
> That were the Instruments of this thy writeing
> Or else the Stool whereon thou sat'st inditing:
> And so might have bin neer that lovely breech
> That never yet was troubled with the Itch.[14]

This is very close to the coarse style Cotton adopts for his imitation of Scarron. The excruciatingly bad rhymes, the deliberate use of vulgarisms, the irregularities of metre became part of the stock-in-trade of Restoration burlesque poetry, and in many ways Smith must be considered the father of this particular style of burlesque. He was equally at home with the octosyllabic couplet as with heroic verse and Butler must have been familiar with his work, for the resemblance between the methods of the two poets is often striking. *Wit Restor'd* begins with a series of octosyllabic verse letters, a sub-genre much favoured by the court wits of the Restoration and even attempted by Dryden. The verse letters in *Wit Restor'd* were addressed to Smith's friend and fellow burlesque poet, Sir John Mennis, when Mennis was in the North fighting against the Scots (presumably in the early 1640s). One, for instance, describes the ruses Smith has to get up to in London to avoid his creditors. These include having to escape from his

lodgings and travel to where he will not be known in order to
persuade a tavern-owner to give him credit for dinner:

> To mend my commons, clad in jerkin,
> On Friday last I rode to Berkin,
> Where lowring heavens with welcome saucst us
> As when the Fiends were sent for *Faustus*
> Such claps of thunder, and such rain,
> That Poets will not stick to feign,
> The gods with too much Nectar sped,
> Their truckles drew, and piss'd a bed,
> And that they belsh'd from stomack musty
> Vapour, that made the weather gusty.
> Well, 'tis a sad condition, where
> A man must fast, or feed in fear.[15]

It is interesting to note again Smith's interest in Marlowe here·
Not only does Smith anticipate Butler's verse style in this passage,
but the poet's assumption of the role of clown, the comic butt of
the poem, is a role reflected in Butler's close relationship to his
clown-hero in *Hudibras*. This same self-mockery is a feature of
Rochester's burlesque poetry. Rochester himself is the comic butt
of both the *Imperfect Enjoyment* and the *Ramble in St James's Park* as
well as of shorter poems like *To the Postboy*. The negativeness of
burlesque shows in nothing so clearly as in this characteristic loss
of confidence in the dignity of the poet.

Although Smith's particular brand of coarse burlesque seems to
set the tone for most of the burlesque to follow in the Restoration
period, it is not itself totally unanticipated. Richard Corbett's
poems contain a considerable amount of burlesque including the
famous *Iter Boreale* that travesties Horace's *Journey to Brindisium*
(Satires I, v). Corbett's poem was written around 1620 and describes a journey to the North of England. In this poem the poet
is already using those techniques of bad rhyming, off-beat rhyth-
mical effects and distortions of language that are characteristic of
Hudibrastic verse. Corbett's poem, however, is much less eccen-
tric than Smith's poetry and most later Hudibrastic verse. It is
written not in octosyllables but in the more dignified heroic couplet. Much of the poem is genuinely witty, there is much shrewd
observation and occasionally the poem foreshadows the inspired
particularly of Rochester's social satire. Here, for instance, Corbett

is describing the hostess of the Swann Inn at Warwick (Inns and their keepers are a favourite subject of the poem):

> Her whole Behaviour borrowed was, and mixt,
> Half foole, half puppet and her pace betwixt
> Measure and Jigge; her court'sy was an honour;
> Her gate, as if her Neighbour had out-gon her.
> She was barrd up in whale-bones which doe leese
> None of the whales length; for they reach her knees:
> Off with her head, and then shee hath a middle:
> As her wast stands, shee lookes like the new-Fiddle,
> The favorite Theorbo (truth to tell yee)
> Whose neck and throat are deeper, then the belly.
> Have you seene Monkyes Chain'd about the Loynes,
> Or pottle-petts with rings? just soe she joynes
> Her self together.[16]

Clearly this owes a good deal to Jacobean satire, but the poem is not consistently satirical, the attack is haphazard and the point of view uncertainly established. Corbett is primarily concerned to make the reader laugh. The poem led to a spate of imitations of humorous journeys which continued into the Restoration with such poems as Charles Cotton's *Voyage to Ireland in Burlesque*. A special form of this burlesque journey may be represented by the 'ramble' poems of the Restoration such as Alexander Radcliffe's *Ramble* and Rochester's *Ramble in St James's Park*. Corbett's poem gets almost too good-humoured at times for burlesque and, rather than mock its subjects from time to time, is closer to celebrating them, there are even passages of warm commendation. It is common in burlesque, however, to divagate in tone because no positive or consistent attitude is controlling the point of view. We shall see the same phenomenon in *Hudibras*.

If Corbett's poem approaches comic celebration, Cotton's *Scarronides* is consistent in its determination to denigrate its subject matter, the story of Dido and Aeneas. Indeed Cotton's poem differs principally from its model, Paul Scarron's *Virgile Travesty*, in its singleminded reduction of Virgil's story to the level of the gutter. Scarron's poem manages a not unsubtle mixture of the crudely prosaic and the poetic and in many ways resembles the naïve mixture of enchantment and realism often found in French medieval Romances. Ariosto is alluded to in Scarron's poem and it seems to me not improbable that Scarron was attempting the creation of a sophisticated primitiveness in accordance with Italian models. In any case the result is much more pleasing and more poetic than Cotton's heavy-handed application of bathos at every turn. A comparison between their two versions of the same moment in the story of the *Aeneid* will be sufficient to bring out the essential difference and will show how much more Cotton was a disciple of James Smith than of Scarron. In their travesties of Book 1 of the *Aeneid* both poets describe the storm, which, through the wrath of Juno, brings Aeneas to Carthage, and how Aeneas first sees Dido as she dispenses justice to her people. Scarron's description of the moment retains something of the magic of the original in spite of its frequent plunges into bathos:

> Sous un grand dome lambrissé
> Dans un grand fauteuil tapissé,
> S'estant mise bien à son aise,
> On cria trois fois, Qu'on se taise.
> On luy presenta des placets:
> Cent Suisses portans cabassets
> Lors que la foule estoit trop grande
> Adioustoient à la reprimande
> Quelquefois des coups de baston,
> Quand bien elle eust esté Caton
> Elle n'eust pas mieux fait iustice,
> Elle ny prenoit nulle espice,
> La rendoit liberalement,
> Et tousjours équitablement;
> Elle ne prononçoit sentence
> Qui ne fut piece d'éloquence,
> Tout se iugeoit là sans apel
> Tant au Civil, qu'au Criminel,
> Et les affaires non plaidées
> Sans Advocats estoient vuidées:
> Quand quelqu'un estoit convaincu,
> On luy donnoit du pied au cul,
> Si s'estoit pour de grandes fautes
> On luy faisoit briser les costes.
> Enfin chacun estoit traitté
> Ainsi qu'il l'avoit merité. . . .[17]

[When she had made herself quite comfortable on a great up-
holstered chair under a great panelled dome, silence was demanded
three times. She was presented with petitions. Whenever the
crowd got too large a hundred helmetted Swiss guards sometimes
added baton blows to their reprimands. She would not have been
a better magistrate even if she had been Cato, she never took
bribes, giving justice liberally and always equitably; she never
gave a judgment that was not also a set-piece of rhetoric, all were
judged there without appeal, both civil and criminal alike and
cases which were not pleaded without lawyers were adjudged null
and void: when anyone was found guilty he was given a kick up
the arse, if it was for major crimes his ribs were broken. In short
each one was treated as he deserved.]

The deflation here is fairly mild, the humour depends on the use of
anachronism, the use of legal jargon and the occasional dig at
Virgil's style—as in the reference to Dido's eloquence—as much
as in the use of vulgarism. Cotton's imitation is far more willing to
indulge in vulgarism and coarse, bawdy humour. Scarron is careful
to keep his poetic style well-mannered and orderly: Cotton indulges in the boisterous disruptive techniques we have already
met with in James Smith's burlesque poetry:

> Even as a proper Woman showes
> When unto Wake, or Fair she goes,
> Clad in her best Apparel, so,
> Queen *Dido* all this time did show,
> And was so brave a Buxom Lass,
> That she did all i' th' Town surpass.
> Into the midst o' the' Church she marches,
> And there betwixt a pair of Arches,
> Upon a Stool set for the nonce,
> She went to rest her Marrow-bones,
> And on a Cushion stuff'd with Flocks,
> She clapt her dainty pair of Docks. [i.e. buttocks]
>   There *Dido* sate in State each day,
> To hear what any one could say,
> Some to rebuke, and for to smooth some;
> And give out Laws, wholsome, or toothsome;
> To punish such as had Insolence,
> And make them good Nolens, or Volens:

> And there likewise each morning-tide,
> She did the young mens Tasks divide,
> Wherein great Policy did lurk,
> Each knew his Jobbe of Journey-work,
> And fell about it without jangling:
> But that which kept them most from wrangling
> Was that they still drew Cuts to know,
> Whether they should work hard, or no;
> And who had th' longest cut, and th' best,
> Had still more work, then all the rest.[18]

The reference in the last lines puns on the bawdy meaning of 'cut' frequently found in Elizabethan English to stand for either the male or, more normally, the female sexual organs. Needless to say there is no parallel passage in either Scarron or Virgil. Here we get that style of 'anti-poetry' so characteristic of seventeenth-century English burlesque where all the rules of poetic good manners are flouted. Rhymes like Insolence/Volens; nonce/bones and especially those feminine rhymes so beloved of Butler, smooth some/ toothsome; jangling/wrangling. The rhythmic devices, too, recall Butler and their common inspiration, James Smith. The simple and regular rhythm achieved by firm end-stopping of the octo-syllabic line is broken into arbitrarily and often against the emphasis required by the syntax, as in:

> But that which kept them most from wrangling
> Was, that they still drew Cuts to know,
> Whether they should work hard, or no:

Often the normal accentuation of words has to be ignored as in 'Nolēns or Volens'. By this defiance of convention, which has no other purpose than to disrupt accepted and expected pattern, the burlesque poet creates disorder out of order. This is the exact reverse of the proper function of the poet which, in John Dennis' words, was to create order out of disorder:

> The great Design of the Arts is to restore the Decays that happen'd to human Nature by the Fall, by restoring order . . . can any thing be more ridiculous than to imagine, that Poetry itself should be without Rule or Order?[19]

Burlesque is not 'without Rule or Order', but the order exists mainly for the delight of breaking it. In seventeenth-century burlesque we see the delight in the earlier concept of an orderly creation being replaced by the jaundiced, sceptical view of a fragmented universe or, at least, by a view of man's inability to envision a harmonious universe. Most burlesque poets were not aware that they were doing any more than trying to entertain, but the fact that people *could* now so readily be entertained in this way is a symptom of a disillusionment with the concepts of order, rather than a firm confidence that such concepts are so inviolable that they can be safely treated comically. The seventeenth-century poet was fully aware that, as Aubrey put it, 'printing and gunpowder had . . . frightened away Robin good fellow and the Fayries'.[20] Aubrey is not alone in linking the disillusionment with the struggle for power during the Civil War, but the mood had set in before then, as the earlier rise of burlesque might suggest. Bishop Corbett (though not yet bishop) blames the Reformation in his nostalgic and comic Ballad *The Faeryes Farewell*:

> By which wee note the Faries
>   Were of the old Profession;
> Theyre Songs were Ave Maryes,
>   Theyre Daunces were Procession.
> But now, alas, they all are dead,
>   Or gone beyond the Seas,
> Or Farther for Religion fled,
>   Or else they take theyre Ease.[21]

For every generation the Fall of man was some time ago, but in the second half of the seventeenth century they felt they could date it more accurately than most.

To no poet was this mood of disenchantment more temperamentally congenial than to Samuel Butler. If the Fall had not already occurred one feels that Samuel Butler would have had to invent it. It is no coincidence that this morbid, sardonic temperament should have created the most impressive burlesque poem of the century. *Hudibras* is, however, relieved by a farcical action and an exuberance of sardonic invention that makes it more congenial than most burlesque. Butler could be much more unequivocally destructive than he is in that poem. In a poem called a *Satyr upon the Weakness and Misery of Man* Butler presents us with a satire on mankind that outbids all others in its unrelieved gloom. There is a positive delight in piling up insults and denigrations of his own species:

> All this is nothing to the Evils,
> Which *men*, and their confed'rate Devils
> Inflict, to aggravate the Curse
> On their own hated Kind, much worse;
> As if by Nature th' had been serv'd
> More gently, than their Fate deserv'd,
> Take pains (in Justice) to invent,
> And study their own Punishment;
> That, as their Crimes should greater grow,
> So might their own Inflictions too.
> Hence bloody *Wars* at first began,
> The artificial *Plague* of Man,
> That from his own Invention rise,
> To scourge his own Iniquities;
> That if the Heav'ns should chance to spare
> Supplies of constant poison'd Air,
> They might not, with unfit Delay,
> For lingering Destruction stay;
> Nor seek Recruits of *Death* so far,
> But plague themselves with *Blood* and *War*.[22]

Butler goes on to express a view that Rochester was to develop in *his* satire against mankind, that the worst of all man's evils was his own propensity for intellectual speculation:

> Is busy in finding Scruples out,
> To languish in eternal doubt.

Rochester's viewpoint, however, is enriched by ironies quite outside Butler's range. Butler's account of man gives the impression that it is being written by a member of another species. Rochester's poem is built on the irony that the speaker of the diatribe against mankind is himself a man. What concerns us here is that Butler's poem makes use of those same burlesque methods that he uses more comically and more successfully in *Hudibras*. We can hardly call this poem burlesque because it is without comedy, and because, for all its destructiveness of man, its viewpoint is consistent, but both the declared attitudes and the poetic techniques are similar to those of his burlesque poetry.

Hudibras, which is burlesque in our definition, shares with the
Satyr upon the Weakness and Misery of Man an equal fondness for
disruptive techniques and the same underlying contempt for mankind. What makes it burlesque rather than satire is the exuberant
comedy and the lack of a consistent viewpoint. As I have argued
elsewhere, the source of the comedy is very uncertain.[23] On the
one hand we are asked to laugh at Hudibras for his fanatical
Presbyterianism, on the other hand we come to admire him for his
resiliance and even his courage. The ambiguous and confusing
role of the hero is seen clearly in the fight of Hudibras and Ralpho
with the bearkeeper Orsin and his companions. Hudibras is presented as both a courageous, if quixotic, knight errant 'recollecting
wonted courage' (I, iii, 451)[24] and as a cowardly buffoon making
sure he keeps himself out of harm's way as long as possible:

> And placing Ralpho in the front
> Reserv'd himself to bear the brunt. (I, iii, 462)

This is the warrior whose sword had grown rusty for 'want of
fighting' (I, i, 358):

> And ate into it self for lack
> Of somebody to hew and hack

but, oddly enough, whose dagger seems to be in common use:

> When it had stabb'd or broke a head,
> It would scrape Trenchers, or chip Bread. (I, i, 379–80)

Hudibras' behaviour is equally inconsistent, for he is not only the
hot-tempered knight thirsting to go into battle against Orsin,
ready 'with trusty sword and spur,/For fame and honour to wage
battle' (I, ii, 742–3), but he is also the hero who argues:

> In all the trade of War, no feat
> Is nobler than a brave retreat.
> For those that Run away, and fly,
> Take Place at least of th' Enemey (I, iii, 607–10)

Such inconsistencies are, of course, the stuff of comedy if they are
presented *as* inconsistencies. But Butler presents them as irrecon-
cilable contradictions—Hudibras either does use his sword or he
doesn't—Butler *tells* us that he doesn't and shows us that he does.

The case of the ambivalent sword, trivial in itself, is symptomatic of Butler's uncertain attitude to his hero. For Hudibras is both the comic butt and the poet's representative in the poem. Hudibras is both cowardly knave and clown-hero. The voice Butler uses for his own comments is identical with that used by the hero: they both have a scorn for orderliness, decorum, restraint; they are both fonder of clowning with words than establishing meaning. Butler, as poet, is as bent on playing the clown as is his hero:

> They rode, but Authors having not
> Determin'd whether Pace or Trot,
> (That is to say, whether *Tollutation*,
> As they do term't, or *Succussation*)
> We leave it, and go on, as now
> Suppose they did, no matter how.
> Yet some from subtle hints have got
> Mysterious light, it was a Trot. (I, ii, 45–52)

Here Butler is characteristically mocking the function of poet that he is himself engaged in. Such a contradictory attitude stems from the curious inconsistency at the heart of his own thought in which he proclaims his contempt for the very thing he is doing and for the very being he is. At the heart of *Hudibras* lies the curious paradox that it is a poem written to decry poetry, to mock the conventions of patterned orderliness without which poetry cannot exist. Not surprisingly, he elsewhere shows a contempt for poetry and poets.[25] But then Butler shows a dislike for almost everything to do with mankind.

Hudibras remains something of a paradox and because of its popularity it has come to give burlesque, of which it is the most notable example in the language, a paradoxical status. As a masterpiece of comic exuberance, it succeeds for long stretches in hiding those elements of repudiation and negativeness that are, nevertheless, so strong a feature of the poem as a whole that the work has often been mistaken for satire. But the negativeness of *Hudibras* is not that of the satirist, who destroys in order to rebuild. There is little in the poem to suggest an alternative to the mad world of author and hero alike. It has the lack of direction that we have seen as a characteristic of burlesque of a literary kind, and its effect therefore on the reader is to confuse and ultimately destroy the world that it seeks to create.

Rochester's Burlesque Poetry

Rochester was undoubtedly influenced by Butler. In the *Satire against Reason and Mankind*, though a poem of much greater complexity than Butler's *Satyr upon the Weakness and Misery of Mankind*, he deals with similar attitudes. Rochester was also occasionally influenced by the burlesque techniques that Butler and Cotton between them did so much to popularise. Rochester, however, has too much respect for form, for patterned orderliness, to find burlesque methods congenial. His life as a poet is a search for a satisfactory basis for imposing pattern on words, much as his life as a man can be seen as a constant, often desperate and eventually successful, search for a pattern in life itself. In only a very few poems does he abandon the role in which the poet asserts his ultimate control over his material. Even when he himself becomes a comic character in his own poem—as in the *Imperfect Enjoyment* —he remains sufficiently aloof from his material *as poet* to give the poetry an imposed coherence that the experience described does not have. It is not by coincidence that the nearest he gets to the adoption of the denigratory techniques of burlesque proper is in the most nihilistic of all his poems, the *Ramble in St James's Park*, a poem that is more profoundly a poem of repudiation than the paradoxical *Upon Nothing*.

The three poems that are my principal subject in this part of my chapter, the *Imperfect Enjoyment,* the *Ramble in St James's Park* and *Signior Dildo*, all seem to have been written close together (Vieth allots them to the years 1672–3). All three have as their central concern the mockery of the one human experience that elsewhere in his poetry he holds up as meaningful: human love:

> That Cordial drop, Heav'n in our *lap* has thrown,
> To make the nauseous draught of life go down.

We have already seen how in the anti-platonic love poetry Rochester can deride the values he elsewhere upholds for human sexual experience. In his burlesque poetry he goes further than in most of his lyrics, especially in the *Ramble*, by showing love as a degrading experience and, therefore, an archetypal situation for demonstrating the fatuousness, the essential meaninglessness, of all human experience. The *Ramble* in particular is a nightmare

8

vision of the betrayal by man of the one value that can give him the illusion of a meaningful existence, a theme which is taken up again in *Artemisia to Chloe*, but there given less despairing treatment.

As in *Hudibras*, poet and protagonist are clearly related in the *Ramble*. By using an indecorous Hudibrastic verse form Rochester associates himself as poet with the clown-hero whose role is to express the humiliation forced on him by his mistress' undiscriminating promiscuity. The theme is not unlike that of the *Imperfect Enjoyment*. In both poems the hero (the poet himself) is sexually humiliated and swears revenge on the source of his humiliation. But in the *Imperfect Enjoyment* the offending member is the man's own member, while in the *Ramble*, the mistress herself is the ostensible enemy. *Imperfect Enjoyment* treats the humiliation much more lightly than the poet is willing or able to do in the *Ramble*. The mistress who chooses to fornicate with three 'asses' in preference to the poet becomes not simply a particular example of love's betrayal but a symbol of womankind as betrayer:

> Whoever had been by to see
> The proud Disdain she cast on me,
> Through Charming Eyes, he wou'd have Swore
> She dropt from Heav'n that very Hour,
> Forsaking the Divine Aboad
> In scorn of some despairing God.
> But mark what Creatures Women are,
> So infinitely Vile and Fair.

The promise of heaven, a promise fulfilled in some of the lyrics, turns out to be a 'hell in heaven's despite' (to quote Blake). The experience which in the lyrics is seen (on occasions) as 'everlasting rest', the love that snatches the 'livelong minute' and 'makes us blest at last' turns out, not only to be the source of humiliation and frustration, but an indication of the absurd compulsions which lead men and women to this humiliation and disappointment. For Corinna is not the real villainess of this poem; like the poet, she is the victim of the universal compulsion to seek a humiliating and nauseous sexual satisfaction. The poem is a protest against the tyranny of sexual drives. Rochester sees *St James's Park* not as a fashionable place for assignations, but as a sacred grove where we are tormented and humiliated by sexual compulsions which there possess us. It is a vision of man, and indeed all nature, possessed by Dionysian frenzies:

> There, by most Incestuous Birth,
> Strange Woods spring from the teeming Earth:
> For they relate, how heretofore,
> When Ancient *Pict* began to Whore,
> Deluded of his Assignation,
> (Jilting it seems was then in fashion),
> Poor pensive Lover in this place
> Wou'd Frig upon his Mothers Face;
> Whence Rows of Mandrakes tall did rise,
> Whose Lewd tops Fuck'd the very Skies.
> Each imitated Branch do's twine
> In some Love Fold of Aretine:
> And nightly now beneath their Shade
> Are Bugg'ries, Rapes and Incests made,
> Unto this All-sin-sheltring Grove,
> Whores of the Bulk and the Alcove,
> Great Ladies, Chambermaids and Drudges,
> The Rag-picker and Heiress trudges;
> Car-men, Divines, great Lords and Taylers;
> Prentices, Pimps, Poets, and Gaolers,
> Foot-boys, fine Fops, do here arrive,
> And here promiscuously they Swive,

The picture of humanity, men equally with women, rich equally with poor, rushing like Gaderene swine under the compulsion to fornicate promiscuously is seen to apply not only to his own generation, but to belong to us as a species. We merely follow our barbaric ancestors. Humanity, it seems, is obeying a law of nature itself and human sexual compulsions are merely the human expression of a force that has caused strange woods to spring from the 'teeming Earth'. The reference to the ancient Picts masturbating on the earth in their sexual frustration links human sexuality to the natural world and the primitive world of the savage to the human world of Rochester's contemporaries. Rochester nicely mixes the language of his own day ('Jilting it seems was then in fashion' and the 'poor pensive lover') with the reference to the primitive Frigga the Scandanavian goddess of fertility.[26] (The slang word 'frigg', meaning 'to masturbate' or 'achieve orgasm' is clearly

derived from the name of the goddess and the capital letter in the
1680 version of Rochester's poem, unusual with a verb, suggests
that the editor is preserving Rochester's intention of associating
the verb with the proper noun—this reading is obscured in the
Gyldenstolpe reading given by Vieth.) The mythological element
in the description is re-enforced by the grotesque account of the
mandrakes that rise from the impregnated earth-mother in turn to
continue the universal obligation that all things must reproduce
themselves. That human beings in their turn 'imitate' the inter-
twining limbs of the natural world to seek for one another in
'buggeries, rapes, incest' merely shows that humanity is as caught
up in the compulsion as every other part of nature. Again,
Rochester associates primitive and sophisticated, mythic and
natural, (the trees of the Park as mandrakes, the branches as the
limbs depicted in Aretino's postures) to give us a vision of a world
impelled by a blind fury of fornication.

The poet's anger and frustration, therefore, is not against
Corinna, primarily or ultimately, but about the humiliation of
being caught up in this blind compulsion. His resentment is not
against Corinna's promiscuity as such (for who can escape the
universal law) but that her choice of fornicating companions alights
on vain, brainless creatures that cannot even see the absurdity of
the madness by which they are afflicted:

> Some Pow'r more patient now relate
> The Sence of this surprizing Fate.
> Gods! that a thing admir'd by me,
> Should taste so much of Infamy!
> Had she pick'd out to rub her Arse on,
> Some stiff-Prick'd Clown, or well hung Parson,
> Each Job of whose Spermatick Sluce
> Had fill'd her Cunt with wholsome Juice,
> I the proceeding shou'd have prais'd,
> In hope she had quencht a Fire I rais'd:
> Such nat'ral freedoms are but Just,
> There's something gen'rous in meer Lust;
> But to turn Damn'd Abandon'd *Jade*,
> When neither *Head* nor *Tail* persuade?
> To be a *Whore* in understanding,
> A Passive *Pot* for *Fools* to spend in,

> The *Devil* plaid Booty sure with thee,
> To bring a Blot of Infamy.

The poet does not complain here that the lady is doing what is natural. Had she fornicated with 'clown' (country yokel) or parson, both assumed to be sexually able and therefore suitable for assuaging the pangs of nature, the poet would have had no objection. Instead she chooses the feeble and stupid and so 'whores her understanding', neither satisfying her tail (her sexual drive) nor her head (her liking for someone intelligent, but also her sense of the ridiculous). Both clown and parson for different reasons would supply satisfaction at both ends—to the head because the absurdity of a fine lady fornicating with such unfashionable people would suitably heighten the absurdity of the whole proceeding.

D. H. Griffin argues that the 'libertine' (the poet's *persona*) in this poem contradicts himself by refusing Corinna the sexual liberty he himself demands and that we are meant to see Rochester's poem therefore as an ironic comment on the libertine point of view.[27] This presupposes a detachment that is alien to the tone of the poem. The burlesque method is deliberately used to avoid such an impression. There is nothing in the poem to suggest that the libertine's anger is not the poet's anger, no formal control that can be measured against the libertine's railing. The point of the poem, as I have argued, is that we are all victims of this sexual madness and the poet is complaining not about Corinna as a person but about Corinna as the feminine representative of the sexual principle that so dominates mankind. The poet is obsessed by the nightmare of being totally absorbed in the world's cunt, and Corinna becomes the devotee of the fertility goddess Frigga. Drawn into this world of sexual frenzy, detachment becomes impossible and the poet's fear is that he has lost what control he may once have had. The detachment of poetic artistry even has been lost. The madness of the final curse on Corinna has been brought about by a vision of the pervading power of sexual compulsion, and the curse attempts the impossible: to hold back the sexual powers that control us. Corinna's preference for the stupid and the sexually incompetent merely demonstrates the overwhelming power of the sexual itch. The poem ends, therefore, with a frenzy of hatred against this power and the human centre of this power, the feminine genitalia. The poem is a hymn of hatred at man's

humiliation by the White Goddess in her aspect of devouring
sow.[28] The mad poet, like the mad King Lear, would like to 'dry
up the agent of increase', hoping:

> You may go Mad for the *North Wind*
> And fixing all your hopes upon't
> To have him Bluster in your *Cunt*.
> Turn up your longing Arse to th' Air,
> And Perish in the wild despair . . .
> But my Revenge will best be tim'd,
> When she is *Mari'd* that is lim'd,
> In that most lamentable State,
> I'll make her feel my Scorn and Hate;
> Pelt her with Scandals, Truth, or Lies,
> And her poor Cur with Jealousies.
> Till I have torn him from her *Breech*,
> While she whines like a *Dog-drawn Bitch*.

The frenzy of hatred is absurdly excessive addressed merely to the
reasons stated, that Corinna has preferred three fops to him. But
the return to a grotesque level, in which the cunt (now thought of
as something like a cave) is blasted by the north wind and in which
human love is compared to dogs refusing a bitch in heat, shifts the
emphasis back from the personal to the general, reminds us that
the anger is directed not simply at Corinna and her three fools, but
at the ludicrous predicament mankind is driven into by the search
for sexual satisfaction.

The *Ramble in St James's Park* is the most frighteningly nihilistic
of all Rochester's poems. The more frightening because its subject, human sexuality, is of such crucial importance in Rochester's
search for existential meaning. The burlesque methods proclaim a
world of frantic lust that turns love into hate and over which the
poet has lost all control. The poem is grimly comic, however, in
that he sees the predicament as inherently absurd. The sardonic
humour constantly reminds us of the incongruities between our
ideals of love and the obsessive quality of our sexuality. There are
superb juxtapositions of the polite and the crude, the natural and
the unnatural, that bring us up sharply against the difference
between our dream of love and the actuality of our lust:

> One in a strain twixt Tune and Nonsense,
> Cries, *Madam, I have lov'd you long since,*

Permit me your fair Hand to kiss:
When at her Mouth her Cunt says Yes.

The bad rhyme is an inspired way of revealing the anatomical distortion required. Samuel Butler never wrote two more sardonic
couplets.

Both *Imperfect Enjoyment* and *Signior Dildo* are burlesques of a
lighter vein. In both, greater detachment is obtained through the
exertion of tighter formal control: the heroic couplet in *Imperfect
Enjoyment*, a tetrameter four-line stanza in *Signior Dildo*. Both make
merry over the oddities of human sexual behaviour. In the *Imperfect Enjoyment* the subject is that treated in the lyric the *Fall*, the
failure of the male member to rise adequately to the sexual occasion. In *Signior Dildo* the thrust is at a feminine target. Although
both poems have it as their first aim to make the reader laugh, in
both Rochester is on one of his favourite subjects, the laughable
frailty and unreliability of the one pleasure that is worth living for.
The subject of *Signior Dildo* is also related to that of the *Ramble in
St James's Park*, the avid demands of womankind for sexual satisfaction. But in this poem it is treated much less as a threat and
much more as a comic condition of human intercourse (both
sexual and otherwise). The burlesque also contains some element
of literary parody that is absent from both the *Ramble* and the
Imperfect Enjoyment, for the story of the invasion of the polite circles
of English society by a foreigner who threatens to oust the native
English product from its rightful place is told in the manner of the
street ballad. The metre Rochester adopts for his four-line stanza
is basically anapaestic tetrameter with iambic admixture, and there
are a considerable number of variant lines that give the rhythm the
characteristic uncertainty of accent of the street ballad. The main
purpose of this element of parody is perhaps to suggest that English ladies must rally to their own flag—or at least their own flag-
poles—a patriotic call of the type heard from the ballad singers.
The actual occasion of the poem, as David Vieth informs us, was
the arrival of James, Duke of York's new Duchess with her
Italian entourage. Signior Dildo (the dildo was an artificial penis
usually made of wood and leather) is said to be a gentleman who
arrives with the Duchess. As his merits become known among the
fashionable ladies they begin to compete for his favours, and the
poet suggest that the men who cater for the ladies' sexual appetites

will soon be out of a job. The middle section of the poem gives
Rochester an opportunity for naming some of the more notorious
of the female lechers of fashionable society, though the purpose of
this is less in the hope of reforming than of pointing out the
prevalence of promiscuous behaviour among the women. There is
little satirical content in the poem, the poet enjoying the absurdity
of a situation he basically asks us to accept. The great success of
Signior Dildo naturally causes resentment among the gentlemen
who are being excluded from their accustomed favours:

> A rabble of pricks who were welcome before,
> Now finding the Porter denied 'em the door,
> Maliciously waited his coming below
> And inhumanly fell on Signior Dildo.

The Englishmen pursue the foreign interloper along Pall Mall to
the dismay of the women who cry out 'for heaven's sake, save
Signior Dildo'. The Italian is only saved because the English are
impeded from outstripping him by the extra weights they have
and that the dildo is free from. This extremely funny burlesque
poem (shocking only to the very impure) shows perhaps better
than any other of Rochester's poems his ability to see the absurdity
of human behaviour. Such comic detachment, achieved primarily
through the element of parody, surely puts paid to those sugges-
tions that would see in his grimmer explorations of human
sexuality a pathological element that prevented him from getting
such matters into focus. It is the reader who cannot enjoy *Signior
Dildo* for the splendid comic poem it is, who is failing to respond
with maturity to the poetry.

Signior Dildo is at the other extreme of light-hearted burlesque
from the highly denigratory burlesque of the *Ramble*. The *Imperfect
Enjoyment* comes somewhere in between. It is perhaps as funny as
Signior Dildo, but with a rather more serious purpose than simply
enjoying the vagaries of human sexuality. For, like the *Ramble,* it
is about sexual disappointment, though the role of the villain is
now taken over, not by the lady, but by the recalcitrant penis,
which turns out to be quite as unreliable and treacherous as
Corinna was in the *Ramble*. The curse to which this 'trecherous,
base deserter' of the poet's flame is subjected at the end of the
poem has not the force of genuine malevolence. This is mainly

because the poem is written in an orderly heroic couplet giving a firm sense that the poet is in command of affairs.

As R. E. Quaintance has shown, in an interesting article on the *Imperfect Enjoyment* poem as a minor seventeenth-century genre,[29] Rochester's poem is one of the last of a series of French and English poems on the subject of sexual disappointment that have as their ultimate origins Ovid's *Amores* (III, vii) and sections 128–40 of Petronius' *Satyricon*. Quaintance lists five such poems in French and five in English, three of which are close adaptations of French modes. Rochester's poem seems to lean rather more closely on Petronius than Ovid, for it is from Petronius that he gets the elaborate curse on his inadequately virile member that ends the poem. Compared to other examples, Rochester's poem is less concerned with rousing erotic feeling in the reader and more concerned with the after effects of his sexual failure. The result is to considerably increase the comic element, with the poet himself as the comic butt as he strives in vain to cooperate with his lady in getting the obstinate penis to try again after its premature ejaculation. Rochester's poem contains the strongest burlesque element compared to other examples. Etherege's version, itself an adaptation of a French poem, *La Iovissance Imparfaite* by Charles Beys published in 1651, has a somewhat moralistic tone as he blames the lady for putting up too much resistance. As in Rochester's poem, the problem is premature ejaculation, though Rochester puts the blame on his own over-eagerness. Rochester's lady could hardly be more cooperative. Etherege spends far more time describing the foreplay as the lover tries to persuade the lady to allow him access, only to find she has left it too late:

> Alas, said I, condemn yourself, not me;
> This is the effect of too much modesty.[30]

Etherege's poem is of the witty, masculine kind, familiar from anti-platonic, lyrical poetry, where the lady's coyness is the subject of complaint.

Aphra Behn's poem, *The Disappointment*, on the other hand, is spiritedly feminist and puts the blame fairly and squarely on the man's lack of control. Like Etherege's poem, Mrs Behn's is an adaptation of a French model, in this case a poem called *L'Occasion perdue recouverte* by Cantenac, published around 1660. Whereas Cantenac's poem ends happily, however, with a successful second attempt, Mrs Behn, like Etherege and Rochester, ends her poem with the lovers' disappointment. Aphra Behn's poem, published along with Rochester's poems in the *Poems on Several Occasions* of 1680, but possibly written before Rochester's poem, could well be an answer to Etherege. Like the lady in Rochester's poem, Aphra Behn's Cloris is highly cooperative, and it is the lover who fails 'the blessed minutes to improve'. This gives Mrs Behn the opportunity to build up the erotic tension, for the disaster does not occur until more than half way through the poem (in Rochester's poem it has happened by line 15 in a 72 line poem). It also enables her to blame the lover for selfishness in trying to prolong his pleasure unreasonably:

> Ready to taste a *Thousand* Joys,
> Thee too transported hapless Swain,
> Found the vast *Pleasure* turn'd to Pain:
> *Pleasure*, which too much Love destroys.[31]

This is somewhat ambiguous (it is not clear whether love is destroying pleasure or pleasure destroying love), but in any case Mrs Behn has no doubt it is the lover's fault and she has her fair nymph show her displeasure by stalking off 'Leaving him fainting on the gloomy bed' while he is 'damn'd to the Hell of Impotence'; a spirited feminist ending.

The villain of Rochester's poem is neither the lover nor his mistress, but the wayward penis. As in the *Ramble* we are asked in this poem to see men (and women) as victims of a power which neither can control. Rochester's curse on his penis is primarily aimed at its unpredictability; his complaint, like that against Corinna in the *Ramble*, is that it humiliates him and makes him look a fool:

> Stiffly resolved, twou'd carelessly invade
> *Woman* or *Boy*, nor ought its fury staid,
> Where e're it pierc'd, a Cunt it found or made.
> Now languid lies in this unhappy hour,
> Shrunk up and Sapless, like a wither'd Flower.[32]

But the vehemence of the curse in the *Ramble* is considerably modified here by the unmistakable mock heroic element. The lance-like weapon 'stiffly resolved' to force its way through the thick and thin of either sex presents us with a comic image rather

than an image of genuine threat. It is the absurdity of man's vulnerability that is exposed here (along with the offending weapon).
It is still burlesque because the poet has no remedy to suggest or
imply for his comic humiliation, it is incident to all men we must
assume. But the poet's ability to laugh gives the conclusion a certain amount of detachment. And this applies even as the language
of abuse rises (unlike the object abused) to a crescendo at the end
of the poem. The very exaggeration prevents us from taking the
curse too seriously:

> But if great *Love*, the onset does command,
> Base Recreant, to thy *Prince*, thou dar'st not stand.
> Worst part of me, and henceforth hated most,
> Through all the town a common fucking post,
> On whom each *Whore*, relieves her tingling *Cunt*,
> As *Hogs*, or *Goats* do rub themselves and grunt,
> May'st thou to rav'nous *Shankers*, be a *Prey*,
> Or in consuming *Weepings* waste away.
> May *Stranguaries*, and *Stone*, thy *Days* attend,
> Mayst thou ne're Piss, who didst refuse to spend,
> When all my Joys did on False thee depend.
> And may *Ten Thousand* abler *Pricks* agree,
> To do the wronged *Corinna*, right for thee.

The absurdity and the humiliation is in having to depend on such
a meagre and uncooperative object for 'all our joys'. Man is as
much at the mercy of the God Priapus as on all the other equally
wayward and malicious gods.

If the three poems we have so far been discussing represent
people as victims of Priapus the *Maim'd Debauchee* represents an
attempt to fight back. The result is again rather absurd, but at
least man is not merely the passive victim of his sexual compulsions. As in the other burlesque poems we have been discussing
the emphasis is on the comedy of sexuality. In the earlier poems,
however, the characteristic denigratory note of burlesque is
apparent, two of the poems ending with elaborate curses and the
third, *Signior Dildo*, containing a series of denigratory portraits of
lecherous women. In none of these poems are different, superior
standards being asserted even by implication; the *Ramble* might
suggest that Corinna's promiscuity is reprehensible but it also, as I
have argued, seems to see it as inevitable. The guilty penis is

certainly offensive in the *Imperfect Enjoyment* but Rochester is the last to suggest seriously that the offending member should be struck off. The comedy is that we are so attached to so unreliable an aid, just as in *Signior Dildo* the comedy comes from the ladies' avidity for a piece of wood and leather. But in the *Maim'd Debauchee* there is a more deliberate ambiguity. Two quite distinct sets of values are placed side by side, the heroic and the erotic, and it is not at all clear whether we are meant to approve or disapprove of either. As in *Signior Dildo*, there is an element of literary parody in the *Maim'd Debauchee*. The stanza form is that used by William Davenant for his epic poem *Gondibert,* which Dryden in his turn used for *Annus Mirabilis*. Perhaps Rochester was thinking of Dryden's poem in particular because the poem opens by comparing the maimed debauchee to an old Admiral looking back at his heroic exploits. The effect of this opening simile is to convey the ambiguity of mock heroic; we are uncertain whether the comparison of the lecher to the admiral heightens the status of the former by association or lowers it by contrast. Are we to see the impotent lecher urging on the younger men to heroic feats of love as a man heroically defying old age or as a nasty old voyeur corrupting the young? For there is something admirable in the speaker's determination to die as he has lived, living up (as far as he can) to his libertine principles:

> My Pains at last some Respite shall afford,
> Whilst I behold the Battens you maintain,
> When Fleets of Glasses sail about the Board,
> From whose Broad sides Volleys of Wit shall rain.

> Nor shall the sight of Honourable Scars,
> Which my too forward Valour did procure,
> Frighten new-listed Souldiers from the Wars:
> Past Joys have more than paid what I endure.

The ambiguity is not just a question of general interpretation here, but stems from the juxtaposition of detail. Are not the scars (presumably caused by venereal disease) more likely to frighten the new recruits than encourage them or (by analogy with fighting men) will it stimulate the young men to equal heroism? Rochester steers a fine course between two opposing interpretations here, as he does in the *Song of the Young Lady to her Ancient Lover*. The source of the comedy is in the incongruity between two ways of looking at things—the heroic and the hedonistic—which are juxtaposed by being equated and yet are essentially opposed. The poem is centred on a paradox that is developed further in the last stanza:

> Thus Statesman like I'll saucily impose,
> And safe from Danger, valiantly advise,
> Shelter'd in impotence, urge you to Blows,
> And being good for nothing else, be wise.

The identification of heroic and libertine values here is complete and *contrasted* with the unheroic and unlibertine attitude forced on admiral and debauchee alike by old age.

Rochester's delight in controlled paradox is apparent in much of his work. It is central to the *Satyr against Reason and Mankind* and *Upon Nothing,* both of which poems share some of the uncertainty and ambiguity of the burlesque poetry: indeed, *Upon Nothing* could almost as well be treated here as in the chapter on satire. In paradox Rochester saw the contradictoriness of man's general situation, his need to find meaning in a meaningless world, his need to find spiritual fulfilment in carnal pleasure, his attempt to understand the feelings that his understanding destroyed. These paradoxes are central to Rochester's view of the world and in the *Maim'd Debauchee* he demonstrates the relativity of our judgments and the impossibility of seeing experience singly or seeing it whole. Burlesque is an expression of this comic uncertainty. But Rochester was not content to remain in uncertainty and the satires show him attempting to build a structure of coherent thought and feeling on the shifting grounds of relative and uncertain judgment. The *Maim'd Debauchee* by its strict command of form and its superbly controlled juxtaposition of contradictory ideas is, more than any of the other burlesque poems, an assertion of the poet's ability to create a coherent structure out of uncertainty.

The Lampoons and Personal Satires

But before we turn to the satire proper we can briefly examine an important group of poems that share with burlesque the purpose of denigration and destruction, but where the comic tone of burlesque frequently gives way to a tone of hatred. In his conversations with Gilbert Burnet, Rochester admitted that he considered

malice an important element in satire, though his major satires are
noticeably free from it.[33] Butler too shared this view:

> There is nothing that Provokes and Sharpens wit like Malice
> and Anger. . . . And hence perhaps came the first occasion of
> calling those Raptures Poeticall Fury. For Malice is a kinde of
> Madnes (For if Men run mad for Love, why should they not as
> well do so for Hate?) And as mad men are say'd to have in their
> fits double the Strength they had before, so have Malitious men
> the wit. He who first found out Iambiques; and before with all
> his wit and Fancy could not prevayle with the Father of his
> Mistress to keep but his Promise with him; had no sooner
> turned his Love into Hate, but he forced him with the bitterness
> of his New Rhimes so to hang himself. So much Power has
> Malice above all other Passions, to highten wit and Fancy, for
> Malice is restles, and never findes ease untill it has vented it self.
> And therefore Satyrs that are only provok'd with the Madnes
> and Folly of the world, are found to conteine more wit, and
> Ingenuity then all other writings whatsoever, and meet with a
> better reception from the world.[34]

Butler goes on to link the power of satire with witchcraft and
elsewhere expresses a preference for satire over all other kinds.
The link with magic and sorcery is confirmed by modern scholars.
R. C. Elliott in his book the *Power of Satire* points out that many
peoples have institutions where satire is used as a potent means of
establishing conformity or precedence and that satire has been
known at times to have the power to kill.[35] Malice certainly plays a
part in providing satire with its energy and power, but, as I have
been arguing earlier, satire as a literary form must be seen as
ultimately constructive, and if malice is used to destroy, charity
must be used to rebuild. So at any rate did seventeenth-century
commentators on satire believe.[36] I have chosen to follow
seventeenth-century theory by considering such destructive lampooning separately from satire because I think it is closer to
burlesque in the negative impulses that motivate it.

Rochester's lampoons certainly are powerful enough at times to
do considerable damage to his opponents' reputations and it must
have taken a great deal of resilience not to succumb to his on-
slaughts. On at least two occasions Rochester found himself engaged in fierce verbal battles with opponents as tough as he was.

Such flyting matches were not uncommon in the seventeenth century, though few had the vehemence of Rochester's disputes with Sir Carr Scroope and John Sheffield, Earl of Mulgrave. The details of his quarrels with these men are not of great importance, but it is important to account, if we can, for the power of the invective which he hurls at his opponents.

Scroope's relationship with Rochester seems to have been originally amicable, for the lyric Scroope contributes to Etherege's *Man of Mode* beginning 'As Amoret with Phyllis sat' contains a complimentary reference (apparently) to Rochester under his usual soubriquet of Strephon. Rochester's allusion to Scroope as the 'purblind knight' in the *Allusion to Horace* is far from complimentary, however, Rochester accusing him of picking 'silly faults' in his verse. Rochester compounded the insult in writing his mock version of Scroope's lyric 'I cannot change as others do', which contains an even worse insult on the lady Scroope was addressing. Scroope replied with a poem *In Defence of Satire* in which he not only states the case for the moral purpose of satire, but turns on Rochester as an example of unlicensed malice. Satire, writes Scroope, should have a reforming purpose:

> So when a vice Ridiculous is made
> Our Neighbours Shame keeps us from growing bad.[37]

Poets have a special responsibility in satire since they have a special power:

> Those and a Thousand Fools unmention'd here
> Hate Poets all becaus they Poets feare.[38]

Having outlined the proper function of a satirical poet, he presents a portrait of Rochester as far more dangerous than the genuine satirist because he uses his influence immorally:

> He that can Rail at one he calls his Friend
> Or hear him absent wrong'd and not defend,
> Who for the sake of some ill natur'd jest
> Tells what he should Conceale, invents the rest.
> To Fatall midnight frolicks can betray
> His brave Companions Life then run away,
> Leaveing him to be murder'd in the Street
> Then putt it off with some Buffoon conceipt,

> This, This is he, you shou'd beware of all,
> Yet him a witty pleasant Man you call,
> To whett your dull Debauches up and down
> You seek him as Topp Fidler of the Town.

This is powerful stuff, the central charge referring, as Vieth points out, to Rochester's involvement in a brawl at Epsom in June 1676. Rochester's reply, *On the supposed Author of a Late Poem in Defence of Satyr*, is a ferocious attack on Scroope that spares neither his abilities nor his person. The central idea is that Scroope has been singled out by God as an illustration of divine malice:

> To Rack and torture thy unmeaning brain
> In Satyrs Praise, to a low untuned strain
> In Thee were most Impertinent and vain,
> When in thy person we more clerely see
> That Satyr's of Divine Authority,
> For God made one on Man when he made Thee,
> To show there are some Men as there are Apes
> Fram'd for meer Sport, who differ but in shapes . . .[39]

In picturing Scroope as a sport of nature Rochester conjures up his familiar view of an arbitrary God who holds man at his mercy. Scroope has been given in an exaggerated form that contradictoriness that Rochester sees so frequently as the lot of all men: a man devoted to love and beauty who nature has made excessively ugly, a fool who wants to be thought wise, a man of fashion who is despised, and, worst of all, one who is despised by women, the ultimate horror (as we saw in the *Ramble*) for those who prize love's truth:

> While every comeing Mayd where you appear
> Starts back for Love and straight grows chaste for fear,
> For none so poor or prostitute have prov'd
> Where you made Love, t'endure to be belov'd.[40]

In Scroope 'are all those contradictions joyn'd' that make man supremely ridiculous. This makes Scroope the antithesis of being if being resides in loving. Even 'coming' women (the sexual pun is obvious) retreat at sight of him, he is the anti-lover incarnate. The phrase 'starts back for Love' is a nice and unexpected paradox. Rochester's scathing attack depends on two elements for its purpose, the assumption that heterosexual love—unavailable to Scroope because of his ugliness, stupidity and gracelessness—is the one experience that gives meaning to life and the assumption that divine malice has settled on Scroope to show its power. Scroope thus becomes a type of deformity and rejection; the invective succeeds in mythologising its subject. Scroope has become an ideal type of the ridiculousness of man.

Scroope, however, was not yet defeated. He replied with an epigram that seems every bit as venomous as Rochester's attack:

> Raile on poor feeble scribler, speak of me
> In as bad Terms as the world speaks of Thee,
> Sitt swelling in thy hole like a vex'd Toad,
> And full of pox, and Mallice, spitt abroad
> Thou canst blast no Mans Fame with thy ill word,
> Thy pen is een as harmelss as thy sword.[41]

Not yet content, Rochester replied again with *On Poet Ninny*. The invective of this poem is less convincing. Scroope is characterised as one who is impotent both in his writing and in his love, but now the emphasis is on the pathetic quality of the man rather than his deformity. He is the 'Melancholy Knight', a 'fool of fancy', a man of 'harmless Mallice and of hopeless Love' and although his ugliness is again mentioned the effect is rather that we should pity him than be in awe of him as a monster. Pathos does not mix well with invective. We are rather more likely to ask why Rochester has wasted his energies on so insignificant a man than commend his courage for attacking a monster who needed to be destroyed. Destructive satire (as Dryden found in *Absalom and Achitophel*) needs a formidable opponent to justify (and perhaps aid) the use of such powerful verbal weapons.

To a modern reader these ferocious libels might seem wholly barbaric and unjustifiable. It is a mistake, however, to see poetry as a civilised or necessarily civilising art. Barbaric peoples frequently write fine poetry, and the force and energy of a conquering, violent nation can sometimes spill out in a barbaric and magnificent poetry. The Elizabethans, after all, were not without their barbaric side. Poetry involves the patterning of human emotion, and hatred, like destructiveness, is (whether we like it or not) an accredited human response. That there is a poetry of hatred as well as a poetry of love should not surprise us and the critic, rather

9

than wishing it away, has the job of assessing its power. Rochester's malicious poetry is no more justified morally than that of Aithirne, the great Ulster satirist, who threatened King Eochaid that he would satirise the king unmercifully unless he was allowed to bed the queen. The king on that occasion gave way with the words: 'thou shalt have the woman for my honour's sake'.[42] Rochester was no less unscrupulous, but it would be naïve to refuse to give him credit as a poet on moral grounds. The art of poetry is not a rational art, it is an art that channels power through words; and the power of hatred (as is still known in Ulster) is very great.

Among Rochester's most devastating personal attacks are perhaps those on his chief benefactor, Charles II. Rochester's lifelong search, as man and poet, for a proper sense of order, had as its complement a distrust of spurious appeals for order. Charles, even to his most devoted friends, was not a convincing symbol of the divine Orderliness whose vicar he was supposed to be. The falseness, even hypocrisy, of Charles' position was therefore particularly galling to Rochester who hit out the harder that he himself had nothing to complain of. Indeed some of Rochester's venom in these poems (as elsewhere) probably stems from self laceration. For wasn't Rochester himself implicated in the deception by which Charles maintained the fiction that he was the upholder of the nation's morals and religion? Certainly he complains of those aspects of Charles' behaviour—his lubricity, his idleness, his privileged position—that might equally have been thrown at his own head. Gilbert Burnet tells us that the King was handed the *Satyr on Charles II* by mistake when Rochester was too drunk to know what he was doing, and that he was banished from court for his pains.[43] The poem is not without humour, but it is, all the same, understandable that Charles should take offence at lines like:

> Nor are his high desires above his strength,
> His Scepter and his Prick are of a length,
> And she that plays the one may sway the other
> And make him little wiser than his Brother.
> I hate all Monarchs and the Thrones they sit on,
> From the Hector of *France* to the Cully of *Britain*.[44]

This is hardly serious satire because Rochester is not seriously complaining of Charles' sexual prowess—on the contrary he seems to enjoy exaggerating it. Rochester's main purpose here (as so often) is to relish the incongruity of a symbol of human dignity and magnificence devoting himself to such undignified pursuits. The poem is burlesque lampoon. Charles becomes yet another example of man's absurd vulnerability to women and his own pintle. The other extended comment on Charles is the lampoon called *The History of Insipids*. Vieth has argued that the poem is by John Freke but more recently Pinto has defended his original ascription to Rochester in a convincing article and the matter must still be regarded as open.[45] Its merits as a poem are considerable and it is difficult to credit it to an otherwise largely unknown poet.

Rochester's quarrel with John Sheffield, Earl of Mulgrave, was altogether a more savage business than is revealed by these half admiring or at least tolerant lampoons on Charles. Like the dispute with Scroope the dispute with Mulgrave came late in Rochester's career and its origins are equally obscure. Three poems by Rochester are concerned in this controversy: *A Very Heroicall Epistle in Answer to Ephelia, My Lord All-Pride* and the *Epistle from M.G. to O.B. upon their Mutual Poems*. Of these the first and third are examples of *prosopopœia*, the use of a dramatic *persona*. The device involves making the person satirised speak in his own person, a common device in earlier satire. Rochester uses it to superb comic effect in his *Very Heroicall Epistle*. This poem is an 'answer' in reply to a complaint by Ephelia which Etherege had devised under the title *Ephelia to Bajazet*. Etherege's poem is written in the form of the complaint of an abandoned mistress to her lover (after the pattern of Ovid's *Heroides*). In Rochester's poem Bajazet (that is, Mulgrave) purports to defend himself from the charge and he does so in terms of the most outspoken male arrogance. Bajazet is conceived as an over-bearing and vain man, who imagines himself irresistible to women. The element of satire is obtruded through exaggeration that is deft enough for the ironic intention of the poem to have been mistaken for direct and unambiguous statement. Pinto, for instance, sees both this poem and the *Epistle from M.G. to O.B.* as statements of Rochester's own point of view.[46] Of course there is no way of proving Rochester's intention in either poem, though the evidence that has been mustered by J. H. Wilson,[47] James Thorpe[48] and David Vieth[49] seems to me to favour the hypothesis that in both these poems Rochester's intention was to characterise Mulgrave satirically. Even if this hypothesis is incorrect, however, the fact is that the exaggerated boastfulness, the vanity, the sexual fantasy are comic and make us laugh at the speaker, whether he is thought of as 'Mulgrave' or 'Rochester'. Whether the poems are therefore irony or self-irony, even unconscious self-irony, makes no difference to the reading of the poems themselves.

There can be no doubt about the merit of the poem itself. Bajazet is a magnificent monster of egotism, wallowing in male sexual fantasies as he dreams of taking the place of an oriental despot in his harem:

> Oh happy Sultan! Whom we barb'rous call,
> How much refin'd are thou above us all.
> Who envies not the Joys of thy Serail?
> Thee like some God! the trembling Crowd adore,
> Each *Man*'s thy Slave, and *Woman-Kind* thy Whore.
> Methinks I see thee underneath the Shade,
> Of Golden Canopy, supinely laid,
> Thy crowding *Slaves*, all silent as the Night,
> But at thy Nod, all active, as the Light.

The satire is effective just because the picture is so tempting. Bajazet's sensual fantasies are likely to afflict any man, as Christopher Sly finds after he is thrown out of the tavern by the hostess in *The Taming of the Shrew*. Rochester undercuts the sensual indulgence, however, by exaggerating the posturing just beyond what the reasonable man can allow himself:

> Each Female Courts thee with a wishing Eye,
> While thou with awful Pride, walk'st careless by;
> Till thy kind Pledg, at last marks out the *Dame,*
> Thou fancy'st most, to quench thy present flame.
> Then from thy Bed, submissive she retires,
> And thankful for the grace, no more requires.
> No loud reproach, nor fond unwelcome sound,
> Of *Women*'s Tongues thy sacred Ear does wound;
> If any do, a nimble *Mute* strait ties
> The True-Lovers-knot, and stops her foolish Cries . . .

It is quite beyond belief that the subtle ironist of *Artemisia to Chloe* would fail to see the funny side of this. And if we had any doubt at all that Bajazet is being mocked here the fact that this is *presented* as sexual fantasy surely dispels it. For this is not a description of Bajazet himself but of the Sultan he wishes he were. Bajazet is a would-be Sultan not a Sultan in reality. Bajazet's daytime personality is far cruder and less attractive as he tells the distressed Ephelia that taking her virginity is no more to him than changing his gold:

> The boasted favour, you so precious hold,
> To me's no more than changing of [my] Gold.
> What e're you gave, I paid you back in Bliss,
> Then where's the Obligation pray of this.

This is not sexual fantasy, but brutish insensitivity. Rochester creates a completely different tonal quality for the early part of the poem with its piggish abruptness compared to the smooth couplets of the fantasy section. Compare, for instance, the first of my quotations from the poem with these lines from the early part of the poem and note the tortuousness of the syntax, and to a lesser extent the rhythms, compared to the later lines:

> Well Manner'd, Honest, Generous and Stout,
> Names by dull Fools to plague Mankind found [out]
> Should I reguard, I must my self constrain,
> And 'tis my *Maxim* to avoid all pain.

It is quite wrong to argue, as Griffin does, that Mulgrave represents the libertine viewpoint in this poem.[50] Libertinism was a naturalistic doctrine which prided itself on its honesty (hence the French description of the libertine as *l'honnête homme*) and on its generosity. Libertinism encouraged egotism only in the sense that it fostered personal sensation as opposed to the abstractions of reason. Mulgrave's egotism is a monstrous obsession whose object is to 'avoid all pain', that is to avoid sensation (compare this to the idea expressed in *The Mistress* that 'pain can ne'er deceive' or in *Woman's Honour* (it is preferable to have the pain that ensures some pleasure rather than not to feel at all). There can be no doubt that we are meant to reject Bajazet's point of view.

The irony of the poem would perhaps be even clearer to the Restoration reader than it is to us because of its use of imagery. The imagery of the early part of the poem revolves around the kingship imagery of the sun. Bajazet sees himself as the centre of

everything as the sun was to the solar system and the King to his
people:

> In my dear self I center ev'ry thing,
> My Servants, Friends, my Mrs and my King.
> Nay, *Heav'n* and *Earth* to that one point I bring.

Here he openly challenges the King by including him as one of his
satellites and in the last line the imagery goes further and antici-
pates the element of blasphemy found in the later passage of fantasy. Shortly he is to compare himself directly to the Sun and then,
again with an element of blasphemy, to a comet. For it was well
known that comets were sent by God as a warning to mankind. By
the end of the poem Bajazet's fantasy has brought him to the use
of the royal 'we'. In the later part of the poem the element of
blasphemy becomes more pronounced; the Sultan's nod is clearly
an echo of God's *fiat Lux*, for already the Sultan has been described
as 'like some God' whom the 'trembling Crowd adore'. The
Sultan too has a godlike ability of receiving the joys of love 'without the pain', his sexual gifts are described as 'grace', his ear is
'sacred'. It is only when the nimble janissary steps out to throttle
an insufficiently submissive female that the harsh reality of
Bajazet's real personality brings us back to earth. Of course,
Rochester was not averse to a bit of blasphemy; still less to mocking Kings himself, as we have seen; but Mulgrave is not showing
a dislike of Kings here, he is wanting to become one. This is
genuine satire discussed here only because it is part of a group of
poems attacking Mulgrave. For here alternative standards are
implied. Bajazet's boastfulness is seen to be absurd and the implication is a plea for common sense and realism in the attitude of
men towards women: an attitude typical of Rochester's letters and
much of his love poetry, as we have seen. The second poem of the
group, *My Lord All-Pride*, however, brings us back to harsh, non-
comic lampooning. This is one of the last of Rochester's poems
and shows his anger and frustration at its peak. Vieth considers
it to be a response to Mulgrave's attack on Rochester in *An Essay
on Satire*, which Rochester is thought to refer to in a letter of
November 1679. Rochester apparently thought the *Essay* largely
Dryden's work. There is some suspicion that the attack on Dryden
in Rose Alley in December 1679 was arranged by Rochester as a
punishment for Dryden's part in the collaboration with Mulgrave.

The *Essay on Satire* attacks Rochester openly, rehearsing the accusations against him that had become credited to him over the years, his treachery, his lewdness, his malice, his cowardice. Mulgrave then turns to the poetry:

> Sometimes he has some humor, never witt
> And if it rarely, very rarely hitt
> Tis under so much nasty Rubbish layd
> To find it out's a Cindar woman's trade.[51]

and so on. Rochester's revenge was obtained both in *My Lord All-Pride* and in the *Epistle of M.G. to O.B. My Lord All Pride* aims to do what Rochester had done in *On Poet Ninny,* create a grotesque monster out of his victim. The portrait, however, sticks rigidly to the physical and Rochester fails to create a typical figure as he does with Scroope. Even so the poem has a good deal of venomous energy:

> Against his starrs the Coxcombe ever strives;
> And to be something they forbid, contrive,
> With a Red nose, splay foot and goggle eie,
> A Plowman's Looby Meen, face all awry
> With [stinking] breath and every loathsome mark
> The Punchionella setts up for a spark. [52]

In *An Epistolary Essay from M.G. to O.B. upon their Mutual Poems,* the last of his extended poems, Rochester tries the technique of *prosopopœia* that had proved so successful in the *Very Heroicall Epistle*. In doing so he employs a technique of ironic indirection that allows both comic contrast between surface and indirect meaning and a set of right standards to be implied in contrast to the stated standards of the speaker. It must be admitted, however, that the two levels are insufficiently demarcated, so that the poem lacks clarity. This has led to critics interpreting the poem in opposite directions, much as the *Very Heroicall Epistle* has been treated, but in this case with much more reason. Critics such as Pinto argue that the poem is not ironic at all and is an expression of Rochester's own view. Against this Vieth and others have argued that the poem is a satire on Mulgrave in which the stated arguments are being mocked. There is some evidence that the divergence of opinion began early, for we find two titles for early copies that suggest these two different readings. The majority of copies have the title I have given the poem, or something like it, but some, including the Gyldenstolpe MS version and the Portland MS, head it *From E:R to E:M* that is, presumably, from the Earl of Rochester to the Earl of Mulgrave. This second title might suggest that early copiers considered that Rochester was speaking in his own person in the poem. Vieth's interpretation of the title *From M.G. to O.B.* as standing for 'from Mulgrave to Old Bays' (a common nickname for Dryden who, as we saw, collaborated with Mulgrave) seems plausible. What are we to make of these contradictions? Griffin tries to mediate between the two positions by suggesting that we can see the poem as both containing advocacy and irony for the position adopted by the speaker:

> An *Epistolary Essay* can be read as a knowing and playful celebration of an egotistic theory of writing, a theory consisting of a number of principles, most of them reasonable in themselves, but here pushed to and beyond their usual logical limits . . . the poem is not simply an ironical satire on its speaker, whoever he is.[53]

The difficulty with this critical stance is that it requires irony to do more than it can. Irony is a very frail device, for it is dependent on the poet creating a divergence between what is being said and the tone of voice in which it is said. As soon as we begin to intrude meant statements into a basically ironic statement then the tone of voice must change; the irony, that is, is destroyed. If Rochester intended to have it both ways in this poem then he intended the impossible, but I don't think he did. I think the intention was as Vieth states it, but the intention has not been fulfilled. Nor is the alternative title necessarily a difficulty for this interpretation, for the title *From E.R. to M.G.* could simply be asserting that Rochester's poem is being aimed at Mulgrave.

We can never prove intention. It is important, however, to decide on probabilities. We must look at the poem without prejudice to either viewpoint and see what impression the speaker has on us in the light of what we know of Rochester's ideas and especially his notions on poetic inspiration—the main subject of the speaker's peroration. The writer of the epistle, M.G., is primarily concerned to justify his writing, on the egotistical grounds that he likes doing it, he thinks it is good and that no-one else need read it if they do not wish to. He is indifferent to public fame, indeed despises it, and is determined to please himself. Some of this does sound like Rochester himself. Rochester is by no means modest in his poetic self-confidence and he certainly despised the rabble and 'common fame' as much as M.G. At the end of the *Allusion to Horace* his scorn of the rabble is every bit as acid as M.G.'s and equally he scorns criticism:

> . . . when the poor fed *Poets* of the *Town*
> For Scraps and Coach room cry my Verses down.

Not only this, but M.G. is clearly a witty, intelligent man, who is given some fine lines:

> The World appears like a great Family,
> Whose Lord opprest with Pride and Poverty,
> (That to a few great Bounty he may show)
> Is fain to starve the num'rous Train below.
> Just so seems Providence, as poor and vain,
> Keeping more Creatures than it can maintain.
> Here 'tis profuse, and there it meanly saves,
> And for one Prince, it makes Ten Thousand Slaves.
> In Wit alone 'thas been magnificent.
> Of which so just a Share to each is sent,
> That the most Avaritious are content;
> For none e're thought (the due Division's such)
> His own too little or his Friend's too much.

The view of Providence as 'poor and vain' fits well into Rochester's view of the waywardness of the gods, and the irony that the only thing we get in abundance is wit because no man thinks he lacks any is certainly worthy of Rochester at his best.

Yet there surely can be no doubt that M.G. in this poem is meant to be a comic butt. The egotism of M.G., as Griffin points out, echoes the egotism of Bajazet in the *Very Heroicall Epistle* and it is inconceivable that Rochester could be referring to his own verse in giving M.G. the lines:[54]

> In all I write, shou'd Sense, and Wit, and Rhime
> Fail me at once, yet something so Sublime
> Shall stamp my Poem, that the World may see
> It cou'd have been produc'd by none but me,
> And that's my End, for Man can wish no more
> Than so to write as none e'er writ before.

Rochester's poetry studiously *avoids* the sublime. It is remarkable
for its realism and its repudiation of the sentimental. Nor is it
conceivable that Rochester should admit to the possibility of 'wit
and rhyme' failing him. Wit (primarily meaning intelligence) is the
thing he most prides himself on and for which he was admired
by others, and lack of wit (witness the three fops in the *Ramble*) is
always scorned. Further, Rochester's poetic method, with its almost obsessive fondness for imitation, that is, the use of earlier
models as a basis for his own poems, is wholly against the concept
that literature should be completely original, what 'none e'er writ
before'.

This portrait of M.G., moreover, fits well with that given of
Mulgrave by Robert Wolseley in his defence of Rochester in the
Preface to Valentinian.[55] Wolseley rounds on Mulgrave (he names
him as the author of the *Essay upon Poetry*) for denying Rochester
wit, 'whose Name was the very Mark it pass'd by'. Mulgrave is
described as one of 'a sort of men, who have been always so in
Love with themselves, as never to be able to see any merit or hear
any praise but their own, . . . they persist in an untoward spiritless
Vein of Rhiming, being perhaps too considerable (in their own
opinions) to design the pleasing any Body but themselves'.[56]

There are further reasons for thinking that M.G.'s point of view
is to be repudiated. As Griffin points out, M.G. contradicts himself. At one point he is claiming enthusiastic inspiration and
appealing to the sublime, but earlier in the poem he appeals to
standards of common sense. In the third line he is claiming to have
written 'in Poetic Rage'; by line 12 he is assuring us:

> 'I'm none of those who think themselves inspir'd,'

only to return to the idea of inspirational verse at line 45. If these
contradictions are Rochester's we must charge him with gross
incompetence; if, as I believe, they are Mulgrave's they reinforce
the impression of a blustering, dogmatic personality.

But the most crucial argument must remain one of the tone of
voice in which M.G. is made to speak (he is of course *writing*, but
the metaphorical extension will be allowed). The speaker is not
merely egotistical (Rochester could be that), he is brash and crude:

> Perhaps ill Verses ought to be confin'd
> In meer good Breeding, like unsav'ry Wind:

Were Reading forc'd, I shou'd be apt to think
Men might no more write scurvily, then stink:
But 'tis your choice whether you'll read or no;
If likewise of your smelling it were so,
I'd fart just as I write, for my own Ease,
Nor shou'd you be concern'd unless you please.

Rochester can be equally outspoken and coprophilic when speaking in his own voice, but almost invariably it is when he is heaping disapproval on someone, not when he is advocating something. This alone would suggest that this is meant to be taken satirically. But there is also surely a comic inconsistency between M.G.'s aspiration towards the sublime in poetry and the scatology he does in fact produce. In short I believe we are meant to find M.G. both witty and disgusting. Rochester is not denying his intelligence or his haughty pride (which Rochester to some extent shared) but he is presenting him in addition as boastful, blustering, coarse and inconsistent. The combination, however, turns out to be too nicely balanced for us to get a clear picture of the subject. Satire demands caricature, the reduction of a character to its salient faults. Rochester has failed to restrain his own inventiveness sufficiently, so that M.G. appears more intelligent, wittier than, as a satiric butt, he should. The lack of consensus among the critics turns out to result from a lack of clarity in the poem.

The poems of Rochester we have been discussing in this chapter show him at his most destructive and pessimistic. In these poems his iconoclastic self, the man who smashed Charles II's expensive sundial, is uppermost. The aristocrat, the formal courtier, the searcher after meaning is not much in evidence. The impulse to destroy triumphs to a large extent over the impulse to construct. This iconoclasm was an essential part of Rochester's nature and without it he could not have written either with the honesty, the force or the clarity that is characteristic of him as a poet. But if he was an unbeliever he was also one who wished passionately to believe, and his finest poetic achievements are those where this honesty is turned to positive good. In his major satires he is able to construct out of this mood of unbelief a world of words that, through its coherence, defies the forces of disintegration.

FIVE

Satire in the Seventeenth Century

Rochester's major satires, *Timon, Tunbridge Wells, The Satyr against Reason and Mankind, The Allusion to Horace* and *The Epistle from Artemisia in the Town to Chloe in the Country* were all written, according to Vieth, about 1674 and 1675. If we ask what models Rochester had for satire at this date the answer in two cases out of the five can be quite precise: the *Allusion* is an imitation or adaptation of the tenth satire of the first Book of Horace's *Satires, Timon* follows Boileau's third satire *Le repas ridicule* fairly closely. (Boileau's poem is itself dependent to some extent on Horace's eighth satire of the second Book of *Satires*.) In an edition of 1715 (where it is attributed to the Duke of Buckingham) *Timon* is described as 'a Satyr, in Imitation of Monsieur Boileau'. *The Satyr against Reason and Mankind* may be related to Boileau, in this case the eighth Satire, though the two poems are vastly different in purpose. *Tunbridge Wells* has no known direct source, while the epistle of *Artemisia*, though having no direct source, would seem to be in general an exercise in the Horatian epistle. Horace and Boileau then are certain influences and we know from Burnet's *Life* that Rochester admired Boileau most 'among the French'. This, however, is not the whole story. The divergences in method and subject matter from both these models are considerable and there are other satirists, both native and foreign that we need to take into account. To get a clear picture both of Rochester's debt to other satirists and his originality we shall need to go back some way.

Earlier English Satire

English satire earlier in the seventeenth century, with the most notable exception of Ben Jonson's, had been dominated by the view that the word satire was related to the Greek Satyrs, those strange, mythic creatures of the woods, half men and half goats or horses. The importance of this association (though it was in fact based on false etymology) is that it led to the belief that satire should be coarse in tone, rough in method and aggressive. This was felt to be appropriate in accordance with the principle of decorum that suggested that the kind of verse whose object was to attack vice should have an appropriately aggressive, rough style. This view led early seventeenth-century satirists to use Juvenal and Persius as models, who were supposedly more appropriate for a coarse medium than Horace. Late Elizabethan and Jacobean formal satire is thus characterised by a harshness of tone that results from a distortion of formal rhythms and syntax which makes reading them both difficult and (mostly) unrewarding. In addition the Elizabethan satirist assumed a *persona* according to that same principle of decorum which decreed that the speaker should be suitable to the style and subject presented. Later Elizabethan satiric *personae* are usually as rough, and generally as unpleasant, as the things they attack. Something of the gnarled language and biting tone of these satires can be gauged from this example from Marston's *Scourge of Villanie* (1599) where he adopts a *persona* with the uncompromising name of Kinsayder (gelder):

> I cannot hold, I cannot I indure
> To view a big womb'd foggie clowde immure
> The radiant tresses of the quickning sunne.
> Let Custards quake, my rage must freely runne.
> Preach not the Stoickes patience to me,
> I hate no man, but mens impietie.
> My Soule is vext, what power will 'th desist?
> Or dares to stop a sharp fanged Satirist?
> Who'le cool my rage? whole stay my itching fist,
> But I will plague and torture whom I list?
> If that the three-fold walls of Babilon
> Should hedge my tongue, yet I should raile upon
> This fustie world, that now dare put in ure
> To make Jehova but a coverture,
> To shade rank filth. . . .[1]

Already here several of the key features of later formal satire appear. There is first of all the character of the satiric *persona* itself: an irate, more than slightly mad, creature who bites and scratches to 'plague and tortue' his victims. That we are perhaps not meant to take such a character too seriously is suggested by the reference to 'quaking custard' that Jonson rather humourlessly rebukes in *Poetaster* (v. i). Then there is the suggestion that it is the type rather than the individual under attack. The stylistic features also reappear later—the uncompromising scurrility of the language, the jerky irregular rhythms, which counterpoint the rhymed pentameter couplet that is to become the almost invariable metre of serious formal verse satire throughout the seventeenth century and on into the eighteenth. Many of these characteristics survive, if with some modification, in Rochester's satire.

The reasons for the use of these harsh techniques is already apparent in Thomas Drant's introduction to his translation of Horace in 1566:

> A Satyre is a tarte and carpying kynd of verse,
> An instrument to pynch the pranks of men,
> And for as much as pynching instruments do perse,
> Yclept it was full well a Satyre then.
> A name of Arabique to it they gave:
> For Satyre there, doothe signifie a glave.
>
> Or Satyra, of Satyrus, the mossye rude
> Uncivile god: for those that will them write
> With taunting gyrds and glikes and gibes must
>   vexe the lewde,
> Strayne curtesy: ne reck of mortall spyte.
> Shrouded in Mosse, not shrynkyng for a shower
> Deemyng of mosse as of a regall bower.
>
> Satyre of writhled waspyshe Saturne may be namde
> The Satyrist must be a waspe in moode,
> Testie and wrothe with vice and errs to see
>   both blamde
> But courteous and frendly to the good.

Drant is here hedging his bets about the etymology of the word satire, but, from whatever angle, he arrives at the same conclusion: that satire demands a rough style to convey harsh truths.

That the Elizabethans did not take the form too seriously is suggested by Everard Guilpin's treatment of the conventions in *Skialetheia or a Shadowe of Truth* (1598) where, in the conclusion to the epigrams he apologises for 'this mad-cap stuff' and says his reader will be justified in using his pages to wrap up soap:

> And justly to; for thou canst not misuse,
> More then I will, these bastards of my *Muse*:
> I know they are passing filthy, scurvey lies,
> I know they are rude, harsh, and unsavory rimes
> Fit to wrap playsters, And odd unguents in,
> Reedifiers of the wracks of Synne.
> Viewing this sin-drowned world, I purposely,
> Phisick'd my *Muse*, that thus unmannerly,
> She might beray our folly-soyled age,
> And keepe *Decorum* on a comick stage,
> Bringing a foule-mouth Jester who might sing
> To rogues . . .[2]

Satire was generally regarded, along with most comic forms of literature, as a lowly kind by theorists and practitioners alike. We are reminded that Boileau in 1663, though already widely known and praised as a poet, was excluded from the royal bounty because satire was not thought important enough to warrant financial reward.[3]

That the satirist was thought of as playing the part of morose clown is confirmed by the adaptation of these satirical techniques to the stage. Jonson and Marston both create characters who mouth scurrility as a general protest against widespread corruption. But the most influential of these early dramatists on the Restoration period would seem to be one with whom we would now scarcely associate satire at all: William Shakespeare. Not only does Rochester name one of his satirical characters after the most spectacular of Shakespeare's scourging satirical characters, Timon, but in the *Allusion to Horace* explicitly singles out Shakespeare and the deftness of his satire:

> A jest in scorn points out and hits the thing
> More home than the morosest Satyr's sting.
> Shakespeare and Jonson did herein excel,
> And might in this be imitated well.

Admittedly he is unlikely to be thinking of Timon or the scourging satiric *persona* in these lines, but rather, as becomes an Horatian
poem, alluding to Shakespeare's lighter essays in the mode. He is
presumably thinking primarily of the lighter comedies here. But it
shows unmistakably Rochester's association of Shakespeare with
satire and suggests that it is quite unnecessary to look in obscurer
quarters to explain the title of Rochester's poem *Timon* and the use
of Timon in the poem as Rochester's satirical mouthpiece.
Rochester was quite widely read, but he was not a scholar and
Vieth's suggestion that he might have had the Greek poet Timon
of Phlius in mind seems unlikely. Shakespeare's *Timon*, especially
in its portrait of Apemanthus and in the scenes of Acts 4 and 5
after Timon's flight from Athens, clearly makes use of satirical
techniques derived from formal satire. As we shall see, there are
specially good critical reasons for associating Shakespeare's and
Rochester's Timons. Apemanthus, described in the 1623 Folio list
of characters as 'a churlish philosopher', functions as the principal
satiric commentator in Shakespeare's play while Timon's satiric
outbursts in the latter half of the play show him responding angrily
to a situation in which he is the principal sufferer. Their conversation in Act 4 Scene 3 presents us with the relative merits of the
impartial and the partial satirical stance:

APEMANTHUS: I love thee better now than e're I did.
TIMON: I hate thee worse.
APEMANTHUS: Why?
TIMON: Thou flatter'st misery.
APEMANTHUS: I flatter not, but say thou art a caitiff.
TIMON: Why dost thou seek me out?
APEMANTHUS: To vex thee.
TIMON: Always a villain's office or a fool's.
          Dost please thyself in it?
APEMANTHUS: Ay.
TIMON: What, a knave too?
APEMANTHUS: If thou didst put this sour, cold habit on
          To castigate thy pride, 'twere well; but thou
          Dost it enforcedly.

Apemanthus is suggesting that he is the true satirist here because he is disinterestedly speaking the truth. The difference
between the two characters is the difference between the poet

himself and the satiric *persona* he adopts. The *persona* is presented as indulging his personal spleen, while the very use of a dramatic character by the poet suggests detachment and disinterestedness. The role of the satirist himself is related to the role of the preacher of *contemptus mundi* literature: to show the weakness of mankind and the absurdity of pride. Timon's impure, selfish satire, on the other hand, can often sound remarkably like that of the scourging satirical *persona* of the formal satire:

> It is the pasture lards the wether's sides,
> The want that makes him lean. Who dares, who dares,
> In purity of manhood stand upright,
> And say 'This man's a flatterer'? If one be,
> So are they all; for every grise of fortune
> Is smoothed by that below. The learned pate
> Ducks to the golden fool. All's obliging;
> There's nothing level in our cursed natures
> But direst villainy.

Perhaps Rochester's use of Timon's name as the title of his poem, however, most obviously refers to the feast at the beginning of Act 3 Scene 6 where Timon in his disgust with all his erstwhile friends invites them to a dinner and then presents them with dishes of hot water:

> You knot of mouth friends! suche and likewarm water
> Is your perfection. This is Timon's last,
> Who, stuck and spangled with your flatteries,
> Washes it off, and sprinkles in your faces
> Your reeking villainy. Live loathed and long,
> Most smiling, smooth, detested parasites,
> Courteous destroyers, affable wolves, meek bears.
> You fools of fortune, trencher friends, time's flies
> Cap-and-knee slaves, vapours and minute-jacks!
> Crust you Quite o'er!

Rochester's *Timon* begins in a jaundiced mood of satirical disgust, and ends its feast, as this scene of Shakespeare, in uproar. But the most important connection is in the kind of satiric *persona* Rochester has adopted in his poem. Like Shakespeare's Timon, Rochester's satirist is caught up with the action he is satirising and is thus given an equivocal position as both commentator and

participant. This is not, of course, Shakespeare's only excursion
into scourging satire. The character of Thersites has the same
function of satirical commentator in *Troilus and Cressida* as has
Apemanthus, except that he is more of a clown and less of a
philosopher.[4] Dryden, interestingly enough, reworked *Troilus and
Cressida* (published in 1679) keeping Thersites as a railing satirical
commentator, while Shadwell almost at the same time was producing his version of *Timon*. That interest in Shakespeare's vehement satires on man had revived in the Restoration period is further attested by Wycherley's handling of the malcontent satirist in
The Plain Dealer. This play is almost exactly contemporaneous
with Rochester's great satires, and poet and playwright, of course,
knew each other. Rochester reserves his highest commendation
for Wycherley in the *Allusion to Horace*. Like Rochester's *Timon*
Wycherley's play is an adaptation of a French model, in this case
Molière's *Le Misanthrope*. But a comparison of the two plays shows
that Wycherley deliberately coarsened the character of Molière's
hero, Alceste, giving him not only an angry misanthropy but an
angry style of speaking, more like that of the scourging satirists of
the Elizabethans, and Timon in particular, and less like the philosophical misanthropy of Alceste. Molière's polished rhyming couplets, too, are in effect quite unlike Wycherley's hard-hitting prose
dialogue. Wycherley's play shows other signs of Shakespearean
influence in the use of the quasi-allegorical figure of Fidelia in a
role with similarities to that of Fidele in *Cymbeline* and in its highly
moral, idealistic ending, where the hero, Manly, and his Fidelia
pair off to the comic bliss of eternal marriage in the true Shakespearean manner. Molière's play ends with the misanthrope totally
unconvinced by arguments intended to convert him, asserting his
milder, but profounder, aversion to mankind.

    Elizabethan satirical methods, however, did not only influence
Restoration literature in this direct way. Many of the qualities of
this early satire survived in the satire of the first half of the seventeenth century. After late Elizabethan formal satirists like Donne,
Joseph Hall, Marston and Guilpin, the early years of the seventeenth century saw only feeble attempts at verse satire and mostly
at a more popular level. There are two interesting satires of
Edward Herbert's dated 1608, but these were not published until
1664. The voluminous George Wither and such minor figures as
Nicholas Braithwaite can be passed over. When satire emerges

again as a serious poetic form it is to show a combination of popular and elite forms that attest both the continuity of Elizabethan influence and fundamental change.

The Popular Tradition

Harold Love has argued that Rochester's satire is a blend of popular and elite satirical techniques.[5] This may be true of some of the minor satire, especially the lampoons, but it is not, I believe, true of the major satires, which it seems to me contain little of the popular element. Such a mixture, however, is found very definitely in the most popular poet of the 1640s who provides a link between Elizabethan and Restoration satire, John Cleveland. John Peters in his justly praised book on early English satire makes a fundamental distinction between a native tradition of 'complaint' and a learned tradition of satire. The Elizabethan satire we have been looking at is very much part of a learned tradition. But throughout the period, we must suppose that a vigorous popular tradition of complaint existed side by side with the learned. One of the characteristics of this popular tradition is its concern with personalities and with topical events. The learned tradition (as we have seen) liked to claim it was attacking vice rather than the vicious, though the distinction was not always easy to maintain. The topicality of popular satire, however, meant that it was less likely to survive and that its practitioners were less concerned with its survival after the events that called it forth had passed into history. It seems unnecessary to conclude that such outbursts of popular indignation as occurred on the assassination of George Villiers, Duke of Buckingham in 1628, for instance, were, in Brian Morris' words, as isolated as 'the lonely North Atlantic island of Rockall'.[6] The fact that most of these particular satires remained in manuscript until they were published under the auspices of the Percy Society in 1850 surely suggests why so few have survived. They remained in manuscript for so long until rescued by antiquarians because almost as soon as they were written they ceased to attract any but antiquarian interest. A glance at the manuscripts in any case suggests that the satire in them is not an isolated phenomenon. The British Museum Additional MS 5832, one of the sources of the nineteenth-century edition, is a later seventeenth-century collection of political satires made for Dr (later Archbishop) Tenison. It includes satires both before and after the events of 1628. There is, for example, a satire against the Scots by Robert Codrington whose title refers to the 'tumultuous sedicion in Scotland, 1639';[7] there is a poem said to be from the time of James I which stanza by stanza satirises the Northants gentry—a note says it was written before 1615. Something of its flavour can be obtained from these lines:

> Watson he waights on good Ale, and then he tells a bawdy
> tale:
> But most of all when Brooks is by: both are perfect in knavery
> And both do love a Bawdy House, and Strange (sic) Ale for to
> carouse.[8]

As this is not an unfair example of the poem's worth the reader will think it is not all that surprising that it was never printed. Yet another poem of the same MS goes back much further, it is a satire on Richard Fletcher, bishop of London, who died in 1596.[9] A note in the MS says it was made 'by some of the gang of Martin Marprelate'. The satires in this and other manuscript collections are both personal and abusive, as may be judged from a poem *On the Duke of Bucks and his Kindred*, stanza 4 of which reads:

> Old Abbott Anthony
> Thinks he hath well done,
> In leaving Sodomy
> To marry Sheldon.
> She hath a buttock plumpe,
> Keep but they Tarse whole
> She will hold up her Rump
> With her black arse-hole.

Rochester (like many another Restoration poet) could write in this time-honoured manner when he wanted, as he does in this poem on the much celebrated Duchess of Cleveland:

> Quoth the Dutches of Cleveland to Mrs Knight,
> I'd fain have a Prick, but how to come by 't,
> I desire you'll be secret, and give your Advice
> Though Cunt be not Coy, Reputation is Nice.

This, however, is mere ephemeral court scandal and must be distinguished totally from Rochester's major satire, which is true to neo-classical theory in being largely about types and problems rather than personalities. Rochester's satiric methods, too, differ widely between his excursions into popular satire and those of his formal satire. The little jibe at the Duchess of Cleveland, like much popular satire, including the examples just quoted, is in a lyric form (in this case a rather complicated stanza that alternates anapaestic lines with lines that combine iambic and anapaestic feet). The formal satire, however, is almost invariably in heroic couplets and there is both a greater concern with regularity of metre and rhyme and with the proprieties of vocabulary. This is not to say that Rochester (like Pope later) altogether neglects popular elements in his formal satire (both *Timon* and *Tunbridge Wells* borrow occasionally from popular example) but in general there is a clear and unmistakable difference in both attitude and manner between the kinds in Rochester's work.

Cleveland, Cowley and Marvell

The situation is quite different in the two most important satirists between Jacobean times and Rochester: John Cleveland and Rochester's satiric master, Andrew Marvell. Cleveland's satires, as both his most recent editors, Brian Morris and Eleanor Withington, and his most recent historian, Lee Jacobus, point out, arose from the confusions of the civil war. They are, therefore, highly topical and highly partisan. But while this topicality relates them to the popular satirical tradition the method that Cleveland uses is much closer to that of the formal verse satirists. As Morris and Withington point out, the poetic *persona* Cleveland adopts, especially in the angry later satires, is clearly related to the Elizabethan scourger, even though Cleveland's close personal identification with the attitudes presented means that he is less able to think of his *persona* as a dramatic character than Marston or Guilpin are able to do with their satiric mouthpieces.[10] Not that this detachment was always obvious in Elizabethan satire (the difference between Apemanthus and Timon is not always very clear). The Elizabethans never exploited the idea of the dramatic role of the satirical commentator to the full, even in their drama, where the scourger is often given a primarily choric function. Marston in the *Malcontent,* however, attempts to overcome this problem by giving Malevole-Altofronto two roles, that of observer as Altofronto and that of participant in the action as Malevole. Shakespeare, as we

see in *Timon*, hits on the solution of dividing his satirists by giving
one a choric function (Apemanthus) and one a partcipatory
function (Timon). Restoration satire, and Rochester in particular,
tends to use the device of *prosopopœia* more distinctly, just as it uses
formal structural devices, as a means of ironic placement of what
is being said. Cleveland's satiric structures are episodic like those
of most Elizabethan formal satire. It was Marvell's major contribution to the development of verse satire to use architectonic
structure (in *Last Instructions to a Painter*) as a means of 'placing'
and commenting on the subject matter of the satire. Rochester, as
we shall see, sometimes follows Marvell in this and sometimes the
looser French methods.

Cleveland's connection with Elizabethan formal verse satire can
be summed up in terms of the use of the scourging, satiric *persona*,
in his use of linguistic techniques to create roughness and the
impression of anger, in the use of the rhymed iambic pentameter
as his basic metre (the heroic couplet), in his transferring petrarchist wit and paradox to satirical use and in the loose, episodic
structures of his poems. His satire relates to the popular tradition
primarily in its partiality, topicality and perhaps in its scurrility.

Cleveland's best and most celebrated satire is that blast against
the Scots, *The Rebell Scot,* that can still warm any self-respecting
Englishman's heart. Even Dryden, to whom Cleveland's poetic
methods were anathema, approved of those devastating lines:

> Had Cain been Scot, God would have changed his doome,
> Not forc'd him wander, but confin'd him home.

Such satiric wit and vigour, however, is often lost in the obscurity of the particular allusions and in the perversities of language. *The Rebell Scot* was written in fury at the part played by the
Scots in securing the defeat of Charles I's armies by the Parlia-
mentary forces. Cleveland was not only incensed by this stab in
the back (as he saw it) by foreigners, but by what he saw as their
treason against their own king (for Charles himself was a Scots-
man). The poem possibly dates from the invasion of England by
Scottish forces in January 1644. In it Cleveland adopts the ferocious voice of the scourging satirist and he adopts the devices of
language which, as we have seen, were thought necessary to
accommodate the point of view:

Come keen *Iambicks*, with your Badgers feet,
And Badger-like, bite till your teeth do meet.
Help ye tart Satyrists, to imp my rage,
With all the Scorpions that should whip this age.
Scots are like Witches; do but whet your pen,
Scratch til the blood come; they'l not hurt you then.
Now as the Martyrs wer inforc'd to take
The shapes of beasts, like hypocrites, at stake,
I'le bait my Scot so; yet not cheat your eyes,
A Scot within a beast is no disguise.

Here we have the same sharp-fanged satirist as in Marston's satire, the same general comment on the depravity of the age, the same desire to plague and torture the satiric victim. Cleveland's metre, too, is the rhymed iambic pentameter favoured by the Elizabethan satirists. Cleveland is more successful than they, however, even than Donne in his satires, in counterpointing the formal iambic metre against the rhythms demanded by the syntax. Like all the earlier formal satirists Cleveland uses a double, counterpointed system of rhythmic control, formal and syntactic; but he manages to keep his basic iambic pattern without either letting it become too dominant (and therefore too smooth for satire) or too abrupt and broken and thereby losing rhythmic control. Marston, Hall and Guilpin tend to the earlier fault, Donne to the latter. This enables Cleveland both to express forceful anger and show that he remains very much master of the situation. The basic technique is to keep the line length accurately decasyllabic and also to allow the syntactic pauses to coincide fairly frequently with the pentameter line (the majority of the lines throughout the poem are end-stopped). Divergences from the metrical norm are obtained by the inversion of feet and the use of weakly stressed syllables in strong positions, thus:

Come keen/*I am*/*bics*, with/your Bad/gers feet
And Bad/ger-like/bite till/your teeth/do meet.
Help ye/tart Sat/yrists, to imp/ my rage,
With all/the Scorp/ions that/should whip/this age.

Here the first three lines each have one inverted foot (a trochaic in

place of an iambic foot), but the lines are basically iambic even
though the iambic rhythm is put under strain by the need to accent
such comparatively weak accents as 'with' in line 1, 'like' in line 2
and 'Sat' in line 3. A contrast with Donne's use of metre in his
satires is revealing: in the second satire Donne, in 110 lines, has
exactly the same number of run-on lines as end-stopped lines
(using Grierson's edition), in the fifth satire he has 54 on-running
lines as against only 37 end-stopped lines (occasionally the on-
running even splits words in half). Cleveland's poem (in Morris
and Withington's edition), on the other hand, has 96 end-stopped
lines and only 30 on-running lines. These figures are only rough
guides, of course, not only because the present writer is not very
good at counting, but also because one man's end-stopping is
sometimes another man's overflowing. With this warning, however, it seems that this is a fair demonstration of just how much
more Cleveland is concerned with metrical control than Donne
and how the undoubted vigour of his lines is achieved by vari-
ations within the line. The Restoration satirists take Cleveland's
techniques even closer to complete metrical regularity by decreas-
ing the number of strong accents on comparatively weak syllables
and using on-running lines as the principal means of counterpointing metrical with syntactic rhythms. Both Rochester and
Dryden in this way manage to impose very firm artistic control
without losing the vigour that comes from the tension between
the two rhythmic principles. Cleveland's tendency to assert the
dominance of the metrical line and the couplet leads the way to
that combination of control and energy that is one of the glories
of Augustan verse satire.

Cleveland's achievement in the *Rebell Scot* undoubtedly showed
the way to develop a satire that was both vigorous and relevant to
contemporary needs, but Cleveland's satire is too frequently tied
to particularity and too concerned with local effect to have found a
satisfactory answer to the problem of giving particularity general
significance and showing full artistic control by giving over-all
shape to the poem. Cleveland's *Rebell Scot*, like most of the Elizabethan formal satire before it, tends to move from aphorism to
aphorism, from thrust to isolated thrust. There is neither narrative
not architectural unity in Cleveland's poem and one has the feeling
that it could both have gone on longer or stopped shorter without
being substantially different. This tends to show, I think, that

Cleveland's view of satire is a largely negative one, that is as attack, but not as providing an alternative constructive viewpoint. Of course Cleveland *implies* an alternative viewpoint, but there is not much in the poem itself to give that viewpoint backing. Cleveland's satire is often close to burlesque.

The Rebell Scot is in any case one of the more orderly of Cleveland's satires, the earlier satires show even more extreme examples of the concept of satire as destruction. A satire called *Smectymnuus or the Club-Divines* illustrates this. Smectymnuus was the outlandish pseudonym (made up of their initials) of five clergymen who had issued a tract on church government—a tract, incidentally, that Milton was to defend. Cleveland, however, is not interested in the tract as such, but in the oddity of the pseudonym: it is rather typical of him as a poet to be more interested in the shadow than the substance. His satire therefore consists of a witty attempt (which deliberately fails) to etymologise the title. Another satire, *The Mixt Assembly*, was written to attack the Westminster Assembly of Scots and English, which met in July 1643 and which was formed to discuss the introduction of Presbyterianism as the national church of England, in return for Scottish support in the Civil War. The poem is especially interesting because its technique of representing the assembly in terms of grotesque disorder is that copied by Marvell in *Last Instructions* for his attack on the Westminster parliament. Again Cleveland is not interested in the issues at stake, but simply in destroying the credibility of the meeting. Cleveland settles on what comes to be a characteristic Restoration satirical device of imaging disorder through a decorum of disorderly presentation. And like Marvell's poem later, Cleveland's satire describes the assembly in terms of sickness and sexual depravity. The grotesque scurrility of lines like these describing the assembly in terms of a 'gay' dance is increased by the waywardness of the language and the obscurity of the reference:

> A Jig, a Jig: And in this Antick dance
> *Fielding* and doxy *Marshall* first advance.
> *Twiss* blows the Scotch pipes, and the loving brase
> Puts on the traces, and treads Cinqu'-a-pace.
> Then *Say and Seale* must his old Hamstrings supple
> And he and rumpl'd *Palmer* make a couple.
> Palmer's a fruitful girl, if hee'd unfold her,

The midwife may find worke about her shoulder.
Kimbolton, that rebellious *Boanerges,*
Must be content to saddle Doctor *Burges.*
If *Burges* get a clap, 'tis ne're the worse,
But the fift time of his Compurgators.

There are constant references to sexual licence (jig, doxy, the cinque-a-pace—for some unexplained reason a dance frequently associated in Elizabethan English with bawdy situations—saddle), and to physical distortion and disease (Palmer's hump back, Burges' getting clap—gonorrhea). The legal technicality of 'compurgation' associates Burges' conviction of adultery (for which he would need defence witnesses—compurgators) with the idea of the need for medical 'purgation' after contracting venereal disease. Cleveland's purpose here is to assassinate character, and it is noticeable how his verse tends to form round the unit of the isolated couplet, each couplet acting as a separate barb. The isolation of couplet from couplet helps to give the impression of disintegration, of things falling apart, just as the outlandish references and the imagery of distortion and incongruity help to give us a feeling of alienation from what is being described. What order there is seems to be forced on the material arbitrarily by the form in which it is expressed (the couplet) and does not stem from any inherent capability of the material to find its appropriate form. The element of grotesque distortion is even carried into the outlandish rhyming of words like 'Boanerges' with 'Burges', 'worse' with 'Compurgators'. Cleveland is using burlesque techniques; but this is not burlesque because the viewpoint is constant and well defined. There is no doubt what it is that Cleveland hates, and therefore it is easy to assess, by implication, what he approves of. Cleveland's satire is primarily motivated by hate (though this might, as Jacobus suggests, also imply fascination with his victims). Unlike the satire of the Elizabethans, it deals with matters that are of immediate concern and it cannot afford the luxury of the somewhat ironical, play-acting element that one feels beneath much of the earlier verse. Its negative motivation impels it both towards an increasing tendency to disintegration and disorder and at the same time demands a stricter imposition of a formal order. The tension between the images of disorder and the forced orderliness of the couplet explain much of the intensity as well as the obscurity of Cleveland's satire. Restoration satire takes a further step towards the imposition of order on recalcitrant material by imposing architectonic shape over-all. One of the great achievements of Restoration satire is to find techniques that will embody an alternative viewpoint to the one under attack. Dryden achieves this supremely in *Absalom and Achitophel* and Rochester achieves it in both the *Satyr against Mankind* and *Artemisia*. For Rochester, however, it was a uniquely difficult problem because he could not bring himself (until he was on his deathbed) to believe that such orderliness was inherent in the nature of the universe; it was simply a compulsive search for order that led him to adopt an orderly method.

An interesting satire by Abraham Cowley, published in the year before Cleveland wrote the *Rebell Scot*, 1643, already shows a tendency towards the use of ordering techniques approaching the Restoration manner. Cowley's *Puritan and the Papist*, though it from time to time makes gestures towards a Clevelandesque scurrility, is really a much better mannered poem than had been previously allowed in satire. Cowley characteristically writes a poem about the middle way between the excesses of Puritanism and Popery. His theme is that the extremes are mirror images of each other—though he finds more distortion in the Puritan image. Like Cleveland's satire it deals in personalities and topicalities, but, unlike Cleveland, Cowley manages to embody his sense of the middle way in the orderliness of a couplet which tends to assert balance and reasonableness rather than barbed hostility:

> They [the Catholics] an unprofitable zeal have got,
> Of invoking Saints that hear them not.
> Twere well you did so; nought may moe be fear'd
> In your fond prayers, than that they should be heard.
> To them your Non-sense well enough might passe,
> They'd ne're see that i' the' Divine Looking-glasse,
> Nay, whether you'de worship Saints is not yet knowne,
> For ye' have as yet of your Religion none.

The technique of balancing opposites is used by Rochester (as in the conversation between the satirist and the 'formal Band and Beard' of the *Satyr Against Mankind* (lines 104–109)) and is a key device of Pope's satire. Cowley is here using an ordering technique to comment on the disorderliness of his material and help to bring it into proper focus.

It was Andrew Marvell, however, who in the Restoration
showed how an architectural order could be used to enrich satiric
meaning. Marvell's early satires, like *Flecknoe* (1646?) and the
Character of Holland (1653) are not to be distinguished in this way
from Cleveland's satire. The *Character of Holland* attempts to stig-
matise Holland in the way that the *Rebell Scot* stigmatises Scotland,
but Marvell's natural good temper and optimism and his inability
to create the verbal tensions Cleveland achieves leaves us with a
badly written set of jokes rather than a concerted attack. Perhaps
at this stage of his career he really did regret the new taste for
satire, where, as he writes in his poem to Richard Lovelace:

> He highest builds, who with most art destroys,
> And against others' fame his own employs.

This preference for building something solid rather than something that will merely destroy certainly shines through his greatest
satire, the *Last Instructions to a Painter* (1667). Marvell is careful to
construct an over-all unity to the poem that reflects the central
theme, that the King must be the unifying presence of his kingdom:

> But Ceres corn, and Flora is the spring,
> Bacchus is wine, the country is the King.

Marvell in the final address to the King takes off his satiric robes
and asserts the values that have been implied in the satire throughout. He also places right in the centre of the poem a passage in
praise of Archibald Douglas, the 'loyal Scot' who was willing to
die in defence of the ships the Dutch were attacking. Douglas
embodies that heroic virtue which the satirical verse surrounding
his portrait denies the English. He functions, therefore, both as a
means of defining what the English lack and as a central assertion
of value in the poem.[11]

To distinguish between the satire and the positive assertion of
virtue Marvell moves in his verse between a cacophanous, disruptive language modelled on Cleveland and a genuine use of the
heroic couplet to embody the heroic. The verse itself, therefore,
frequently enacts the orderliness it describes. Marvell's contribution to Restoration satire is to provide it with the shapeliness and
the orderly verse techniques that will allow positive attitudes to be
stated as well as implied. Rochester, who was himself compli-

mented by Marvell (according to Aubrey) as 'the only man in England that had the true veine of satire' learnt much from the older poet. Above all he learnt of the possibility of conceiving his satires as structures rather than as a series of consecutive lines. He must also have been helped towards evolving a more restful, mannerly style than the scourging satirist tradition had encouraged. Marvell's couplets can still sound uncomfortably like the biting iambics of Cleveland:

> When grievance urged, he swells like squatted toad,
> Frisks like a frog, to croak a tax's load;
> His patient piss he could no longer hold than
> An urinal, and sit like any hen;
> At table jolly as a country host
> And soaks his sack with Norfolk, like a toast;
> At night, than Chanticleer more brisk and hot,
> And Sergeant's wife serves him for Pertelote.

The use of Chaucer in this passage (as in others) suggests how much Marvell is writing in the native traditions; yet his ability to encompass a more orderly language in satire must have helped to confirm Rochester's decision, unanticipated in English satire before Marvell, to use a mannerly style in his major satires. The reason he does this will become clear when we look more closely at them in the next chapter, but that such a choice was neither inevitable nor, indeed, likely needs to be stated here. Looking back from our vantage point in the twentieth century we take it for granted that Dryden's and then Pope's use of a polished cultivated style for satire is the right one. Indeed it was customary to think (as Pope did) of Rochester's use of the couplet as somewhat rough and irregular. 'He has very bad versification sometimes' Pope remarked to Spence.[12] But Rochester had not the advantage of reading even Dryden's satire, let alone Pope's, before he wrote his own. The satire in English that he would have read was dominated largely by the Elizabethan tradition of the scourging satirist and it would be taken for granted by most people that Drant's view that 'a satyre is a tarte and carpying kynd of verse' was the correct one, for it was still generally assumed that satire was connected with the Satyrs. Oldham, who was Rochester's protégé, was still writing scourging satire after Rochester's death, though he had learned enough from his master to modify his tone in the direction of civility. On several occasions Pope is concerned to contrast Rochester's comparative delicacy with Oldham's roughness.[13] Even Dryden, in the lines to Oldham's memory (1683), acknowledges that 'Satyr' does not need smoothe versification. The fact that Dryden takes the trouble to spell out the incorrectness of the traditional etymological explanation of the word satire in his *Original and Progress of Satire* as late as 1693 suggests that the old view is still widely current. Isaac Casaubon, Dryden's authority, it is true, had made the discovery in his *De Satyrica* as early as 1605, but it had clearly not become widely accepted or even widely known, else there would be no point in belabouring the point in 1693. Even as late as 1700 Samuel Cobb praises Oldham for adopting a style 'like Satyrs rough' and an anonymous author a year later comments on the absurdity of having Epic and 'Satyr' expressed in the same 'heroic mein' and that polished verse is inappropriate for satire.[14]

The French Connection

Rochester's practice then is a considerable departure from the native tradition, though he still owes much to it. It is true that in Ben Jonson's satirical epistles a gentler, Horatian manner is used, but this was too sophisticated and difficult a style to find much following in the seventeenth century—it requires the utmost refinement of language, and as satire became more topical so such refinement seemed less relevant or appropriate to the needs of the day. Jonson's subtle, discursive language of the epistles, was not, I believe, Rochester's model. But if we look across the English Channel to what Rochester was reading in French in the late 1660s and early '70s we find much that will help to explain further Rochester's satiric technique. It is worth noting that Marvell calls Rochester the only man 'in England' who wrote satire correctly. Marvell's knowledge of French poetry was certainly considerable and the inference that other poets elsewhere were writing satire correctly seems reasonable. We know for certain that Rochester was reading the work of his young contemporary, Nicolas Boileau-Despréaux because, as I have said, he used Boileau's third satire extensively in writing *Timon*. He may also have used Boileau's fourth and eighth satires in writing the *Satyr Against Mankind*. Boileau's eighth satire is, in a different sense from Rochester's poem, a satire against mankind. There are a few lines of Boileau's poem which remind us of Rochester's satire. Boileau, for instance, writes of restless man caught in a vortex that takes him unceasingly from thought to thought:

> Mais l'Homme sans arrest, dans sa course insensée,
> Voltige incessamment de pensée en pensée,
> Son cœur toûjours flottant entre mille embarras
> Ne sçait ni ce qu'il veut, ni ce qu'il ne veut pas.[15]

[But man without ceasing, in his mad career, is swept incessantly from thought to thought, his heart always irresolute amidst a thousand obstacles, knows neither what he wants or what he does not want]

which seems to be echoed in Rochester's poem in:

> Stumbling from thought to thought, falls headlong down
> Into doubt's boundless Sea . . .

And later, when Boileau is demonstrating the superiority of animals over man (125–152), he seems to find an echo in Rochester's lines on the same topic (114–140). In this case, though both poets are voicing commonplaces of the theriophilic tradition, there are some lines that seem quite close. Boileau writes:

> L'Homme seul, l'Homme seul en sa fureur extrême,
> Met un brutal honneur à s'égorger soi-même. (151–152)

[Man, man alone in his extreme ferocity exhibits a brutal honour in cutting his own throat.]

Rochester writes:

> Birds feed on Birds, Beasts on each other prey,
> But Savage man alone does Man betray . . .

Boileau's fourth satire, which in theme is in some ways closer to Rochester's *Satyr Against Mankind*, seems to be echoed in the lines of Rochester translating a choric speech from Seneca's *Troades*. The libertine, writes Boileau, holds that these ancient ideas of demons and flames are suitable for frightening women and children; that it is to encumber themselves with superfluous cares and that in fact all the pious are mad. This is considerably nearer Rochester's version than the original Latin, which has no mention of 'flames' (Rochester's 'fiery jails') nor (not surprisingly) of the Christian 'demons' (Rochester's 'foul fiend') nor of the feebleness of the people who believe in them. Rochester's lines, like Boileau's, are unmistakably of the Christian tradition (for even the grisly dog Cerberus can be found in Dante):

> For Hell and the foul fiend that rules
>   God's everlasting fiery jails
> (Devised by rogues, dreaded by fools),
> With his grim, grisly dog that keeps the door
>   Are senseless stories, idle tales,
>   Dreams, whimseys, and no more.

Seneca's lines on the other hand are firmly placed in the Graeco–Roman tradition:

> Taenara, et aspero
> Regnum sub domino, limen et obsidens
> Custos non facili Cerberus ostio,
> Rumores vacui, verbaque inania,
> Et par sollicito fabula somnio.

[Taenarus and the kingdom under its harsh lord (Pluto), the dog Cerberus who blocks the way and guards the difficult approach— all are inane words, empty lies and like the action of a terrifying nightmare.]

None of these parallels adds up to anything like proof that Rochester was borrowing these specific lines. The vexed problem of Rochester's exact sources, especially for the *Satyr Against Mankind*, has received a great deal of attention, most recently by D. H. Griffin in his book on Rochester.[16] The conclusion at which modern scholarship has arrived is that while no precise source has been found the poem is a tissue of ideas culled from a wide variety of sources. When Rochester was not using a specific source (as, for instance, he does in *Timon* and the *Allusion to Horace*) his method was to weave together ideas and verbal reminiscences that he held in what seems to have been a retentive memory. Burnet tells us in the *Life*: 'sometimes other men's thoughts mixed with his composures, but that flowed rather from the Impressions they made on him when he read them, by which they came to return upon him as his own thoughts, than that he serviley copied from any'.[17]

The problem at issue here, however, is not what Rochester's precise sources may or may not have been, but what in general he would have learnt from his undoubted knowledge of French poetry and Boileau in particular. To understand this Boileau's position in the French tradition of satire must be briefly described. When he wrote the Satires that Rochester read, Boileau was a young man in his late twenties. If Rochester met him on his visit to France in 1661–2 Rochester would have been only 14 years old, Boileau 25. On the return journey from Italy in 1664–5 Rochester might have heard of the six satires that Boileau had by then written (nos. 1–7 in modern editions but *excluding Le Repas Ridicule* that Rochester used for *Timon*). He could have obtained a copy of these six in a pirated edition that appeared late in 1665 and in an authorised edition that appeared on 6 March 1666, which included *Le Repas Ridicule*. Boileau was not yet 30 when these satires were issued and the Boileau we think of today, the pillar of the neo-classical establishment, the author of *Le Lutrin* and the *Art Poéti-que*, had not yet appeared. The young Boileau was a very different character, a quarrelsome, heterodox young man, who frequented the *Croix-Blanche*, a literary club where he met such notorious *libertins* as the ancient poet Jacques Vallée des Barreaux, as well as more respectable, sceptical minds like Molière and La Mothe le Vayer and the gourmand brothers du Broussin, one of whom became the chief satirical butt of the third satire. A hostile commentator described Boileau in 1666 as a 'declared parasite, *farceur*, impious blasphemer in places where drunkenness and debauchery abound'.[18] This was an exaggeration, but there was enough truth in it to make the attack plausible. His brother Gilles (another of Boileau's enemies) gives a not dissimilar picture:

> Il était en ce temps fort dissipé dans le monde . . . il n'eut pas fort grand souci de dire son bréviare avec l'application qui étoit nécessaire, ni de mener une vie telle que doit un bénéficier selon les règles exactes du Christianisme.

[He was at this time a dissipated man of the world . . . he was indifferent about saying his breviary with the necessary application, nor did he lead the kind of life befitting a beneficed clergyman according to the exact rules of Christianity.]

More important than his personal behaviour at this time were his literary affinities. These early satires contain a tradition of Horatian satire that goes back to the early years of the century and whose greatest exponent is the poet Mathurin Régnier (1573–1613). Régnier was a great opponent of the father of French neo-classicism, Malherbe, and it is ironic that Boileau was later to assume Malherbe's neo-classical mantle. Both Régnier and the young Boileau, fifty years later, though their practice relates to Horace, felt freer to develop their own techniques and attitudes than the neo-classical doctrines of strict imitation allowed. In English the difference would be that between a strict imitator of Horace like Jonson and the much freer use Rochester makes of the Latin poet. But the English did not develop a *tradition* of Horatian imitation until later, and the contrast between the two countries in this respect is between the English 'Juvenalian' tradition (as it was understood) of rough satire and the more polished French Horatian satire.

Rochester learnt from both traditions and therefore his satire partakes of both. In particular he learnt to modify the harshness of English versification towards the greater mellifluousness of the French couplet. He learnt to use a more 'correct', polished language than had generally been allowed in English satire. He learnt (perhaps from Régnier directly) a greater sense of realism, so that, like Régnier's and Boileau's satire, the pictures he describes of contemporary life are not grotesque as they are in Cleveland and Marvell, but often convincingly realistic portraits. And he learnt that satire need not be confined to the narrow range of subjects, mostly moral or topical, of the English tradition, but could range into philosophical and wider social matters. Two further qualities of Rochester's satire may owe something to the French tradition: the use of reported conversation and in particular the use of an *adversarius* to whom the satirist puts his case (though there are signs of this technique in some Elizabethan satire and it could have come directly from classical example). Finally something is owed to French satire in Rochester's use of a wider range of satiric *personae* than the Elizabethan formal tradition allowed. Rochester's invention of a satiric character to speak the satire, however, Artemisia, Timon, the Maim'd Debauchee, 'Mulgrave' in the *Heroicall Epistle in Answer to Ephelia* and in *M.G. to O.B.*) could have developed from the use of *prosopopœia*, the art of character representation well understood by English rhetoricians and English poets. A popular satire in BM MS Sloane 826 is entitled *Prosopopœia on the* [*Duke of Buckingham*] and has the Duke address us directly to condemn himself out of his own mouth, just as Mulgrave does in the *Heroicall Epistle*.

Boilaeu's satire does not evince all these qualities, but from it Rochester could certainly have learnt a gentler use of language and of metre than was customary in English satire as well as a greater realism in the treatment of his scenes. Satire 3, *Le Repas Ridicule,* is perhaps the most realistic of all Boileau's satires and much of this realism survives in *Timon.* Boileau wrote the satire towards the end of 1665, about a year after he had completed the previous satire, *L'Embarras de Paris,* which is now placed sixth in the satires. It seems to record a definite break with his friends of the *Croix-Blanche* (though not with Molière) and marks the beginning of a soberer, more moralistic phase than is expressed in the earlier satires. The subject of attack is the gourmand the Abbé du Broussin, who is represented in the poem by the initial P while the Adversarius (A) represents the voice of the poet. The satire is an imitation of the eighth satire of Horace's second book and rather closer to Horace than Régnier's imitation in his eleventh satire. Like Horace's satire Boileau's reports a conversation between the poet and a diner who tells the story of a previous day's feast. But while Horace treats his interlocutor with respect, Boileau mocks him by allowing him to present himself as a fussy, greedy man. For Horace the joke is shared between the two conversationalists and revolves round the absurdities of the host and his other guests. Rochester is perhaps closer here to Horace than Boileau, though by giving Timon the tone of voice of the scourging satirist he makes Timon's position somewhat equivocal—we are not really sure whether to be for him, as we are for Horace's Fundanius, or against him, as we are against Boileau's P. In this Rochester is perhaps closest of all to Régnier than anyone else, and as Griffin believes the ending of the poem is a direct borrowing from Régnier, perhaps this is a conclusive reason for accepting Régnier as a direct influence on Rochester.[19] Régnier describes the events as happening to himself while Timon (who, like Rochester, is a poet) has the same friends as the poet (Sedley, Buckhurst, Savile). Régnier's satirist, however, is more obviously meant to represent the attitudes we are to assume ourselves. It is interesting that in Satire eight Régnier has a fop address him on his poetic talents (lines 25–39) rather as does Rochester's fool in *Timon.* Taking into account the coarsening of tone that is due to the influence of the English scourging satirist tradition (and Shakespeare's *Timon* in particular) Rochester's satiric *persona* is fairly close to Régnier's.

Both Régnier and Rochester concentrate on the absurdities of the
dinner and the diners and we can on balance take the attitudes of the
satiric *personae* as those endorsed by the poets. Something of Roches
ter's greater roughness and energy, too, comes over in Régnier's
poem, though Régnier is more closely tied to stock description (as,
for instance, in the *description* of the pedant, lines 139–242) and his
poem is less able to reflect the general disgust with mankind that
informs all Rochester's major satires.

Both French poets, however, working in the Horatian tradition
of French formal satire, are careful to adopt a comparatively cultivated tone and both present us with a more carefully modulated
couplet than Rochester. Rochester keeps some iambic feet in the
English camp, as it were. Let us compare the three poets, however,
in related passages of the three poems to show how the language
is used. All three modern poets (unlike Horace) end their satires
with the dining place in an uproar, plates and food are thrown, the
guests start fighting. Régnier's fight, like Boileau's, begins over a
literary argument, Rochester's (knowing his countryment were
less likely to get themselves worked up over books) has them fight
over whether the French are cowards or not. Here is Régnier's
description of the opening of the fight (lines 369–383):

> Et sembloit que la gloire en ce gentil assaut
> Fust à qui parleroit non pas mieux mais plus haut.
> Ne croyez en parlant que l'un ou l'autre dorme:
> 'Comment, vostre argument,' dist l'un, 'n'est pas en forme.'
> L'autre tout hors du sens: 'Mais c'est vous, malautru,
> Qui faites le sçavant et n'estes pas congru'.
> L'autre: 'Monsieur le sot, je vous feray bien taire:
> Quoy? Comment? est-ce ainsi qu'on frape Despautere?
> Quelle incongruité! vous mentez par les dents!
> —Mais vous!' Ainsi ces gens à se picquer ardents,
> S'en vindrent du parler à tic tac; torche, lorgne,
> Qui casse le museau, qui son rival éborgne,
> Qui jette un pain, un plat, une assiette, un couteau,
> Qui pour une rondache empoigne un escabeau;
> L'un faict plus qu'il ne peut et l'autre plus qu'il n'ose . . .[20]

[And it seemed that the glory in this noble fight would go to him
who spoke not best, but loudest. You can believe we neither slept
during this argument. 'Why,' said one of them, 'your argument is

badly presented.' The other, beside himself, replied, 'It's you, you misshapen idiot, who plays the scholar and is off the track.' The other says, 'Fool, I will shut you up, what? how? is this the way to quote Van Penteran's grammar? What absurdity! You lie in you teeth! But you . . .!' So these people go on quarrelling vehemently, speaking against each other click-clack, ding-dong, some thump each other in the jaw or put out their rival's eye, others throw bread, platters, plates, knives, others grab stools as shields, one of them does more than his strength allows, the other more than he dares.]

For all the slangy rumbustuousness of this passage (and it has a superb force and energy) the impression is given that the poet-satirist is very much in charge of the poem. His scornful attitude is one of superiority and there is no doubt that we are meant to agree with him. He sums up his wisdom and their foolishness in pithy 'sentences' like that of the last line I quote: 'one does more than he can: the other more than he dares'. The combatants are pedantic, boorish fools. It is they that supply the disruptive element to the verse—the slangy language, the breaks in the smooth-flowing rhythmic patterns. It is the poet-satirist (poet and satiric *persona* are virtually one) that provides the controlling ordering patterns: the characteristic end-stopping of French hexameter verse is here clearly illustrated, giving the rhythm a formal regularity that is rarely met with in English before Waller and, in satire, before Dryden. By later French neo-classical standards, however, this verse is highly irregular both in its rhythmic freedom and in its use of coloquial language. A comparison with Boileau's satire (even though it is Boileau before his complete conversion to neo-classical correctness) will illustrate how much more concerned he is with strict orderliness.

Boileau's diners also find themselves in dispute on literary matters (this seems to be Régnier's invention, it is not in Horace). And, as in Régnier's satire, Boileau's third satire ends with the disputants coming to blows. Even the debate, however, is at a rather higher level of expression, if not of content, than Régnier's (let alone Rochester's) [200–216]:

'Il est vrai que Quinaut est un Esprit profond',
A repris certain Fat, qu'à sa mine discrete
Et son maintien jaloux j'ai reconnu Poëte:

'Mais il en est pourtant, qui le pouroient valoir.'
'Ma foy, ce n'est pas vous qui nous le ferez voir'
A dit mon Campagnard avec une voix claire,
Et déjà tout boüillant de vin et de colere.
'Peut-etre', a dit l'Auteur paslissant de couroux:
'Mais vous, pour en parler vous y connoissez-vous?'
'Mieux que vous mille fois', dit le Noble en furie.
'Vous? Mon Dieu, mêlez-vous de boire, je vous prie',
A l'auteur sur-le-champ aigrement reparti.
'Je suis donc un Sot? Moi? vous en avez menti.'
Reprend le Campagnard, et sans plus de langage,
Lui jette pour deffi, son assiette au visage:
L'autre esquive le coup, et l'assiette volant
S'en va frapper le mur et revient en roulant.[21]

['It is true that Quinault is a profound wit', a certain fop replied,
whom I recognised as a poet by his sober appearance and envious
disposition: 'but he is, however, one of those who might deserve
to be one.' 'My god, you'll not be able to convince us of it,' said
the rustic distinctly, already boiling over with wine and anger.
'Perhaps,' said the author, paling with anger, 'But what do you
know that gives you the right to talk about it?' 'A thousand times
more than you,' said the noble rustic in a fury. 'You, by God, I'd
stick to your drinking, if I were you,' the author straightway snaps
acrimoniously. 'I'm a sot then, am I? you're a liar,' replied the
rustic and without more words throws a plate in his face in
defiance: the other dodges the blow and the flying plate hits the
wall and comes rolling back.]

This is (like Horace's) a rather higher class gathering than those
described by Régnier and Rochester, though an aristocratic class
distinction occurs only in Rochester's poem. Boileau's satiric observer—though it is not clear from this passage—has already been
established as a ridiculously pernickity gourmet. Here he acts less
as a disgruntled participant than as a disgusted observer. Boileau's
manner is also the most decorous of the three poets. Compared to
both Régnier and, even more, Rochester the language (given the
circumstances) is not excessively rough and colloquial and the prevailing artistic control is much in evidence. Even more than in
Régnier's poem the couplets assert a civilised judgment on the
festal barbarities, with the added subtlety that the observer

himself has already been ironically undercut. The satiric observer's later comment on 'cette lutte barbare'—this barbarious struggle—has added piquancy when we consider the extreme and absurd fastidiousness of his character. The passage in Boileau owes much to Régnier but is generally politer in tone and handled with greater irony.

Rochester is closer to Régnier in most respects and in general his language is harsher, less precisely controlled, more vehement even than Régnier. The satiric *persona*, though closely related to the poet, has also much of the Elizabethan scourging satirist about him, and this gives the poem a smouldering anger that seems to make these idiotic proceedings typical of what the satirist expects of man in general. Rochester's stance, therefore, is ultimately much more unsettling than either Régnier's (who is a sensible man among idiots) or Boileau's who—himself a sensible man—presents us with one kind of idiot (the over-fastidious) in the company of idiots of a different sort (the under-fastidious). Boileau's method is ultimately to establish a balance: between the extremes we find the truth. Rochester's method is ultimately to establish uncertainty about our values, to secure distrust and displeasure. We shall return again to this poem in the next Chapter, but let us hear now something of Rochester's version of the fight:

> 'Damn me!' says Dingboy. 'The French cowards are,
> They pay, but th'English, Scots and Swiss make war.
> In gaudy troops at a review they shine,
> But dare not with the Germans battle join.
> What now appears like courage is not so:
> 'Tis a short pride which from success does grow.
> On their first blow they'll shrink into those fears
> They showed at Cressy, Agincourt, Poitiers.
> Their loss was infamous; honour so stained
> Is by a nation not to be regained.'
> 'What they were then, I know not, now th'are brave.
> He that denies it—lies and is a slave,'
> Says Huff and frowned. Says Dingboy, 'That do I'
> And at that word at t'other's head let fly
> A greasy plate, when suddenly they all
> Together by the ears in parties fall:
> Halfwit with Dingboy joins, Kickum with huff.

Their swords were safe, and so we let them cuff
Till they, mine host, and I had all enough.

These are comparatively weak lines, not only less impressive than
those of the two French poets, but much less dynamic than earlier
parts of the poem. The use of expletives like 'does', 'do', 'all'
weaken the effect and the syntax is often unproductively inelegant.
The lines serve to illustrate well, however, what Rochester learnt
from French example. The use of direct speech, rare in English
satire before, here results in a sense of actuality that helps to place
both characters and scene before our eyes. The language is now
perspicuous, if tough; the witty, paradoxical style of Cleveland
and Marvell has given way to something closer to the neo-classical
clarity of the late Augustans. The couplet is characteristically the
unit of both rhythm and syntax together. Orderliness is now at
least as much the concern of the poet as attack and destruction.
And the poem as a whole is organised in a new way, for the poem
tells a story (a story borrowed from the French writers) whereas
earlier English formal satire is held together by its themes. Even
Marvell's *Last Instructions,* although it has a narrative element, is
organised primarily in terms of its thematic content. There are
many much better lines in the poem than those I have quoted,
where Rochester is able to combine the vigour of Régnier with the
control of Boileau, but we shall need to discuss the full poem later.

Philosophical Satire

Rochester learnt from French example one other quality that has
not yet been illustrated: that satire could broaden its subject to
include philosophical matters. I have already suggested that *Timon*
has philosophical implications that are not adumbrated by Régnier
or Boileau in their related poems, even though they are only present in a rather shadowy fashion. The philosophical implications
become stronger in *Tunbridge Wells* and *Artemisia to Chloe* where
Rochester's theme is the disorderly nature of man and his universe
and where the problem is how to impose some kind of order. It is,
however, in the *Satyr Against Reason and Mankind* that Rochester's
satire is most intellectually challenging. The themes that Rochester deals with in this poem he partly obtains from Hobbes and
Montaigne but partly from those several French satirists who had

dealt with the problem of the fundamental nature of man and his relation to the natural world, especially to animals. Possible sources are Boileau's eighth satire and also his fourth. The eighth satire, as Antoine Adam points out, is essentially a Christian *vanitas* poem expressing the foolishness of man's pride in his own abilities.[22] Boileau's poem is in the long tradition of Augustinian thought which seeks to humble man so that he can the better worship God with humility.[23] Boileau purports to show that man, for all his proud arrogance, is no better than the animals. Needless to say there is nothing of a Christian purpose in Rochester's poem, though in the first section of the poem (lines 1–122) he borrows anti-rationalist arguments to undermine the Christian rationalist (the 'formal band and beard') in a similar way to Boileau's treatment of the rationalistic 'Docteur' and then goes on to use theriophilic arguments, which Boileau also uses, in the second section of the poem (123–173). Rochester's ultimate purpose is to stand the Augustinian argument on its head by suggesting men are so depraved that the only hope is in the use of the kind of spiritual abstractions that the Augustinian tradition finds demonstrative of man's vanity. In the last section of the poem the poet is forced to the conclusion that only a life led according to abstract 'laws' (219) has any chance of overcoming man's sinfulness and searches for a man:

> 'Whose passions bend to his unbiased mind' (186)

and

> 'Whose pious life's a proof he does believe
> Mysterious truths, which no man can conceive.'

These ideas are part of the age-old tradition of Christian optimism that suggests that man can overcome his propensity for evil, though in Rochester's poem they remain putative and largely ironic. *If* you can find a man like this, says the satirist, I shall recant my paradox (217). The paradox itself can be presented as:

(i) That man's reasoning tendency prevents him from living (being) because it abstracts him from feeling, he should therefore aim to return to nature and so to natural feeling.

(ii) That man's natural feelings are so depraved that he would be better to live a life divorced from them.

The first argument is frequently met with among libertine writers in the seventeenth century. The second argument probably derives from Hobbes in Part 1 of *Leviathan* where man's life in nature is described in the famous phrase as 'solitary, poor, nasty, brutish and short'. This view of man without civilisation, however, clearly derives from the Augustinian view of man without God as a depraved creature, and Boileau's satire, as Antoine Adam argues, is part of that tradition.

The libertine argument can be found in French satire. Régnier's sixth satire is an attack on 'honour', conceived of as an absurd abstraction which prevents people from leading the natural life (93–96):

> Qui nous veut faire entendre, en ses vaines chimeres,
> Que, pour ce qui nous touche, il se perd si noz meres,
> Noz femmes et noz sœurs font leurs maris jaloux,
> Comme si leurs desirs dependissent de nous.

[which tries to make us believe in its vain chimaeras that, in so far as it affects us, it is lost if our mothers, wives and sisters make their husbands jealous, as if their desires depended on us].

That this abstraction is a result of urbanisation is made clear in the contrast that is drawn between a society devoted to abstraction and the simple life of the countryside 'before Saturn was superseded by Juppiter' (131), that is, in the libertine's golden age. Since then mankind has been plagued with hunger, hypocrisy, blasphemy, plague, venereal diseases, brothels—but all these are nothing compared to Honour: (155, 159–168):

> Ce fier serpent qui couve un venim soubs des fleurs
>
> .   .   .
>
> Mais ce traistre cruel, excedant tout pouvoir,
> Nous fait suer le sang soubs un pesant devoir,
> De chimeres nous pipe et nous veut faire acroire
> Qu'au travail seulement doibt consister la gloire,
> Qu'il faut perdre et someil et repos et repas,
> Pour tâcher d'aquerir un suget qui n'est pas,
> Ou, s'il est, qui jamais aux yeux ne se decouvre
> Et perdu pour un coup jamais ne se recouvre,
> Qui nous gonfle le cœur de vapeurs et de vent,
> Et d'exces par luy mesme il se perd bien souvent.

[(Honour), this fierce serpent which breeds venom under the flowers . . . But this cruel, all powerful traitor, makes us sweat blood under a heavy load, entices us with mirages and tries to make us believe that glory must consist only in hard work, that one must forego sleep, repose, food to try to gain something that does not exist, or, if it does, which no eyes have seen and which if it is lost for a minute it is never recovered, which inflates our hearts with dizziness and wind and which loses itself very often in its own excesses.]

Rochester too can be eloquent on the foolishness of following the will-o'-the-wisp of honour. But Régnier here is using this abstraction to stand for a general tendency in the human mind: to follow abstraction rather than the reality of actual things. Régnier ends his poem wittily by going off to dinner with the comment that few are willing to talk in abstractions when food is to be had. The tendency of this satire, as of the first part of Rochester's satire, is to pour scorn, in the libertine manner, on man's propensity for abstraction and hold up libertine materialism as the choice of common sense.

Another French poet whose work Rochester must surely have known is the famous libertine poet Théophile de Viau (1590–1626). Théophile's defiant unorthodoxy which (reputedly) led to a death-bed conversion has much to remind us of Rochester. Théophile's open religious scepticism led to his imprisonment and trial. In his first satire—which begins very much like a satire against mankind—Théophile argues that animals are happier than men partly because they do not reason: they live a life of practicality, avoiding abstractions: (31–38):

> Elle ignore le mal pour en avoir la peur,
> Ne cognoist point l'effroy de l'Acheron trompeur.
> Elle a la teste basse, et les yeux contre terre,
> Plus pres de son repos, et plus loing du tonnere:
> L'ombre des trespassez n'aigrit son souvenir,
> On ne voit à sa mort le desespoir venir:
> Elle compte sans bruit et loing de toute envie
> Le terme dont nature a limité sa vie . . .[24]

[he (the animal) is too ignorant of evil to have fear of it, and the story of deceitful Acheron does not give him cause to fear, she keeps his head low and his eyes to the ground, nearer to repose and further from (the divine) thunder: the shadow of sin does not embitter his memory, one does not see him despairing at death: he expects without complaint and without enviousness the length of life which Nature has granted him.]

The lesson to be drawn from this is the libertine lesson that the closer we can get to the animal world of nature the happier we will be (85–90):

> J'approuve qu'un chacun suive en tout la nature,
> Son Empire est plaisant, et sa loy n'est pas dure:
> Ne suivant que son train jusqu'au dernier moment
> Mesmes dans les malheurs on passe heureusement.
> Jamais mon judgement ne trouvera blasmable
> Celuy-là qui s'attache à ce qu'il trouve aimable . . .

[I approve of each person following Nature in all things, her Empire is pleasant and her law not harsh: if one follows her ways only one lives in happiness until the last moment, even in misfortune. I shall never find blameworthy a person who holds to what he finds pleasurable.]

The avaricious, the ambitious follow 'a vain title of wind', those who consider their honour, especially military honour, are fools. Even love is more trouble than it is worth (175–180)

> Je pense que chacun auroit assez d'esprit,
> Suivant le libre train que Nature prescrit.
> A qui ne sçait farder, ny le cœur, ny la face,
> L'impertinence mesme a souvent bonne grace:
> Qui suivra son Genie, et gardera sa foy,
> Pour vivre bien-heureux, il vivra comme moy.

[I believe that everyone would have enough wit if he followed the free way of life Nature prescribes. On a person who does not know how to paint either his face or his heart impertinence itself often sits well. He who follows his natural bent and keeps faith with himself will live happily and live like me.]

Théophile's libertine naturalism provides Rochester with one half of his paradox. The originality of Rochester's poem is to pit the libertine argument *against* the theriophilic argument that is usually used to support the libertine case. The libertines liked to argue that

man could find happiness if only he returned to nature and used
the contrast between the happiness of animals and the unhappiness
of men to encourage man to live a more natural life. By setting
libertine against theriophilic argument Rochester creates a logical
impasse that not only shows the parlous state of man as neither able
to think *or* feel his way out of trouble, but also throws doubt on
the capabilities of human thought. The *Satyr against Mankind*,
therefore, is essentially a poem in the tradition of philosophical
scepticism that aimed to demonstrate the limitations of the human
mind in solving metaphysical problems. This scientific scepticism
was, of course, very influential during the Restoration period and
informs, for instance, Hobbes' philosophical work and much of
Cowley's poetry.

The tradition of philosophical scepticism, however, is also represented among the French satirists, where it derives in part from
Montaigne. Both Régnier and Boileau write satires where the
limitation of human reason is the principal subject. In Satire 5
Régnier argues that values are relative (lines 41–46):

> Ainsi c'est la nature et l'humeur des personnes
> Et nous la qualité, qui rend les choses bonnes.
> Charnellement se joindre avecq' sa paranté,
> En France c'est inceste, en Perse charité,
> Tellement qu'a tout prendre, en ce monde ou nous sommes,
> Et le bien et le mal depend du goust des hommes.

[Thus it is the nature and disposition of the individual not the
quality of the thing itself which makes things good. To have
sexual intercourse with your relations is incest in France and
charity in Persia, so we see, all things considered, that in this world
both good and evil are according to men's taste.]

Régnier then launches into a defence of his own amorousness by
presenting a similar view of love to that presented by Artemisia in
Artemisia to Chloe. We are all subject to ageing, however, and he is
quite willing to accept that he might change his mind in old age.
He concludes (251–254):

> Mais puisque c'est le tans, meprisant les rumeurs
> Du peuple, laissons là le monde en ces humeurs
> Et si selon son goust un chacun en peut dire,
> Mon goust sera, Bertault, de n'en faire que rire.

[But since such are the times, let us, despising the gossip of the people, leave the world to its humours and if everyone is to decide according to his taste my taste will be, Bertault, to do nothing but laugh.]

This detached view of the satirist who laughs at the contradictions inherent in man's nature is an attitude central to some of Rochester's work.

In Satire 14 Régnier returns to the same subject of the relativity of human judgment. The opening of the poem has an angry energy comparable to that of Rochester's satire (1–10):

> J'ai pris cent et cent fois la lanterne en la main,
> Cherchant en plein midi parmi le genre humain
> Un homme qui fust homme et de faict et de mine
> Et qui peust des vertus passer par l'estamine;
> Il n'est coin et recoin que je n'aye tanté
> Depuis que la nature icy bas m'a planté:
> Mais tant plus je me lime et plus je me rabote,
> Je croy qu'à mon avis tout le monde radote,
> Qu'il a la teste vuide et sans dessus dessous,
> Ou qu'il faut qu'au rebours je sois l'un des plus fous.

[Time after time I have taken my lantern in my hand to search in broad daylight among human kind for a man who was a true man in deed and stature and whose virtues would suffer close examination, there isn't a corner or a cranny that I have not tried, since nature put me down here on earth: but the longer I file away and polish my style it seems to me that either the world drivels, that it is empty-headed and upside down, or on the contrary, that I must be one of the most foolish.]

The small lantern of reason, however, is helpless to sort out the complexities of human nature. Everyone sees things from his own subjective point of view, as 'people see the land slipping away and not their boat'. Reason itself is an unreliable guide. Reason is a strange beast (155–158):

> Ainsi ceste raison est une estrange beste,
> On l'a bonne selon qu'on a bonne la teste,
> Qu'on imagine bien du sens comme de l'œil,
> Pour grain ne prenant paille, ou Paris pour Corbeil.

[Thus this reason is a strange beast, reason is all right if we have a clear head, it is supposed to have as much perception as the eye, not taking chaff for grain, nor Corbeil for Paris.]

Boileau's fourth satire adopts a similar viewpoint. Men have an almost infinite capacity for deceiving themselves (38–40):

> En ce monde il n'est point de parfaite sagesse.
> Tous les hommes sont fous, et malgré tous leurs soins,
> Ne different entre Eux que du plus ou du moins.

[There is no perfect wisdom in this world, all men are fools and in spite of all their efforts differ only slightly one from the other.]

The wisest are those who don't even realise they are wise (54) but who realise their own shortcomings. The worst evil of all is often our reason which prevents our desires from functioning naturally (114–116):

> Souvent de tous nos maux la Raison est le pire.
> C'est Elle qui farouche, au milieu des plaisirs,
> D'un remords importun vient brider nos desirs.

[Often reason is the worst of all our ills, it is reason which brutally, in the midst of our pleasures, comes to check our desires with unwelcome remorse.]

This libertine notion that thought inhibits our natural selves occurs not only in Rochester's *Satyr*, but in lyrics like 'What cruel pains Corinna takes' and *The Fall* (where it is handled philosophically) and is a theme of *The Imperfect Enjoyment*. In Boileau's poem the libertine element was even stronger originally, for Boileau suppressed the most outspoken libertine lines in the published version of 1666:

> Jouissez des douceurs que demande votre age,
> Et ne vous plaignez pas ces innocens plaisirs
> Dont l'argent, tous les jours, peut combler vos desirs.

[Enjoy the pleasures your age calls for and do not find fault with those innocent pleasures in which money can always gratify your desires.]

Rochester's *Satyr* is very different in tone from Boileau's fourth satire, rather closer to Régnier's. Rochester develops his paradox not only intellectually, as an impasse between two interpretations of man's nature, but as a clash between the anger that man's impossible situation generates in the satirist and his powerlessness to do anything about it. It is the satirist who ends by looking lame and absurd. However, the purpose here is not to interpret the *Satyr* critically, but to give some idea of the traditions of verse satire from which Rochester is borrowing. Without understanding what Rochester inherits we cannot be in a position to understand what he does with his inheritance.

Rochester's satiric inheritance, then, is varied and complex. He retains from the English tradition of the 'scourging satirist' the use of an independent *persona* who is sometimes (in *Timon, Tunbridge Wells*) unbalanced and coarse. Accordingly he retains some of the tough roughness of the style that had become associated with this kind of satire. But this roughness is considerably modified towards a more controlled, smoother use of the heroic couplet, a modification that can be accounted for by French influence. The delight in obscurity and wit that characterises much earlier English satire is also modified under the influence of the greater French clarity of style, though Rochester retains a liking for the paradox that is also a feature of earlier English writing. From French example he obtains a greater sense of actuality than is evinced by any earlier English satirist (except the Francophile Chaucer) as well as a willingness to discuss broader philosophical themes than are usually thought fitting in English satire.

SIX

Upon Nothing: Rochester's satire

True Genius, like the *Anima Mundi*, which some of the Ancients believ'd, will enter into the hardest and dryest thing, enrich the most barren Soyl, and inform the meanest and most uncomely matter; nothing within the vast Immensity of Nature, is so devoid of Grace, or so remote from Sence, but will obey the Formings of his plastick Heat, and feel the Operations of his vivyfying Power, which, when it pleases, can enliven the deadest lump, beautifie the vilest Dirt, and sweeten the most offensive Filth; this is a Sprit that blows where it lists, and like the Philosopher's Stone, converts into it self whatsoever it touches; Nay, the baser, the emptier, the obscurer, the fouler, and the less susceptible of Ornament the Subject appears to be, the more is the Poet's Praise, who can infuse dignity and breath beauty upon it, who can hide all the natural deformities in the fashion of his Dresse, supply all the wants with his own plenty, and by a poetical Demonianism, possesse it with the Spirit of good sence and gracefulness, or Who (as Horace says of Homer) can fetch Light out of Smoak, Roses out of Dunghils, and give a kind of Life to the inanimate. . . .[1]

So Robert Wolseley writes in defence of Rochester's poetry in his *Preface to Valentinian*, 1685. Wolseley was primarily concerned here to defend Rochester's lyric poetry against Mulgrave's charge that it made up in bawdy what it lacked in wit. Wolseley asserts a fairly common argument among seventeenth-century critics that: 'it never yet came into any man's Head, who pretended to be a Critick . . . that the Wit of a Poet was to be measur'd by the worth of his Subject' and he quotes the example of Virgil's *Georgics* to support the contention. Such an assertion had been made many

years earlier (probably some time in the 1630s) by Philip Massinger in his praise of James Smith's burlesque poetry:

> It shewd more art in Virgil to relate,
> And make it worth th'heareing, his Gnats fate;
> Then to conceive what those great minds must be
> That sought and found out fruitfull Italie.[2]

As many years, or more, later the Abbé Charles Batteux had much
the same point to make in his *Parallèle de la Henriade et du Lutrin*,
Paris, 1746:

> I should be tempted to believe personally, in considering the
> *Lutrin* and the *Henriade*, that the choice of subject contributes
> nothing towards the success of a poem. One can have a very fine
> poem on a very mediocre subject. One thinks of the *Combat
> between the Frogs and the Rats,* Tassoni's *Rape of the Bucket*, Pope's
> *Rape of the Lock* as perfect works in their genre. The poet is a
> creator, he builds a world upon a point; so it matters little
> whether one sings of a hero or a pulpit; one is only wrong if it
> does not succeed.[3]

Generally this defence of manner over matter refers to light comic
poetry. But Rochester had a tougher, if related, problem on his
hands: how to make poetry out of nothing. Again, earlier poets
had met the problem, as Rosalie Colie has shown in her excellent
account of Renaissance paradox, *Paradoxia Epidemica,* 1966. Writing poetry upon nothing was a popular rhetorical exercise for
Renaissance poets and these were mostly light-hearted poems
playing with contradiction, though poems as distinguished as
Donne's great *Nocturnall upon St Lucy's Day* resulted from the
tradition. Rochester's was a more serious and all-embracing problem: how to construct poetry out of unbelief, how to build a world
on a vanishing point.

Rochester's major satires are an attempt to answer this problem.
We saw in Chapter 4 how Rochester plunges into a world of
negativity and destructiveness in the burlesque poetry and in the
lampoons. The satire proper is often closely related to the burlesque and indeed it is sometimes hard to draw the line between
his burlesque and his satirical poetry. The satire, however, is distinguished by its attempt to construct a coherent world out of the
chaos of experience. This was difficult, because Rochester did not

believe the universe had coherence, or rather he did not believe that men were capable of discovering what, if any, coherence the universe possessed. It is comparatively easy to play with ideas about negativity if you are convinced it is merely play, it is much more difficult to find the meaningful in an apparently meaningless world. What was a comic paradox to the poets who believed in the orderliness of God's universe, became grim irony in Rochester's world.

It would perhaps be as well to say something about what we know of Rochester's metaphysical viewpoint here. Our chief evidence for his views on the nature of the world are to be got from his conversations with Gilbert Burnet just before his death. Burnet recorded these conversations in his *Life of Rochester*, 1680, naturally giving his own Christian gloss on Rochester's views. Rochester makes it clear in these conversations that while he was not, strictly speaking, an atheist, he thought God was unknowable to the human mind:

> As to the Supreme Being, he had always some Impression of one: and professed often to me, That he had never known an entire *Atheist*, who fully believed there was no God.[4]

Generally it is to the capabilities of the human mind he addresses his scepticism throughout these conversations. Man's mind was too limited to have any clearer notion of God than that he was 'a vast power, that had none of the Attributes of Goodness or Justice we ascribe to the Deity'.[5] The idea that one could not know what God was like, but could know what he was not like, stems from Rochester's belief that the world as he knew it could hardly have been the creation of either a good or a just God. He seems to have assumed that the deity was a largely impersonal force:

> When he came to explain his Notion of the Deity, he said he looked on it as a vast Power that wrought every thing by the necessity of its Nature: and thought that God had none of those Affections of Love or Hatred, which breed perturbation in us, and by consequence he could not see that there was to be either reward or punishment. He thought our Conceptions of God were so low, that we had better not think much of him: And to love God seemed to him a presumptuous thing, and the heat of fanciful men.[6]

As Burnet replies to him, this makes God look synonymous with Nature. Certainly it suggests that man was essentially on his own, unloved and uncared for, in a universe he could not understand. It was not that necessarily the universe was meaningless, but that man could never know what that meaning was or if there was one. All man's thoughts and feelings about God Rochester put down to 'the effect of a heat in Nature'. At times he seems to suggest that religion is simply a creation of man's psychological needs. The desire to believe in God, which Rochester admits he shares, is no indication one way or the other that there is any substance in the belief: 'They were happy that believed: for it was not in every Man's power'![7] If man is to all intents and purposes on his own in an incomprehensible universe there are no principles that can govern his conduct and no coherences he can discover, except those that he can devise for himself. Of these devices, love, as we have seen, offered both the most rewarding and the most easily disappointed sense of meaningfulness. The betrayal of love is the main theme of *Artemisia to Chloe*. But there were two other defences against succumbing to total chaos: reason and laughter. Rochester employs both in his poetry extensively. There is a strong streak of rationalism in Rochester's work in spite of his rational scepticism. *The Satyr against Reason* is, paradoxically enough, conceived in syllogistic form and Rochester's chief scorn is often reserved for the stupid and the irrational. His conversations with Burnet show that his concept of moral, and therefore of social, order was essentially a rationalistic one. He could not believe in divine sanctions, but he seems to have believed in rational curbs on behaviour:

[he] was very much ashamed of his former Practices, [i.e. behaviour] rather because he had made himself a Beast, and had brought pain and sickness on his Body, and had suffered much in his Reputation, than from any deep sense of a Supream being or another State: But so far this went with him, that he resolved firmly to change the Course of his Life; which he thought he should effect by the study of *Philosophy*, and had not a few no less solid than pleasant Notions concerning the folly and madness of Vice: but he confessed he had no remorse for his past Actions, as Offences against God, but only as Injuries to himself and to Mankind.[8]

This, of course, is the voice of Rochester at the point of break-down and being reported by someone whose aim was to make the breakdown complete. In his stronger days, however, his tendency was to seek rational answers if they could be found. Certainly his aristocratic upbringing led him to a respect for the orderliness which reason seemed to offer. When reason failed, however, (as it so often did) it was an equally aristocratic quality to find detach-ment in laughter.

Rochester's conversations with Burnet are not the only source of information on Rochester's *Weltanschauung*, but they are the most explicit and the most extensive account of his own point of view. We must remember, however, that they are being reported by someone who was not only totally opposed to such sceptical views but was writing his account specifically to give himself an oppor-tunity to refute the heresies Rochester was promulgating. Burnet received his reward in this life in obtaining the bishopric of Salisbury. If God has any sense of humour and/or irony he will by now, no doubt, have rewarded Rochester in the next life. Roches-ter's viewpoint, as recorded in the *Life*, therefore, needs to be read with caution, all the more because it was expressed at the end of Rochester's life when he was seriously ailing and had long since passed his peak as a poet. The poetry sometimes seems to express a more aggressive agnosticism and a more derisive scepticism of human abilities.

Rochester's Satires: Upon Nothing

Rochester's major satires divide themselves into two distinct groups: there are the social and literary satires, *Timon, Tunbridge Wells*, the *Allusion to Horace* and *Artemisia to Chloe*, and there are the philosophical satires, *Upon Nothing* and the *Satyr against Reason and Mankind*. In this division *Artemisia* holds something of an indeterminate position, because although its subject is, as the 1679 broadside of the poem states on the title page, the 'loves of the town', its implications are more far-reaching than is usually com-prehended in the term social satire. *Upon Nothing*, too, has some-thing of an equivocal status, for though it starts on a metaphysical subject it ends in social satire. It may be thought anyway rather pretensious to consider this poem as philosophical at all, seeing that it belongs to that rhetorical play genre I referred to earlier, the main purpose of which is to produce startling paradoxes. But it is not as 'entirely trivial' as Rosalie Colie maintains and needs to be discussed seriously.[9]

That is not, of course, to say that Rochester's poem is non-comic. Like many of its predecessors Rochester's poem exploits the comic paradoxes in treating 'nothing' as a positive concept. Several such early poems, Rosalie Colie tells us, are collected in a compilation called *Amphitheatrum sapientiae socraticae joco-seriae* (an Amphitheatre of comico-serious Socratic Wisdom) first published in Hanover in 1619 and subsequently in Frankfurt in 1670.[10] These poems are typical of play-rhetoric where the ingenuity in handling ideas totally dominates the ideas themselves. There were examples in English. H. K. Miller lists such examples as Cornwallis' *Prayse of Nothing*, 1616, and an anonymous ballad *Praise of Nothing*, 1625?, 'SS' 's *Paradoxes and Encomiums In the Praise of . . . Nothing etc*, 1653, Billingsley's *Praise of Nothing*, 1658.[11] But although Rochester's poem is comic in its delight in paradox and contradiction it is very far from treating those paradoxes as so many counters in a verbal draughts-game. For Rochester's poem is distinguished by its use of the concept of nothingness, annihilation, 'things that are not', as a metaphor to describe the ultimate meaninglessness of the world with which man has to deal. Griffin notes rightly that sexual imagery plays an important part in the poem in describing the nothingness out of which we are made in terms of a devouring 'hungry womb' (21) whose 'mysteries' only the Divine can 'pry' into or 'pry' open (23), and Griffin links this with the sexual imagery of the lyrics and so to Rochester's personal psychological condition.[12] But there are two important uses of this imagery in the poem that transcend the purely personal, indeed make it irrelevant. Firstly, as Griffin notes, the imagery is confused in seeing 'Nothing' both as male and female ('Nothing' is the 'Elder Brother' of 'shade' in line 1 and *begets* 'Something' in line 5, but has female attributes later). Secondly the description of 'Nothing' as female presents a picture not of human femininity but of the divine female principle that informs the *Ramble in St James's Park*. The womb of nothingness into which matter returns and the bosom which is debarred to mortal eyes are not thought of primarily in physical, but in psychological, terms. Rochester is conjuring up the archetypal image of the earth mother spewing out and then re-absorbing her sons, the White Goddess who demands human sacrifice and whose image, according to Robert Graves, all true poets seek to worship.[13] But these ideas, the confusion of ideas about our origins and the psychological origins of our concepts about the world, find echoes in the passages we quoted from the conversations with Gilbert Burnet. As I pointed out earlier, Rochester believed that our ideas of an after life and of God were products of a 'heat in nature', that is, that they were of psychological origin and indicated nothing about the real nature or even the existence of an after world. We 'embody' the nothing that we know about the after world, through our own physical compulsions—we give it human form, sexual attributes, because it is merely a projection of our own mind, 'whimsies heaped in (our) own brain' as Rochester calls them in the *Satyr against Reason and Mankind.*

Essentially *Upon Nothing* is upon man's inability to know about his origins and purpose. It is not only the sex of 'Nothing' that is confused in the poem; as Griffin again points out,[14] the whole description of the world's genesis is confused, by linking three separate accounts of the world's origins: that 'Nothing' begot 'Something' and then created the world from an incestuous union (stanza 2); that 'Something' was 'sever'd' from 'Nothing' (as Eve from Adam) and, from the power 'Something' was given, created 'Men, Beasts, Birds, Fire, Air and Land' (stanzas 3–4); and that 'Matter', 'Nothing's' 'wicked' offspring, created the world of things in rebellion against 'Nothing'. Such uncertainty, of course, records the varying attempts men have made to explain the origins of the world—all of them, according to Rochester, mere 'Whimsies' of the brain, the results of a 'heat in nature':

> After many Discourses on this Subject [how we know what God wants of us] he still continued to think all was the effect of Fancy: He said, That he understood nothing of it, but acknowledged that he thought they were very happy whose Fancies were under the power of such Impressions; since they had somewhat on which their thoughts rested and centred.[15]

One of the subjects of disagreement with Burnet during the conversations was the contradictions in the Bible.[16] Such a contradiction could be found in the account of man's creation in Genesis. For there are two accounts of the creation there. In Chapter 1 we are told God made male and female in his own image, in Chapter 2 that Adam was made out of the dust of the earth and Eve out of Adam's rib. Two such different accounts merely demonstrate what Rochester thought invariable about man's attempts to understand his origin and purpose: they were subjective and unreliable.[17] Frequently we hear that stress on the subjective notion of experience that we have already noticed as a feature of some of the lyric poetry ('Fair Chloris in a Pigsty' is a case in point). Rochester is discoursing to Burnet on his favourite theme of the compulsion in the human mind to make its own coherence *out of nothing*.

Upon Nothing is informed by this central idea that we have no reliable authority for coming to any conclusions about the world. That we know *nothing* (stanza 10):

> Great *Negative*, how vainly wou'd the Wise
> Enquire, define, distinguish, teach, devise,
> Didst thou not stand to point their dull *Philosophies*.

This (and stanza 9) is the centre of the poem and reaches the heart of its theme (seventeenth-century poetic structure frequently demands a central idea in a central position). The theme is one of complete scepticism: Man knows nothing except that he knows nothing and all human endeavour has to be conducted in that perspective. So the poem goes on to describe the pervasiveness of the idea of 'nothing', its central importance in everything we do, by listing, in the following stanzas, the ways in which this ubiquitous 'nothingness' expresses itself (stanzas 11, 12):

> Is or Is not, the two great ends of Fate,
> And true or false the Subject of Debate,
> That perfect or destroy the vast designs of Fate.

> When they have rack'd the Politicians Breast
> Within thy Bosom [i.e. Nothing's] most securely rest,
> And when reduc'd to thee are least unsafe and best.

The poem is essentially in three parts and each part is logically related. Stanzas 1–7 describe man's attempts to explain his origins in the face of the fact that he knows nothing. Stanzas 8–10, the core of the poem (literally and metaphysically), express explicitly the agnosticism that lies at the centre of Rochester's philosophy. The third part of the poem, stanzas 11–17, illustrates the omnipresence of this general uncertainty in all our doings. Nothing turns out to dominate in King's courts, among Churchmen, among nations:

> The Great *Man*'s Gratitude to his best *Friend*,
> Kings Promises, *Whores* Vows, towards thee they bend,
> Flow swiftly into thee, and in thee ever end.

Everything flows back into the unknown from which it emanated.

Far from being a trivial poem *Upon Nothing* is a masterly, witty and serious exposition of Rochester's fundamental scepticism. It rightly justifies Johnson's high praise, even if we must deny that it is the 'strongest' effort of Rochester's muse. Its tendency is perhaps more strongly agnostic than anything Rochester admitted to Burnet, for it seeks to suggest not only that man knows nothing about his origins, but that his origins are probably in nothing. In this it seems to anticipate the picture of man after death as the 'lumber of the world' described in the translation of Seneca that immediately preceded *Upon Nothing* in the 1680 editions. *Contemporaries* seemed to have seen a connection between the two poems. But for all its profound pessimism the poem does *not* celebrate the triumph of negativity: on the contrary it expresses the possibility of triumph over it. For the very wit and playfulness of the mind that handles the theme expresses the capability of erecting something out of nothing, of building the world upon a point, in a more profound way than Charles Batteux intended. The rhythm of the poem is certainly rough and sometimes uncertain, but the effect of the stanzaic patterning, and especially the determined assertion of the third line Alexandrine, is to give the triumphant ring of creation out of recalcitrant material. Coherence is being found out of the very material of chaos (stanzas 5, 6):

> Matter, the wicked'st off-spring of thy Race,
> By Form assisted, flew from thy Embrace,
> And Rebel Light obscur'd thy reverend dusky Face.

> With *Form* and *Matter*, *Time* and *Place* did join,
> *Body*, thy Foe, with these did Leagues combine,
> To spoil thy peaceful *Realm*, and ruin all thy *Line*.

This is not only a witty account of the 'rebellion' against Chaos which resulted in man's creation, it is an assertion of the role of the poet in that rebellion. For what is poetry but the 'spoiling' of the chaos of words through the imposition of order? Rochester's fondness for the allusive analogy between writing poetry and living has been commented on earlier.[18] His struggle to bring words into an orderly shape is registered through a frequent use of inverted iambic feet (i.e. trochaic feet, as in lines 1 and 5 of the passage quoted) or by supernumerary syllables (as in the penultimate line of the stanza quoted previously). The stately Alexandrine at the end of each stanza, however, reinforces the hold on form by reiterating the rhyme word and rhythmically asserts the triumph of measure. The last line of each stanza is, with only two major exceptions, a regular iambic hexameter (in stanzas 4 and 14 the last line is a regular iambic pentameter) while the heavy end-stopping of all but one stanza gives each stanza a formal close that asserts the stanzaic pattern (this pattern is clearer in the 1680 editions than in Vieth's modern edition). *Upon Nothing*, therefore, picks up the themes implied or stated in the burlesque poetry of the meaninglessness of man's position and asserts its triumph over that negativity in a more decisive way than the language and the ribaldry of the burlesque poems can do. It is for this reason that we must see the poem as satire, a poem attacking man's pretensions and demonstrating our limitations but at the same time asserting the possibility of triumphing, through wit and ingenuity, over these limitations.

A Satyr Against Mankind:

A Satyr against Mankind also bears in several early versions the title of *A Satyr against Reason and Mankind* (the title Vieth adopts).[19] The alternative title is, I think, to be preferred, for the poem is a satire on mankind's power of reasoning, but in a rather different sense from that assumed in the more usual critical readings. Like the poem *Upon Nothing* the *Satyr* is a profoundly sceptical poem. It satirises man's intellectual pretensions, not merely, as did *Upon Nothing,* in asserting the limits of our knowledge, but by demonstrating the weakness of our reasoning processes and the contradictions of our situation. The indignation which, in the curious 'epilogue' to the poem, Rochester says he has 'hurl'd' at mankind's vanity in believing in their reasoning abilities (lines 174–178) is as much anger against the absurdity of man's (and his own) intellectual impotence as against mankind itself. For what distinguishes this poem from any other of Rochester's poems, and indeed makes it unique in the satire of the period, is the intensity of feeling with which Rochester endows his satire. The anger, which is so powerfully expressed, is at the predicament man finds himself in and at that remote, uncaring God who has placed man in his predicament.

The poem seems to have been conceived as a two-part paradox, for in the earliest datable version, that of the 1679 broadside, the poem ends with the couplet that forms lines 172–173 in the longer version of the 1680 edition:

> And all the subject matter of Debate
> Is only who's a Knave, of the first Rate.

Pinto in the notes to his edition of the poem speculates that the final lines, variously called the 'Apology' or the 'Epilogue' in early versions, were written as a retort to an *Answer to the Satyr Against Mankind* which Anthony Wood says was published a month after Rochester's poem appeared. This was variously attributed to a 'Mr Griffith' and Richard Pococke. I think it unlikely that the epilogue was a retort to the *Answer* because it seems to me that the author of that poem misunderstands Rochester's *Satyr*, and the epilogue does not attempt to put the record straight. Rather the added lines seem to round out the *form* of the poem, giving it a tri-partite, syllogistic structure, which to some extent weakens the basic paradox that the poem sets out to assert. For the poem expresses logical impasse and therefore no proper conclusion (as is required by syllogism) is possible. Rochester's desire for formal neatness here to some extent contradicts the tendency of his argument, even though the conclusion is drawn in purely hypothetical terms. It is an interesting example of that stress between formal regularity and emotional and intellectual honesty that informs so much of Rochester's work.

The subjects Rochester treats of in this poem, as I explained in the last chapter, are familiar subjects of discussion in seventeenth-century philosophical debate and in French satirical poetry. The opening section of the poem (lines 1–122) presents us with the traditional theriophilic arguments that were used by Christian pessimists to undermine man's intellectual pride.[20] This section of the poem is conceived of as an imaginary debate between the poet (or his satiric *persona*—the distinction is not clear) and a 'formal

band and beard', a clergyman who takes the then fashionable view
of the Christian optimist that man was made in God's own image
and that his reason is his most god-like attribute:

> Blest Glorious Man! to whom alone kind Heav'n
> An everlasting Soul has freely given,
> Whom his great Maker took such care to make,
> That from himself he did the Image take,
> And this fair frame in shining Reason drest,
> To dignifie his Nature above Beast. (60–65)

The Satirical Spokesman, however, counters this argument with
the accusation that confidence in man's reason revealed the sin of
pride, that reason merely led man astray because it encouraged
him to attempt speculation above his powers (75–79):

> this very Reason I despise,
> This supernatural Gift that makes a *Mite*
> Think he's the Image of the *Infinite*,
> Comparing his short Life, void of all Rest,
> To the Eternal and the ever Blest.

It is for this reason that the satiric *persona* takes up again the argument that begins the poem, that it would be better to be an animal
than human because animals are not led astray by pride in their
reasoning abilities. This theriophilic argument is developed further after the views of the 'band and beard' have been put down in
scorn. Man should aim to be like the animals, using intelligence
for practical purposes, letting reason serve appetite (98–105):

> Thus whilst against false reas'ning I inveigh,
> I own right *Reason*, which I wou'd obey;
> That *Reason* that distinguishes by Sence,
> And gives us *Rules* of good and ill from thence;
> That bounds Desires with a Reforming Will,
> To keep 'em more in vigour, not to Kill.
> Your *Reason* hinders, mine helps to enjoy,
> Renewing Appetite yours wou'd destroy.

Here is the familiar libertine contrast between man acting 'naturally', as his nature prompts, and man as an abstracting animal, who
destroys his own spontaneity by thinking too much on the event.

It is a theme touched on in *The Fall* and in the *Imperfect Enjoyment* that our 'hopes and fears', our propensity for abstraction, help to destroy the 'livelong minute' of actual experience. Rochester describes the tragedy of a disassociated sensibility where the shadow falls 'Between the emotion And the response . . . Between the desire and the spasm'. The libertine answer is to return to nature, to stop thinking and start doing (94–97):

> But thoughts are giv'n for Actions Government,
> Where Action ceases Thought's impertinent:
> Our *Sphere* of Action is Lifes happiness,
> And he who thinks beyond, thinks like an ass. . . .

It should be noticed that the libertine argument here is given absolute priority. The discussion with the 'band and beard' is not a discussion of equals. The rationalistic clergyman is really presented as an Aunt Sally to be swept aside by the force of the satirist's feeling. Rochester gives his satiric speaker the scorn and indignation of the old scourging satirist that he had used in *Timon* and *Tunbridge Wells*. But because the argument is presented with such force and immediacy we do not think of it as presented by a 'spokesman' but by the poet himself. This is deliberate, for the *persona* is the poet in the sense that he represents the emotional conviction of the poem. On the other hand, as we shall see, the *persona*'s point of view is ultimately rejected, indeed made to look absurd. As in the *Ramble* and the *Imperfect Enjoyment* and at a subtler level in *Artemisia,* the poet is assuming the role of clown. The poet is passionately identifying himself with an argument that is to be defeated. It is the poet who is ultimately to be knocked down, because, like the reader, the poet is also one of 'those strange prodigious Creatures, Man': Rochester is at his familiar game of self-laceration.

And the force and immediacy of the poet's argument, sustained over a great part of the first half of the poem, help to persuade the reader to identify with the poet's views. Critics have responded to the opening lines both by admiring the astonishing power of the lines and by assuming that the argument that is presented in them is the poet's viewpoint, to which we are bound to accede. We have, for instance, the picture of Tennyson reciting lines 12–28 of the *Satyr* 'with almost terrible force', lines which are quoted by a greater poet, Goethe, as 'frightening'.[21]

> Where I (who to my cost already am
> One of those strange, prodigious Creatures, Man)
> A Spirit free to choose for my own share
> What Case of Flesh and Blood I'd please to wear,
> I'd be a Dog, a Monkey, or a Bear,
> Or any thing but that vain Animal
> Who is so proud of being rational.
> The Senses are too gross, and he'll contrive
> A Sixth, to contradict the other Five;
> And before certain Instinct, will prefer
> Reason, which fifty time for one do's err . . .

This is an extraordinary combination of rhythmic control and syntactical contortion, producing a tension that exactly voices the force of the indigation that describes man as a prodigy, a spirit 'Cased' in a vain animal. But is it the *poet*'s indignation? Certainly it is not the poet's *argument* that is presented, for the theme of the poem is not, as Griffin would have it, a defence of the paradox, 'that it is better to be an animal than a man'.[22] On the contrary the poet demonstrates during the course of the poem the *impossibility* of a man like himself being an animal and concludes in the epilogue that if there *is* any way out of the dilemma man finds himself in, caught between flesh and philosophy, it is in manufacturing for himself some variety of 'artificial' man (215–224):

> But a meek humble *Man*, of modest Sence,
> Who, Preaching Peace, does practice Conscience.
> Whose pious life's a proof he does believe
> Mysterious Truths, which no Man can conceive.
> If upon Earth there dwell such God-like Men,
> Then I'll Recant my Paradox to them:
> Adore those *Shrines* of *Virtue*, Homage pay,
> And with the Rabble-world their laws obey.
> If such there are, yet grant me This at least,
> Man differs more from Man, than Man from Beast.

The force with which the opening position is stated is so persuasive that it colours response to everything that follows. But this is Rochester's purpose. Having persuaded us to assume the anti-rationalistic scorn that he presents in the first half of the poem, he then confronts us with the impossibility of satisfying the demands he has aroused. The libertine argument that we should return to the natural world of the animals that is so passionately advocated turns out to lead us into a blind alley. The poet's persuasiveness turns out to be a trap which we follow the speaker into.

For the paradox at the heart of the poem is not that animals are better than humans (a very tired theme by Rochester's day) but that rejection of reason forces us to accept a nature that is even more 'unnatural' by animal standards than the life of reason. Up to line 122 we have been presented with a passionate argument in favour of the libertine contention that we should behave as naturally, that is, as much like the other animals, as possible; that the life of feeling and spontaneity demonstrated by the animal world is a life of freedom from the cares and abstractions of our thought; that the taking of the fruit of the tree of knowledge marked our fall from happiness:

> His Wisdom did his Happiness destroy,
> Aiming to know that World he should enjoy . . . (lines 33–34)

Fom lines 123–173, however, we are ironically shown the 'idyllic' picture of what man is like in his natural state. Having been used to support the libertine position in the first half of the poem the theriophilic argument, that animals are superior to man, is now turned *against* the libertine argument that man should be as natural as possible. For man in his natural state is shown to be every bit as nasty as is described in Hobbes' famous description of natural man in Part 1 of *Leviathan*. Man *differs* from the other animals in being by nature unnatural (123–142):

> You see how far Man's Wisdom here extends;
> Look next if Humane Nature makes amends,
> Whose Principles most Gen'rous are, and just,
> And to whose Morals you wou'd sooner trust,
> Be Judge your self, I'll bring it to the Test,
> Which is the lowest Creature, Man or Beast.
> Birds feed on Birds, Beasts on each other prey.
> But Savage Man alone do's Man betray:
> Prest by Necessity, they kill for Food;
> Man undoes Man to do himself no good.
> With Teeth and Claws by Nature Arm'd they hunt
> Nature's Allowance, to supply their Want;
> But Man, with Smiles, Embraces, Friendships praise,

Unhumanly his Fellows Life betrays.
With voluntary Pains works his distress,
Not through Necessity, but Wantonness.
For Hunger or for Love they fight or tear,
Whilst wretched Man is still in Arms for fear;
For fear he arms, and is of Arms afraid,
By Fear to Fear successively betray'd.

In the first half of the poem the theriophilic argument was used to bolster up the idea that we should return to nature and be like all the other animals; that, like them, we should exercise 'right reason', that is, employ our thoughts to satisfy our appetites. Now the theriophilic argument is being used to *contrast* the basic natures of man and beast. Now indeed the argument is that it is better to be an animal, but only in the sense that man's animality turns out to be even less acceptable than his rationality. The two stages in the argument that produces the paradox can be expressed (as I showed earlier) as:

(i)   Man should live a life as natural as the animals by the exercise of 'right reason' (the libertine argument lines 1-122)
(ii) In his natural state man is far more vicious and 'unnatural' than other animals (the Hobbesian argument lines 123-173)

The argument has come to the paradoxical position that *neither* man's reason *nor* his instincts are satisfactory guides to conduct. The argument is at a complete impasse and the headlong persuasion to which we were subjected by the force of the opening lines has led us into a state of intellectual impotence. It is the apotheosis of the poet as clown; as with Lear's fool, comic wisdom has led to impotence and absurdity: the fool's coxcomb hangs limp and useless:

> Women and Men of Wit are dangerous Tools,
> And ever fatal to admiring Fools (lines 41-42)

The reader shares in the feeling of complete stalemate.

And it appears that the original intention was to leave the poem at this point. As an after thought, it seems, Rochester added a third part, a conditional 'recantation' which postulates a way out of the dilemma by combining abstraction and action. This is very much Hobbes' way out of a similar dilemma in *Leviathan*. Having shown man in all the depravity of his natural state in Part 1 of

Leviathan, Hobbes goes on to show how man can rise above his own nature through artifice. By means of his intelligence, his reasoning power, he can construct an 'artificial' social system that will modify his own behaviour. He can become a product of his own artifice. This is what Rochester seems to be suggesting in the curious epilogue to the *Satyr*. He had made a similar mocking suggestion in his lyric *The Fall* where the lover concludes that the fall has deprived him of the ability to offer anything more to his lady than the abstracts of platonic love. In the Epilogue to the *Satyr* he tentatively suggests the possibility of finding a man who really does behave in accordance with the dictates of reason by obeying laws of virtue and piety. But *if* such a man exists (and the mocking tone in which this is presented suggests this is unlikely) then he would differ from most men more than most men from beasts. This last couplet probably echoes a passage in Plutarch's *Gryllus* (an influential text for the theriophilists) where Gryllus, who has been transformed by Circe into a pig, argues that there is less to choose between beast and beast than between man and man.

> I do not think there is such a great difference between beast and beast as there is between man and man in matters of prudence, discourse, reason and memory.[23]

This idea is brought even closer to Rochester's lines in Montaigne and Charron as reported in a letter of Descartes to the Marquis of Newcastle, 1646:

> Although Montaigne and Charron have said that there is greater difference between man and man than between man and beast, there has never been found any animal so perfect that he has used signs to communicate with other animals anything other than had to do with feelings.[24]

Rochester thus ends as he began in theriophilic strain, but his chief purpose in the poem is not to assert the superiority of the animals, but the dilemma of man caught between a vicious nature and a life-denying reason. It is a dilemma that his epilogue does little to resolve.

Yet the poem is not simply destructive, not merely content to present an unsolvable problem. Like so much of Rochester's poetry it has the detachment of a comic stance. It is comic in its unresolved juxtaposition of incompatible ideas and comic in its

13

presentation of those ideas. Rochester has managed to combine into a convincing whole a passionate statement of first libertine and then misanthropic ideas with a comic, aristocratic detachment —Rochester's satiric spokesman is both the lunatic raver at man's predicament and the detached ironist contemplating it. Like the circus clown he is both part of the mess and aloof from it because burlesquing it, using it for his own intellectual ends. And the formal shape of the poem, the suggestion of a syllogistic structure, however incompatible with the paradoxical nature of the poem, expresses that triumph of *imposed* orderliness to perfection, just as the extraordinarily well-controlled couplets insist on an orderliness that the material of the poem is denying.

The Social Satires: Timon

Timon is a more modest affair than the *Satyr against Mankind* not only because it keeps comparatively close to a single source but because its scope at first sight is primarily social rather than philosophical, though on closer inspection the poem is seen to have philosophical implications. The criteria for satiric judgement are the aesthetic criteria of a comedy of manners rather than the philosophical criteria suggested by the *Satyr*. Timon, the poet's satiric spokesman, combines the superior aloofness of the aristocratic observer with the tone of voice of the Elizabethan scourging satirist. Like Chaucer's satire in the *Canterbury Tales* this is snob satire, judging the inferior orders by the standard of the superior. But the tone of voice—so different from Chaucer's insidious ironies—enables Rochester to give his social criticism a wider implication. For although this is not primarily philosophical satire, it has certain philosophical implications that relate it to the *Satyr against Reason and Mankind,* and its use of the scourging satirist *persona* further relates it to the *Satyr* by giving it an angry, scornful tone.

We have already discussed the relationship of Boileau's third satire in the previous chapter, but a summary of their similarities and main differences may be useful at this point. Both poems are presented as a conversation between two fashionable gentlemen, one of whom recounts to the other his unpleasant experience of being invited to a dinner which turns out to be coarsely presented and with coarse, boorish companions. Boileau's reluctant guest, however, is himself presented satirically, the questioner clearly finding his fastidiousness ridiculous. The comedy resides in the contrast between the rude host and his boorish other guests and the excessive fastidiousness of the reluctant guest—designated 'P' in Boileau's satire and quickly recognised by Boileau's contemporaries as a satiric portrait of the gourmet the abbé du Broussin. P's attitudes can be illustrated (and contrasted with Timon's) by an episode during the meal where the gourmet complains bitterly of there being no ice available during the meal (lines 79–86):

> Toutefois avec l'eau que j'y mets à foison,
> J'esperois adoucir la force du poison.
> Mais qui l'auroit pensé? Pour comble de disgrace,
> Par le chaud qu'il faisoit nous n'avions point de glace.
> Point de glace, bon Dieu! dans le fort de l'Esté!
> Au mois de juin! Pour moi, j'estois si transporté,
> Que donnant de fureur tout le festin au Diable,
> Je me suis veu vingt fois prest de quitter la table . . .

[All the time I was hoping to sweeten the effect of the poisonous wine by mixing large quantities of water with it. But who would have expected it? To crown the misfortune of its being so hot, there was not a scrap of ice. Good God, no ice! At the height of summer! In the month of June! As for me, I was so beside myself that, furiously wishing the whole meal to the Devil, I was twenty times on the point of leaving the table . . .]

Rochester reduces the reference to the lack of ice to a passing reference of half a line (85–86):

> And now the Bottle briskly flies about,
> Instead of *Ice*, wrapt in a wet *Clout*.

Boileau deftly portrays the fussy, bad-tempered sybarite, and it is clear we are meant to laugh at him as much as at the boors he describes.

Rochester is equally concerned to convey a realistic picture of contemporary manners. But the point of view of the observer, the reluctant guest, is more difficult to gauge and his character more difficult to estimate. Boileau's *adversarius* (A) presents P in the beginning with unmistakable irony in thirteen lines that clearly mock the gourmet.

Qu'est devenu ce teint, dont la couleur fleurie
Sembloit d'ortolans seuls, et de bisques nourie,
Où la joye en son lustre attiroit les regards,
Et le vin en rubis brilloit de toutes parts?
Qui vois a pû plonger dans cet humeur chagrine?
A-t-on par quelque Edit reformé la cuisine?

[What has become of this complexion whose florid colour seemed nourished by broths and ortalans solely, where pleasure in its shining surface attracted notice and wine shone in every part like rubies (with pun on *rubis*—pimples). Who has been able to plunge you into this bad mood? Has some edict reformed cooking?]

Rochester's *adversarius* (also in the 1680 edition known by the initial A) is given only four lines before Timon takes over, and the tone of those four lines suggests the boisterous mockery of exact equals, the kind of comradely humour with which the rakes of Charles II's court commonly addressed each other in letters and scurrilous verses:

What Tim'n does old Age begin t' approach,
That thus thou droop'st under a Nights Debauch?
Hast thou lost deep to needy *Rogues* on Tick,
Who ne're could pay, and must be paid next Week?

This is the aristocratic camaraderie of the wits who despise the impecunious card or dice sharpers that they are fleeced by. At once we are in the world of Rochester's own London circle and the suspicion of a connection between poet and satiric *persona* is strengthened when Timon goes on to describe himself as admitting that he occasionally writes verse for his 'Pintle's sake' (a passage I quoted as the voice of Rochester earlier). The detached mockery of Boileau's P is lost by an ambiguous presentation of the satiric spokesman, who, though he has some relationship to his author, still seems to be in part a dramatic projection. This seems implied both by his name—which associates him, as I have argued, with Shakespeare's misanthrope—and by his jaundiced, angry tone. The *adversarius* seems to be suggesting that Timon's attitude to the meal could be at least in part the result of personal spleen (a similar role is given to the satirical spokesman in *Tunbridge Wells*). In any case the effect of the close identification of satiric *persona* and author is to give Timon a much greater authority than

Boileau's P and Timon's personality dominates the poem to a far greater extent than Boileau allows for his character. The result is an angrier poem in which the reader is being asked to share to some extent in the anger. But what is the anger about?

Boileau's P gets angry simply because he finds both food and company so distasteful, and it is obvious that we are meant to find this anger excessive and so absurd. Timon's greater toughness makes him less of a victim and more of a satiric observer. Nor is he concerned with the same things; the food is a comparatively minor problem. Its coarseness and lack of delicacy are noted in almost ten lines (lines 73–84) and even these lines are as much an opportunity for Timon to make coarse, sexual comparisons (the beef compared for toughness and size to 'Mother Mosely's arse', the carrots to the Countess of Northumberland's dildo) as to show the inadequacy of the feast. Boileau spends nearly half his rather longer poem having his spokesman describe or allude to the food and its presentation. Rochester's Timon is much more interested in the gallery of fops and fools that surround the table and much of the poem is devoted to their conversation. The most prominent of these diners is the host's wife, a faded beauty who is Rochester's invention entirely; Boileau's dinner is a wholly male affair. Rochester introduces the lady to increase the importance of the theme of sexual aberration that is totally lacking in Boileau's poem (or indeed in the Régnier and Horace satires on the same subject). The lady is one of those resilient old lechers which the Restoration stage rejoiced to portray (lines 45–52):

> In comes my *Lady* strait, she had been *Fair*,
> Fit to give *Love*, and prevent Despair,
> But *Age, Beauties* incurable Disease,
> Had left her more desire, than pow'r to please.
> As *Cocks* will strike, although their *Spurs* be gone,
> She with her old blear Eyes to smite begun:
> Though nothing else, she (in despight of time)
> Preserv'd the affectation of her prime . . .

The theme of sexual striving and sexual impotence runs through the poem. At one point the hostess complains that modern youth is sexually coarse, interested only in Whores and Players (103–104):

> Who were too wild for any virtuous *League*,
> Too rotten to consummate the Intrigue.

This jaundiced view of sexual relations is shared between the lady and Timon himself (whose use of sexual imagery is largely in terms of the unnatural or distorted) and further complicates the relationship of satirist and satirised. Indeed we are in Rochester's characteristic world of uncertain values where the 'disease' of being human afflicts observer and actor alike. The main difference between Timon and the other characters (analogous to that between Rochester as poet and his 'blind' material) is that he realises his absurdity, whereas the others do not. The poem turns out, therefore, to be more than merely a social commentary. It expresses that characteristic disgust with humanity that is also the subject of *Tunbridge Wells* as well as the *Satyr against Mankind*. And this is why Rochester allows the subject of the conversation to shift from the literary discussion to the quarrel about the martial virtues of the peoples of Western Europe, a subject not discussed at either Boileau's or Régnier's dinners. Rochester uses the switch in conversation as a transition passage to the conclusion of the poem (shared by all three poets) that has the diners come to blows with one another. The purpose is to use this custard pie episode, not just as a further comic example of the diners' boorishness, but, by linking it to the international bellicosity, to suggest again that we are seeing man as a whole in his characteristic absurdity. Rochester is anticipating the theme of the *Satyr against Mankind* that man is a pugnacious, aggressive animal whose nature is to fight and kill his fellow creatures. The fight over whether the French are as brave as the English in war, that ends the poem, merely illustrates at a comic level the savagery that is the subject of the conversation. Rochester ends, therefore, unlike his two French models, by implying a far more wide-reaching criticism, extending beyond the inadequacies of social behaviour to a radical criticism of the very nature of man. The actual inventiveness of the poem, as I said earlier, flags towards the end and the fight is not as well presented in *Timon* as in the two French poems, but its scope is wider and the implications more far reaching. As usual Rochester has not used his models slavishly, but as a starting off point for a radically different poem:

Whatsoever he imitated or Translated, was Loss to him. He had a Treasure of his own; a mine not to be exhausted. His own Oar and Thoughts were rich and fine: his own Stamp and

Expression more neat and beautiful than any he cou'd borrow
or fetch from abroad.[25]

Tunbridge Wells

There seems to have been no single source to this second of
Rochester's social satires. Like *Timon* it is ostensibly a comment on
the manners of the day and like *Timon* it reaches out beyond the
subject of social behaviour towards a more general vision of
human depravity. Veith's dating of the two poems suggests that
they were composed very close together (during the spring of
1674) and about eighteen months before the *Satyr against Mankind*.
Certainly the two social satires have much in common, though
Tunbridge Wells shows an advance on *Timon* in the progress towards a more fundamental criticism of mankind and thus justifies
Vieth's placing it between *Timon* and the *Satyr against Mankind*. As
in *Timon* Rochester uses a splenetic, angry, satiric spokesman,
whose eccentricities make us feel there is not that much to choose
between the satirist and the satirised. Rochester is again using the
Elizabethan device of the scourging satirist to undermine our confidence not only in the things seen but in the manner of seeing.
In this poem Rochester's deep rebelliousness finds, for the first
time, a truly adequate formal expression. The spokesman is presented rather more clearly as wayward and comically splenetic
than in *Timon* and the associations with the author are less in
evidence:

> At five this Morn, when *Phoebus* rais'd his head
> From *Thetis* Lap, I rais'd my self from Bed,
> And mounting Steed, I trotted to the Waters,
> The Rendevouze of Fools, Buffons and Praters,
> Cuckolds, Whores, Citizens, their Wives and Daughters.
> My squemish Stomach, I with Wine had brib'd,
> To undertake the Dose that was prescrib'd:
> But turning Head, a cursed suddain Crew,
> That innocent Provision overthrow,
> And without drinking, made me purge and spew.[26]

The mock heroic description of the rising sun—a favourite subject of burlesque from Chaucer to Fielding—here gets the poem
off to a suitable, comic start and emphasises the mood of zany

derision that dominates the poem. The burlesque element is further heightened when we consider that in seventeenth-century bawdy the 'head' and the 'lap' were not the parts of the anatomy that first spring to mind for a twentieth-century reader.

Rochester goes out of his way to heighten the comic role of the satirical commentator not only by having him lash out indiscriminately at everyone he sees, but in having him frenetically move about from group to group, finding each group worse than the last:

> Endeavouring this irksome sight to baulk,
> And a more irksome noise, their silly talk,
> I silently shrunk down to th' lower Walk.

There he finds objects even more absurd and derisory and off he rushes:

> From hence into the upper end I ran,
> Where a new Scene of Foppery began . . . .

He meets a group of clergymen who are assembled to cure themselves of various distempers including the satirical commentator's own complaint: the spleen. Their usurpation of his own ailment causes particular displeasure:

> To charge the Spleen to be their Misery,
> And on that wise Disease bring Infamy.

He hides himself to evade a group of Irishmen, only to find himself overhearing a ludicrous conversation between a fashionable young lady and a fop (the account of this conversation is one of the highlights of the poem):

> Quite tir'd with this most dismal stuff: I ran
> Where were two Wives, and Girl just fit for man . . .

At last he can stand the place no longer, jumps on his horse and rides off. In an earlier account of the poem I likened the behaviour of the satirical spokesman, with his running from place to place, throwing out a stream of witty and scurrilous abuse to all and sundry, to the behaviour of Groucho Marx in films like *A Day at the Races* and *The Big Store*. This still seems to me the best way of describing the zany, clown-like role Rochester gives his spokesman, helping to create an atmosphere of complete absurdity from which no-one is exempt.

D. H. Griffin has complained that the structure of the poem is too loose and uninteresting.[27] But once the role of the satiric spokesman is understood as a general disturber of the reader's peace then the structure is seen as a highly suitable vehicle for Rochester's purpose. Moving restlessly from group to group gives us not only a sense of dissatisfaction, as we can find nothing to approve of, but conveys precisely the feelings of formlessness, of meaninglessness, that helps to assert the basic theme of the absurdity of man. The escape from the tighter narrative structure of *Timon* is in fact a step forward in developing the underlying restlessness that was conveyed in a more shadowy way in the slightly earlier poem. Nor is the lack of progress as he moves from group to group inappropriate, for in a world of absurdity how can progress be made?

And there is no doubt what Rochester's general target is in this poem, it is man himself. As we move from group to group it becomes clear that we are watching the effects of the disease of being human. It is not that he is being unkind to the ugly or to the Irish for what they cannot help, it is that all mankind, the ugly, the fashionably handsome, the beaux, the belles, the learned and the ignorant join in a fantastic rout (85–90):

> But ne'er could Conventicle, Play, or Fair,
> For a true Medly, with this Herd compare.
> Here Lords, Knights, Squires, Ladies and Countesses,
> Chandlers, Mum-Bacon Women and Sempstresses
> Were mix'd together; nor did they agree
> More in their Humours, than their Quality.

This is vanity fair, an indiscriminate medley of humanity without order and without purpose. We pass from this general picture to a detailed account of particular inanity as we listen to the polite conversation of the gallant and the damsel that follows: perhaps the most vivid and brilliant passage of detailed satire in all Rochester (91–114):

> Here waiting for Gallant, young Damsel stood,
> Leaning on Cane, and muffl'd up in Hood;
> That would-be wit, whose business 'twas to woo,
> With Hat remov'd, and solemn scrape of Shooe,
> Bowing advanc'd, then he gently shrugs,

And muffled Foretop, he in order tugs;
And thus accosts her, 'Madam, methinks the Weather,
Is grown much more serene since you came hither;
You influence the Heavens; and should the Sun
Withdraw himself to see his Rays out-done,
Your Luminaries would supply the Morn,
And make a Day, before the Day be born'.
With Mouth screw'd up, and awkward, winking Eyes,
And breast thrust forward; 'Lord, Sir'; she replies
'It is your goodness, and not my deserts,
Which makes you shew your Learning, Wit and Parts'.
He puzzled, bites his Nails, both to display
The Sparkling Ring, and think what's next to say.
And thus breaks out a fresh: 'Madam, I gad,
Your Luck, last Night at Cards, was mighty bad
At Cribbage, Fifty-nine and the next Shew,
To make your Game, and yet to want those Two;
God damn me, Madam, I'm the Son of a Whore,
If in my Life, I saw the like before.'

There is nothing to compare with this in any English satire before it for vivid realism and accurate observation if we except Chaucer. The conventional shackles that had kept satire at least one remove from actuality are here broken and for the first time satire comments directly on life as it is actually lived. Observation has triumphed over dogma and satire can at last compare favourably with the best achievements of stage comedy. Perhaps the most remarkable feature of Rochester's achievement here is in the use of such a formal medium as the heroic couplet for so naturalistic an effect. He does this by allowing a great deal of flexibility in the stressing of syllables within the line, but confines the rhythmic units largely within the couplet or occasional triplet. There is nothing like this in English that comes before it and little as good after. Nothing in English; but Rochester could and certainly did learn much from French example.

Paul Scarron had made a visit to the spa waters at Bourbon-l'Archambault in 1641 and 1642 the subject of a satirical verse letter, *La Legende de Bourbon*. This poem, like Rochester's, gives a series of comic portraits of the people the poet meets and it has a similar loose structure. Scarron's poem, however, is in octosyllabics

and the element of burlesque is stronger. Scarron's identification
of himself with his observer does not allow the ironic distancing
that Rochester's techniques achieve. Some of the detailed portraits, however, (often portraits of actual people) might well have
suggested to Rochester how he might achieve a sense of realism in
his poem, for we must suppose that, like everyone else, he knew
of Scarron's work. Here, for instance, Scarron describes a young
lady who has come to take the waters, like Rochester's two wives
(line 114), in the hope that it will help her to become pregnant:

> Mais j'oubliois par grand oubly,
> Dont j'aurois eu toujours ennuy,
> La Ribandou belle et charmante
> Qui but aussi de l'eau bouillante.
> C'estoit pour avour embompoint
> Qu'alors son gent corps n'avoit point:
> Son Espoux estoit avec elle
> Qui n'est pas si beau qu'elle est belle.
> Dieu luy donne soulagement
> Quand elle aura quelque tourment,
> Et que mauvaise haleine aucune
> Jamais son beau nez n'importune.[28]

[But I forget, in the great forgetfulness that I have always been
afflicted with, the beautiful and charming Ribandou who also
drank the hot water. It was so she could become fatter than her
pretty body was at that time: her husband, who was not as handsome as she was beautiful, was with her. May God give comfort
when she has her pains and may no stinking breath ever offend his
nose.]

Closer in tone to Rochester's poem and indeed in vividness are the
satirical portraits of Régnier's satire. Satire eight, for instance,
contains a detailed portrait of a fop which in spirit is close both to
Rochester's portrait of a fop in *Tunbridge Wells* and the opening of
Timon:

> Il me prist par la main, après mainte grimace,
> Changeant sur l'un des pieds à toute heure de place
> Et dansant tout ainsi qu'un barbe encartelé
> Me dist en remachant un propos avalé:
> 'Que vous estes heureux, vous autres belles ames,

Favoris d'Apolon, qui governez les dames
Et par mille beaux vers les charmes tellement
Que n'est point de beautez que pour vous seullement;
Mais vous les meritz, voy vertuz non communes
Vous font digne, monsieur, de ces bonnes fortunes.'

[He takes me by the hand, after many grimaces, shifting from one foot to another all the time and dancing about like a lame barbary horse says to me, chewing over an idea already digested: 'How fortunate, you are, you fine souls, favoured by Apollo, who govern women and charm them with a thousand fine verses to such an extent that they reserve their beauty for you alone.']

It is not that earlier English satire lacks satiric portraits, but that nowhere before Rochester in English do they attain to the convincing actuality of Régnier's descriptions.

Rochester's ultimate purpose, however, is not simply to describe a fashionable watering place but to use his canvas to image his feelings about mankind. The representative nature of Rochester's characters has already been commented on, but the theme of mankind's inanity becomes entirely explicit at the end of the poem as the zany commentator at last merges indistinguishably with the poet himself (lines 171–180):

> Bless me! thought I, that Thing is Man, that thus
> In all his Shapes, he is ridiculous.
> Our selves with noise of Reason we do please
> In vain, Humanity's our worst Disease:
> Thrice happy Beasts are, who, because they be
> Of Reason void, are so of Foppery.
> Faith, I was so asham'd, that with Remorse,
> I us'd the Insolence to mount my Horse;
> For he, doing only Things fit for his Nature,
> Did seem to me by much the wiser Creature.

Here the moral of our lurch through the spa crowd is stated, and it turns out to be the moral that provides the first premise of the argument of the *Satyr against Mankind*. Man is foolish, absurd, because he is unnatural, if only he could imitate the other animals and simply confine himself to things 'fit for his nature', avoid the abstractions of reason and the ridiculous, artificial affections he would cease to be absurd and become as wise as a horse. Alas, as

Swift was to demonstrate in Book Four of *Gulliver's Travels*, man is no more able to become a horse successfully than he is able to avoid his affinities with the Yahoos. But it is not until the *Satyr* that Rochester faces up to the full nature of this dilemma.

The Allusion to Horace

The Allusion to Horace was the last of the major satires and it is the least interesting. Like *Timon* it has a literary theme, though in this case the literary interest dominates. Like *Timon*, too, the poem is an imitation, in this case of one of Horace's *Satires* (the tenth of the first book). Much has been written about Renaissance 'imitations' of earlier poets, and Rochester's most recent editor claims that Rochester's *Allusion to Horace* is the first such work in the English language and likens it to Pope's later imitations of Horace.[29] In fact the use of earlier verse on which to structure new poems is thoroughly characteristic of Renaissance poetic technique, indeed fundamental to it. Few, if any, Renaissance poets wished to be considered as completely independent of the classical or modern examples it was frequently their aim to emulate. Such imitation helped to guarantee their acceptability and vouched for the serious-ness of their claim to vatic power. H. F. Brooks has given a number of examples of the practice from Wyatt to Rochester's time and beyond and he shows merely the tip of the iceberg.[30] We have already seen how often Rochester makes use of other poets in his lyrics; the practice is exhibited as much in lyric verse as in satire. Wyatt's use of Petrarch in such sonnets as *Who so list to hount* (from Petrarch's sonnet *Una candida cerva sopra l'erba*) and *Was I never yet of your love greved* (from Petrarch's *Io non fu d'amar voi lassato unquanco*), for instance, shows the wide variety of divergence from the model text that was possible as early as the 1520s. *Who so list to hount* is a brilliantly original poem which transforms Petrarch's dream vision into a frightening evocation of the perils of Henry VIII's court, while *Was I never yet of your love greved* is much closer to its original both literally and in tone. 'Imitation' in fact varies almost poem by poem, from using someone else's poem as simply a starting off point for an almost totally new poem to something very close to what we would now call translation. Rochester tends to use earlier poets, as Wyatt most often does, to give him a start-ing point to invent a new poem, in which a knowledge of the original adds comparatively little to our reading of the new work. Such 'imitation' is a technique for getting a poet started, though it will nearly always involve some implication of shared ideas or shared conventions. Rochester's use of particular earlier lyrists in writing his own songs is less important in detail than in his adopting the conventions and attitudes that they share. Other poets might use earlier models more integrally, to highlight values they themselves wished to express or to contrast the values of the past with those of the present. This is Pope's tendency in his use of poetic allusion, whether it is the fragmentary allusion of word or line, or the use of an earlier poem as a subsuming model. This technique, too, was already well known to the Elizabethans. Sidney's use of Petrarch in *Astrophil and Stella* exhibits a clever use of contrast between Astrophil's attitudes and those of the Petrarchan poem Sidney is imitating in such an example as the sonnet 'Who will in fairest book of Nature know' (in imitation of Petrarch's sonnet *Chi vuol veder quantunque po Natura*). The purpose of this poem is to contrast Astrophil's impatient lust with the pure, idealised love Petrarch expresses for Laura in the original poem.

Rochester's use of Horace in the *Allusion to Horace* is not (in spite of the title) of this detailed, allusive kind, though a knowledge of the Latin helps us interpret the poem's precise intentions. Howard Weinbrot in a recent article on the poem, which compares Rochester's poem in great detail to Horace, shows in any case that the term 'allusion' was used in Rochester's day for the kind of loose imitation we have here.[31] Weinbrot argues that Rochester's poem fails to take advantage of the opportunities that a closer imitation would have brought, that Rochester never uses the Horatian satire integrally to his theme.[32] But this criticism is itself to oversimplify what Rochester is doing because it ignores the point that Rochester reads Horace's poem from a standpoint that takes Dryden's response to the Latin poem into account. Vieth's edition draws our attention to Dryden's use of Horace's tenth satire in his *Defence of the Epilogue of the Conquest of Granada* (1672), and Rochester's purpose, I believe, cannot be understood without taking this defence into account.[33]

Horace's poem is both a defence of himself for his judgment on the earlier Latin satirist Lucilius (a poet who wrote about one hundred years before Horace) in satire four of the first book of satires, and an account of the kind of refinements a modern poet should aim for as an advance on Lucilius' methods. An important part of Horace's assessment of Lucilius is the insistence on historical perspective; that Lucilius' coarseness can be explained by the coarseness of his audience and that a modern poet has not this excuse. Horace's principal target is not in fact Lucilius, but those of his contemporaries, who still adopt Lucilius' coarse methods.

> Fuerit Lucilius, inquam
> Comis et urbanus, fuerit limatior idem
> quam rudis et Graecis intacti carminis auctor
> quamque poetarum seniorum turba sed ille,
> si foret hoc nostrum fato delapsus in aevum,
> detereret sibi multa, recideret omne quod ultra
> perfectum traheretur, et in versu faciendo
> saepe caput scaberet, vivos et roderet unguis

[I say Lucilius was affable and urbane, and he was also more polished than you would expect of an author of a new style of writing unrelated to the Greek, and more polished than the mob of more ancient poets: but had he descended by chance on our times, he would file down much of his work and would cut away everything which was drawn out beyond the correct proportion and in writing his verse he would often scratch his head and gnaw his nails down to the quick.]

Dryden takes up this historical stance in his attack on the poets of the previous age in the *Defence of the Epilogue*. And he opens his defence by quoting this satire of Horace and deliberately associating himself with Horace's stance both in tone and in his insistence on the superior refinement of his own day:

> But malice and partiality set apart, let any man who understands English read diligently the works of Shakespeare and Fletcher; and I dare undertake that he will find in every page either some solecism of speech, or some notorious flaw in sense; and yet these men are reverenced when we are not forgiven. That their wit is great, and many times their expressions noble, envy itself cannot deny.

> neque ego illi detrahere ausim
> haerentem capiti multa cum laude coronam.
>
> [Horace I, 10, 48–49]

'But the times were ignorant in which they lived. Poetry was then, if not in its infancy among us, at least not arrived to its vigour and maturity. . . .'[34] The lines from the tenth satire quoted here are echoed by Rochester in the *Allusion* (lines 79–80). Like Horace, Dryden is defending himself against a charge (by Shadwell) that he has arrogantly maligned the great of the past and like Horace he replies, in measured, judicious tones by reiterating his criticism, and explaining the deficiencies of the past age in terms of the coarseness of the audience. Like Horace, too, his chief concern is with the older poets' coarseness in language and sentiment. Just as Lucilius is upbraided for being coarse and abusive and for roughness of language and metre, so Dryden accuses the earlier English poets of crudities in language and style, giving a number of examples to illustrate his points.[35]

Rochester's poem picks up the dispute between Dryden and Shadwell by using Horace's poem to Dryden's disadvantage. Taking on Horace's role himself Rochester inverts the relationship between Dryden and the writers of the past by pillorying Dryden for his coarseness in sentiment and expression and holding up the Jacobeans as superior models. Dryden is not just taking the place of Lucilius in the poem, he is being made to assume the position he gives the older English writers he so arrogantly disparaged. It is Shakespeare, Jonson and Fletcher who provide the real standards in comparison to which Dryden is found wanting. By implication, in comparison with Horaces' poem, it is the past that can teach the present a lesson not, as Dryden assumes, as it was in Horace's day. Horace's poem is being used in witty irony at Dryden's expense. So that whereas Dryden can only appeal to *hoi poloi* ('the Town . . . an audience of clapping Fools'):

> Though ev'n that Talent merits, in some sort,
> That can divert the Rabble and the Court

the poets of the earlier age had the delicacy and sophistication to aim for something better. In place of Dryden's clumsiness Shakespeare and Jonson show true delicacy (28–31):

> A jest in scorn points out and hits the thing
> More home than the moroser *Satyr*'s sting,
> *Shakespear* and *Johnson* did herein excel,
> And might in this be imitated well.

Rochester returns to this contrast later in the poem when, having remarked on Dryden's lewdness and coarseness, he points out that Dryden has criticised the earlier poets on this very point (81–90):

> But do's not *Dryden* find even *Johnson* dull?
> *Fletcher* and *Beaumont* uncorrect and full
> Of *Lewd Lines,* as he calls them? *Shakespear's* Stile
> Stiff and affected; to his own the while
> Allowing all the Justness that his Pride
> So arrogantly had to these deny'd?
> And may not I have leave impartially
> To search and censure Dryden's Works, and try
> If those gross Faults his Choice Pen do's commit,
> Proceed from want of Judgment, or of Wit.

The point of these lines is that it is Dryden who is the Lucilius, not Shakespeare and Jonson, it is the Restoration that has the 'false Judgment . . . of Clapping Fools', not the Jacobeans. Dryden has misapplied his Horace—and of course we are meant to re-apply it. A reference back to Horace's original is indispensable, but only via the use Dryden has made of it. For it is Dryden who is the coarse and unmannerly poet (71–76):

> *Dryden* in vain try'd this nice way of Wit.
> For he to be a tearing Blade thought fit;
> But when he wou'd be sharp, he still was blunt,
> To frisk his frollick Fancy, he'd cry *Cunt,*
> Wou'd give the Ladies a dry Bawdy Bob,
> And thus he got the Name of *Poet-squab.*

This accusation of extreme coarseness is repeated by Shadwell in a continuation of the dispute. In the *Medal of John Bayes* Shadwell embroiders the charge giving chapter and verse to justify his libel:

> Thy [Dryden's] mirth by foolish Bawdry's exprest,
> And so debauch'd, so fulsome, and so odd,
> As
> 'Let's Bugger one another now by God'
> (When ask'd how they should spend the Afternoon)

and Shadwell adds the marginal gloss verifying the quotation, 'At Windsor in the company of several persons of quality, Sir George

Etherege being present'. Any fair judgment of Dryden, of course, will have to admit both his maladroitness in reference to sexual matters and his ponderous sense of humour (he admitted both charges).

Rochester, however, is not merely concerned with Dryden's Lucilius-like coarseness in the *Allusion to Horace*, he is equally concerned to assume the reasonable, judicious tones of Horace himself as Dryden had in the *Defence*. The comparison with Horace's poem in fact has four distinct, though related purposes:

(a) to contrast the refinement of the Jacobeans with the coarseness of Dryden in contradistinction to the contrast between the refinement of the moderns compared to the ancients in Horace's satire.

(b) to suggest that Dryden's viewpoint in the *Defence*, therefore, should be *contrasted* with Horace's exposure of the inadequacies of Lucilius and his generation as its inverse. Dryden should take the place of Lucilius and not of Horace.

(c) to show Horatian balance in judging Dryden as Horace has in judging Lucilius.

(d) to suggest true Horatian standards for judgment in poetry.

Rochester's judgment of Dryden is in fact not unfair. His point that Dryden (and popular Restoration) refinement compares unfavourably with that of Jonson and Shakespeare and their audience would hardly now be disputed. Apart from this, his comments on Dryden are reasonably complimentary, at times generous (77–80):

> But to be just, 'twill to his praise be found,
> His Excellencies more than Faults abound;
> Nor dear I from his Sacred Temples tear
> That Lawrel which he best deserves to wear . . .

This could, of course, as Weinbrot argues, be ironic—it is impossible to disprove ironic readings—but the tone strikes me as a successful attempt to capture the Horatian judiciousness. Nor is this his only concession to Dryden's greatness; he admits that Dryden *has* great popularity and that that argues *some* talent. It is also a mitigating circumstance that Dryden writes in a coarse age (as Horace argues of Lucilius) and Rochester spends a good deal of energy berating most of his contemporaries and giving only very little (if any) unqualified praise. The reference to Etherege is

highly ambiguous (he fails to copy Shakespeare and Jonson, who
have just been praised, though he is 'refin'd' and a 'meer Original'
i.e. 'just a clown' or 'an entirely original' poet?). Shadwell is hasty,
Wycherley slow and is guilty of 'fewer faults than any of the best'.
Waller is almost unequivocally praised—except that he flatters
three Kings, one of whose courts had been derided earlier as being
as unrefined as the rabble. There is also a sly dig at Waller's shift
of allegiance from Cromwell (conquerors) to Charles (Kings).
Even Rochester's personal friends Charles Sackville, Lord Buckhurst, and Sir Charles Sedley are given ambiguous compliments;
Buckhurst's muse is bad natured and obscene, Sedley writes erotic,
pornographic verse.[36] Rochester was never one to flatter the age.

His attempts to suggest Horatian standards for judgment are
the least successful part of the poem. It is interesting that here at
last he throws all his weight against the English Juvenalian tradition in favour of the Horatian. As a satirist Rochester's development was from Butlerian burlesque, to the English Juvenalian
tradition and thence to the Horatian, but he himself was too much
part of the native tradition, and had profited too much from it, to
be wholly convincing as an upholder of restraint and decorum.
Rochester's poetry thrives on the tension between the rebel and
the reasonable man; here he is trying to insist on *noblesse oblige*, but
the Satyr keeps revealing itself through the Horatian toga. If he
objects to Dryden's coarseness he does so in characteristically
coarse phraseology. Nor can he convincingly represent himself as
an upholder of strict stylistic decorum (98–103):

> To write what may securely stand the Test
> Of being well read over thrice at least,
> Compare each Phraise, examine every Line,
> Weigh ev'ry *Word*, and ev'ry Thought refine;
> Scorn all *Applause* the vile Rout can bestow,
> And be content to please those few you know.

This gets as close to 'correctness' as Rochester's heroics ever do
and a lot closer than most of his work, but even here, at his most
Pope-like, he allows a half-rhyme and a curiously misplaced strong
accent on 'can' in the fifth line that belie the concern with the
minutiae of style. More revealing still is the haughty snobbery of
the Restoration aristocrat who despises *hoi poloi* and feels no
obligations are owed by his nobility.

Rochester's great merit as a poet, however, is not a niggling regard for syllabic refinement, but an extraordinary energy and fire and a concern for strict truth, however uncomfortable, that this poem ultimately lacks. It lacks conviction because Rochester assumes the role of Horatian arbiter of taste unconvincingly. It lacks the characteristic fire because it fails, unlike so many of his poems, to reach out beyond its immediate theme to more general truths. As an assessment of his literary contemporaries it is interesting and not lacking in shrewdness, but it remains stubbornly particular, except in its general accusation of the age as lacking in refinement. Of all the major satires this is the only one that confines itself to socio-literary questions.

A Letter fanc'd from Artemisia in the Town to Chloe in the Country

We have now almost a complete picture of Rochester's poetic world. It is a world where there is a constant struggle between dissolution and coherence. Against a backdrop of metaphysical inanity man attempts to construct local harmonies that defy the disharmony of the spheres. Frequently man shows himself a true offspring of that inanity. Yet Rochester's anger at fools and knaves (himself sometimes included) is matched by his defiant attempts to uphold intelligence and sensitivity. His determination to defy the forces of disintegration is expressed in his praise of love in the lyrics as 'the everlasting rest' that makes us 'blest at last', the 'lucky minute' that allows us the brief vision of a heaven whose existence resides only in those glimpses. But even here inanity re-asserts itself, man's hopes and fears destroy the very happiness he dotes on. Nature as a cruel and blind jest centres our sexual instruments in the places of excrement, men's sexual ability depends on an undependable, involuntary organ. As Pope was to write, mankind is the 'glory jest and riddle of the world'. The poet, like the lover, also defies inanity in constructing his harmonies out of metaphysical disharmony. Like the lover, the poet's task is to make something out of nothing (the comparison becomes even closer if we allow ourselves the seventeenth-century bawdy meaning of nothing). Poetry is both sublime and absurd, it is both heroic defiance of the chaos that rules the universe and psychological equivalent of ejaculation or defecation. The poet is both hero and fool.

All these themes are triumphantly brought together in this last poem we have to discuss, the *Epistle from Artemisia to Chloe*. I have reserved it till last, not because chronologically it comes last, (Vieth dates it to around 1675, placing it after the *Satyr against Reason and Mankind* and before *Upon Nothing* and the *Allusion to Horace*) but because it is the summit of Rochester's poetic achievement. It is a social satire in the sense that it describes contemporary manners, but its theme expands outwards towards a vision of man's predicament as damned with the 'nauseous draught of life', caught in a Hobbesian search of power after power where:

> 'Man undoes man to do himself no good.'

Here too Rochester deals with the themes of the power of love and its betrayal by cynicism and greed (40–51):

> *Love*, the most generous Passion of the Mind,
> The softest Refuge Innocence can find,
> The safe director of unguided *Youth*,
> Fraught with Kind Wishes, and secur'd by Truth;
> That Cordial drop *Heaven* in our Cup has thrown,
> To make the nauseous draught of Life go down,
> On which one only Blessing *God* might raise,
> In *Lands* of *Atheists, Subsidies* of praise;
> For none did e're so dull and stupid prove,
> But felt a *God* and Bless'd his Power of Love;
> This only Joy for which poor we were made,
> Is grown, like Play, to be an Arrant *Trade* . . .

Here, too, is the theme of the ambiguity of the poet's role as hero and clown. Artemisia opens her letter to Chloe by pleading her unsuitableness for attempting 'the lofty flights of dangerous poetry' and goes on to address herself in imaginary expostulation (16–31):

> Dear Artemisia, Poetry's a Snare,
> *Bedlam* has many *Mansions*, have a Care,
> Your Muse diverts you, makes the Reader sad,
> You think your self inspir'd, he thinks you Mad.
> Consider too, 'twill be discreetly done,
> To make yourself the Fiddle of the Town.
> To find th' ill-humour'd pleasure at their need:
> Curst when you fail, and scorn'd when you succeed.[37]

> Thus like an Arrant Woman as I am,
> No sooner well convinc'd Writings a Shame,
> That *Whore* is scarce a more reproachful Name
> Than *Poetess*—
> Like Men that Marry, or like *Maids* that Wooe,
> Because 'tis the Worst Thing they can do:
> Pleas'd with the Contradiction and the Sin,
> Methinks I stand on Thorns till I begin.

But above all in this poem Rochester faces the central problem of his poetry: how to construct a poem in defiance of the forces of disorder. For *Artemisia to Chloe* is a triumph of poetic engineering. The story tells of the progressive collapse of the layers of civilization, the layers of those forms and ceremonies by which we relate to one another and without which there can be no meaningful human existence. But out of this collapse Rochester constructs a poem that is a model of structural skill. The forces of disintegration are allowed to be present only as it were by proxy, the stronger the forces of disruption become the further are they distanced by the structural ingenuity of the poem, until at the end the frightening world of the prostitute Corinna is recounted to us at three removes from the reader's actuality. It is not that the forces of disruption have been annihilated, the violence of their presence is certainly felt in the poem, it is that they have been absorbed and turned to good by the poet's art. Poet has triumphed over both rebel and aristocrat in reconciling the explosive and the stable. Let us see more closely how it is done.

The poem is conceived of in three layers. In the opening section Artemisia, who is supposedly writing the verse letter, after some hesitation about her suitability as a poetess, gives an account of the state of contemporary attitudes towards love to her friend in the country (lines 1–72). In the second section Artemisia introduces a 'fine lady' of fashion, who is allowed to speak in her own voice, mostly about her views on men (lines 73–188). This monologue is interspersed with the occasional critical and interpretative comment from Artemisia and leads on directly to the third part. This consists of the fine lady in *her* turn telling us the story of the whore Corinna and how Corinna achieves her revenge on men. By this time we are at three removes from actuality: Artemisia is recounting the fine lady's account of Corinna. But there is, of course, yet another element of indirection: the author's stance. Rochester nowhere intrudes into the poem. The fiction is that the poem is written by Artemisia and the judgments made in the poem are Artemisia's except where the 'fine lady' makes judgments on Corinna. All the judgments are therefore relative to the interpretation we put upon Artemisia. Rochester deliberately keeps us uncertain about the extent to which we are meant to see things from Artemisia's point of view (there is a good deal of modern critical disagreement about it, which illustrates the point). The poet creates this uncertainty because, in a world without ultimate sanctions, it would be dishonest not to. There can be no right and wrong, only better (more coherent) and worse (less coherent).

There is no doubt that Artemisia is the most coherent and self-aware of the three major characters in the poem. She shares obvious qualities with her creator: she, too, writes poetry, she has a lively, intelligent mind, capable of seeing things from a multiplicity of angles—as we have seen, a special characteristic of Rochester as a poet. Griffin has well pointed out her propensity for qualification, as in the opening lines:[38]

> Among the men—I mean the men of Wit,
> (At least they past for such before they writ)
> How many bold Advent'rers for the Bays. . . .

For Artemisia as for Rochester truth is rarely plain and never simple. Her capacity for irony, including a characteristically Rochesterian self-irony, does not preclude her from the kind of direct, impassioned statement in defence of love that I quoted earlier. We have already noticed that this defence echoes sentiments expressed in Rochester's lyrics. Like her creator she is concerned to reconcile reason and emotion; form and spontaneity. One cannot *prove* that Rochester intends us to take her defence of love sincerely. The critic can only appeal to the reader's musical sense in asking him to detect a clarifying regularity in the movement of the verse, point to the impassioned (if sometimes wry) use of metaphor and to the remarkable correspondence of Artemisia's metaphysical stance to Rochester's own. Both share the view of a remote, yet unfriendly God (Artemisia has him contemptuously *throw* the 'cordial drop' of love, which is all he allows us), both see life as essentially unpleasant (a 'nauseous draught'), both see love as a momentary experience of escape from this.

But this is not to say that Artemisia *is* her creator. To start with she is very much a woman and is concerned to remind us of the fact. In this poem Rochester is careful to represent the feminine viewpoint and much of the poem discusses how woman can be revenged on 'her undoer, Man'. In contradistinction to the fine lady and to Corinna, Artemisia avoids this female chauvinism, however. Artemisia blames her own sex for betraying love by treating it as trade or mere amusement, and both the fine lady and Corinna are illustrations for Artemisia of what she deplores. This betrayal is more shameful in women because love is under the guardianship of women—the love deity is usually represented in seventeenth-century art by the triumphant Goddess Venus. Artemisia's femininity, therefore, is crucial to her argument and to what she stands for: the transcendent power of sexual love. So she complains of love's prostitution by people like the fine lady (62–69):

> To an exact Perfection they have brought
> The action Love; the passion is forgot.
> 'Tis below Wit, they tell you, to admire;
> And ev'n without approving they desire.
> Their private Wish obeys the publick Voice,
> 'Twixt good and bad whimsey decides, not choice.
> Fashions grow up for tast, at Forms they strike;
> They know what they wou'd have, not what they like.

Artemisia's complaint against the fashionable of her own sex is that love, which ought to be a genuine expression of personal feeling, has become mechanical and contrived, sincerity is betrayed. The collective rules over the individual. This viewpoint is closely allied to that of Dorimant (the 'Rochester' of Etherege's *Man of Mode*) whose opposite is the totally fashionable and insincere Sir Fopling Flutter whose clothes are his personality. Dorimant, however, presents an aggressive male libertinism, Artemisia's libertinism (she complains of those who are 'deaf to Nature's rule') is noticeably more gentle, more civilised and more feminine. Like Dorimant-Rochester, however, (the identification is that of the critic John Dennis) Artemisia is sufficiently detached and selfaware to see the funny side of her own attitudes. In her, Rochester achieves a balanced, ironic, yet emotionally honest response to the world; a response that combines feeling and form.

Artemisia's viewpoint combines town sophistication and country sincerity; she writes from town to a friend in the country. As in Horace's retirement epistles, Hobbesian 'natural' man is ironically more likely to be found in the town than in the country.

Her balanced view, intellectually aware yet capable of emotional commitment (represented by her willingness to take the plunge into both poetry and love), is now contrasted with the two town women the poem goes on to describe. The fine lady shares Artemisia's intelligence and detachment, but completely lacks her willingness to give of herself. Artemisia introduces the fine lady as an example of the betrayal of love, but the fine lady soon takes over the poem and it is her voice that we hear for most of the remaining lines. The first part of her peroration describes exactly that attitude towards love as fashionable game that Artemisia has decried. We hear her despatch her 'necessary thing' of a husband and launch into a description of the ideal lover—a fool who, unlike the wits, can be easily deceived and manipulated. This is the attitude, we remember, that caused the Rochester of the *Ramble* to rise to such a pitch of angry invective and that causes most pain to Dorimant in the scene of the *Man of Mode* where Loveit pretends to take on Sir Fopling as her lover. It is worth remarking that the fine lady's attack on the men of wit as too observant for their own good is not an attack on intelligence as such, on the contrary, women must learn to outwit men and it is easier to outwit fools than wits. The fine lady thus represents wit without passion, lust without love.

There is no doubt that our response to the fine lady is meant to be disapproving. Artemisia presents her as a caricature: her voice is louder than 'a great-bellied Woman's in a Crowd', she adopts 'fifty Antick Postures', her speech is wildly affected (the affectation is superbly conveyed in Rochester's verse) (95–112):

> Dear Madam, am not I
> The strangest, alter'd, Creature! let me Die,
> I find my self ridiculously grown
> Embarrast, with my being out of Town:
> Rude and untaught, like any *Indian Queen,*
> My *Country* Nakedness is strangely seen.
> How is *Love* govern'd? Love that rules the state—
> And pray who are the Men most worn of late?

This is a superb handling of fashionable jargon; it has the vivid quality of actual speech and is unparalleled among his contemporaries and unrivaled by his successors. The lady 'wears' men as Fopling wears French gloves and Pope's Belinda wears lapdogs. The sterility and absurdity of her behaviour is brilliantly summed up when she turns to compliment her pet monkey in terms that she clearly would refuse not just husbands but men in general:

> Kiss me? thou curious Miniature of *Man*.
> How odd thou art! how pretty! how japan!
> Oh I cou'd live and dye with thee! . . .

The sexual innuendo in the last line suitably highlights the perversions involved in the lady's attitudes. And Artemisia again leaves us in no doubt what she thinks. The monkey, she says, is 'a dirty Chattring Monster'. Artemisia then attempts a summing up of the lady's character, emphasising her intelligence and her lack of any sense of decorum, of form: 'So very Wise, yet so Impertinent'. It is interesting that the fault that Artemisia emphasises is this lack of discrimination, lack of propriety in the lady's conduct. Like Rochester himself, Artemisia's critieria are ultimately aesthetic: how to impose pattern where there is none. In lacking feeling the lady lacks balance, that sense of the interplay of feeling and form that has become Rochester's triumphant achievement in writing the poem. She had, writes Artemisia:

> . . . discerning *Wit*; to her was known
> Ev'ry ones fault, or merit, but her own:
> All the good Qualities that ever blest
> A Woman, so distinguished from the rest,
> Except Discretion only, she possest.

In Coles' *Dictionary* (1676) the word 'Discretion' is glossed, 'a distinguishing', and 'discriminating' is given the same gloss. The fine lady lacks discrimination, she fails to distinguish adequately, because her view of the world is lopsided. She sees the world from the sterile viewpoint of rationality as a place where man outwits man or, more to the point, woman outwits man for fear she herself will be outwitted. Hers is the Hobbesian protection against man's depravity: to keep a clear head. With her, we are in a world that has gone numb with loss of feeling.

The fine lady returns to her monologue, from her monkey, to

take us one stage further into a depravity from which her intelligence keeps her. She opens this new point of her monologue with an apology for decrying intelligent men and again Rochester emphasises *her* intelligence as she does so:

> You Smile to see, me, whom the *World* perchance
> Mistakes to have some Wit, so far advance
> The interest of Fools. . . .

She tells the story of Corinna to explain why women have to beware of intelligent men and in doing this she introduces us to the Hobbesian natural world where 'every man is enemy to every man' (*Leviathan* i, 13). This is the world of unbridled passion against which the fine lady's intelligence protects her. In this frightful world the balance of discrimination is lost not by lack of feeling but by lack of restraint. If the fine lady's world is the barren desert of the rationalist 'band and beard' of the *Satyr against Mankind*, then Corinna inhabits that world described in the second section of the *Satyr* where 'Savage *Man* alone does Man betray'. In *Artemisia* the two opposing worlds of reason and feeling are triumphantly reconciled in the balanced attitudes of the recorder of the scene. The logical impasse of the *Satyr* has become the *discordia concors*, the 'concord in discord', of the *Letter from Artemisia to Chloe*. Artemisia leads us, with the help of the emotionally immune fine lady, into the hell of unbridled human feeling.

Corinna has been betrayed by the man she loves, a wit who:

> 'Made his ill-natur'd jeast, and went away',

leaving the girl, it is implied, with syphilis. Here is a fearful result of surrendering to Artemisia's 'Safe Director of unguided Youth' —but Artemisia's love was 'Fraught with kind Wishes, and secur'd by Truth'. Corinna's betrayal, in true Hobbesian fashion, leads her in turn to seek power over her betrayers. She plots revenge: attracting a rich fool by flattering him, becoming his mistress, taking his money and then poisoning him. The poem ends like the new revelations that Artemisia promises to Chloe by the next post:

> 'Truer than Heaven, more infamous than Hell.'

These melodramatic happenings, however, are acceptable because we see them in an orderly perspective. They illustrate one undeniable extreme of human conduct, a world where greed and rapacity dominate. The fine lady's sardonic comment is that in spite of its apparent chaos the world of Corinna and her booby has its point and plays its part in an over-all pattern:

> Nature, who never made a thing in vain,
> But does each *Insect* to some end ordain,
> Wisely provides kind keeping Fools, no doubt,
> To patch up Vices, Men of Wit, wear out.

Wit, then, ultimately triumphs not because intelligent men get their will more easily than unintelligent, but because intelligence is required to discern, indeed create, pattern. The poem is Artemisia's triumph because she has made a coherent account of the chaos she describes. And her triumph is even more a triumph of her creator. *His* wit, *his* intelligence, *his* commitment in putting pen to paper has defeated the blind chance that almost saw the triumph of those fashionable idiots in the *Ramble*. Rochester's catalogue of idiots is considerable, the fools of the *Ramble*, the string of fops, fools and knaves in *Tunbridge Wells,* the buffoons of *Timon*, the more insidious clever fool, the 'band and beard' of the *Satyr*, Artemisia's fine lady, even the poet himself as he too succumbs to the absurdity of chance in the *Imperfect Enjoyment*. Mankind hovers always on the edge of absurdity, caught up by mindless powers like the sexual daemon that dominates the *Ramble* or the greed of Corinna's world in *Artemisia*. But intelligence, wit, and above all the wit of the poet, can make order out of this inanity. It may be a local victory, but it is better than total defeat. 'Tis all that heaven allows.

Notes

Chapter I

1 Text from V. de Sola Pinto's *Poems by John Wilmot, Earl of Rochester* (2nd edn.) 1964, p. 147.

2 John Sheffield, Earl of Mulgrave, *The Character of Charles II*, 1696. 'I dare confidently affirm it (his religion) to be only that which is Vulgarly (tho' unjustly) counted none at all, I mean Deism.'

3 See *Rochester, the Critical Heritage*, ed. D. L. Farley-Hills, 1972, pp. 40, 138, 197.

4 *ibid.* p. 49.

5 *The English Writings of Abraham Cowley*, ed. A. R. Waller, Cambridge, 1905–6, i, 10.

6 *Critical Heritage*, pp. 193–4.

7 Matthew Arnold, *Essays in Criticism* (Second Series); *English Literature and Irish Politics* ed. R. H. Super, Ann Arbor, p. 181.

Chapter II

1 Quoted by J. Culler in *Structuralist Poetics*, 1975, p. 30.

2 Dryden distinguishes three kinds of translation: metaphrase (literal), paraphrase (conveying the sense of the author in contemporary terms) and imitation (using an earlier work as the point of reference or starting point for original creation) *Essays*, ed. W. P. Ker, i, 237.

3 Josephine Miles, *The Primary Language of Poetry of the 1540s and the 1640s*, Berkeley, 1948, p. 1.

4 *Critical Heritage*, p. 6.

5 For some accounts of Rochester's reading see J. Treglown 'Satirical Inversion of some English Sources in Rochester' *RES* n.s. xxiv (1973), pp. 42–8; J. Hayman, 'An Image of the Sultan in Waller's *Of Love* and a *Very Heroicall Epistle*' *N&Q* (Oct 1968), pp. 213, 380–1; J. H. Wilson, 'Rochester's Valentinian' *E.L.H.* iv (1937), pp. 265–73; D. Vieth, 'Rochester and Cowley' *TLS* 50 (12 October 1951), p. 645.

[6] D. H. Griffin, *Satires against Men,* 1973, p. 174.

[7] S. F. Crocker, 'Certain Aspects of the Background of the Satire against Mankind', *West Virginia Studies III, Philological Papers* vol 2 (May 1937).

[8] See T. H. Fujimura, 'Rochester's Satire against Mankind, an Analysis' *SP* lv (1958), 576–90.

[9] 'The late Lord Rochester, who was very well acquainted with Boileau and who deferr'd very much to his judgement, did not at all believe that the censure of Boileau (on Burlesque) extended to Butler. For if he had he would never have followed his fashion in several of his masterly copies'.

[10] See Griffin, *op. cit.,* especially chapter 4, 'The background to Rochester's Satire'.

[11] V. de Sola Pinto, *Enthusiast in Wit,* 1962, pp. 17–18.

[12] *Critical Heritage,* p. 46.

[13] K. M. Wilson, *Shakespeare's Sugared Sonnets,* Allen & Unwin, 1974.

[14] Edward Herbert, *Occasional Verses 1665,* facsimile edition, Menston, 1969, p. 74.

[15] See especially Jonson's 'Epistle to John Selden', ll. 1–4, *Poems of Ben Jonson,* ed. G. Johnston, Routledge & Kegan Paul, 1954, p. 135.

[16] *English Writings,* i, 75.

[17] John Cleveland, *Poems,* 1653, facsimile edition, Menston, 1971, pp. 70–1.

[18] For reference to other poems with similar opening lines, see chapter 3, p. 64.

[19] See H. M. Richmond, *The School of Love,* Princeton, 1964, chapter 4.

[20] *Purity,* ed. R. J. Menner, Yale, 1920, ll. 697–708.

[21] *English Writings,* p. 150.

[22] *Poems of Edmund Waller,* ed. G. Thorn-Drury, 1901, ii, 47.

[23] Tristan de l'Hermite, *Poésies* ed. P. A. Wadsworth, Paris, 1962, p. 58.

[24] *The Complete Poems of John Wilmot, Earl of Rochester,* ed. D. Vieth, Yale, 1968, p. 83.

[25] *Poems of Richard Lovelace,* ed. C. H. Wilkinson, Oxford, 1930, p. 141.

[26] *ibid.,* p. 139.

[27] *ibid.,* p. 148.

28 F. Lachèvre, *Le Libertinage au 17e Siècle, Disciples et Successeurs de Théophile de Viau,* Paris, 1911, p. 464.

29 Lovelace, p. 42.

30 *The Songs and Sonets of John Donne,* ed. T. Redpath, 1956, p. 92.

31 *Works of Sir John Suckling,* ed. T. Clayton, Oxford, 1971, p. 30.

32 *Critical Essays of the Seventeenth Century,* ed. J. E. Spingarn, ii, 118.

33 Cleveland, p. 79.

Chapter III

1 Pinto, p. 137, ll. 13–14.

2 *ibid.,* p. 98, 120–4.

3 *ibid.,* p. 50.

4 General Prologue, ll. 95-8.

5 William Wycherley, *The Country Wife,* iii, ii.

6 *Critical Heritage,* p. 205.

7 *ibid.,* pp. 40, 138, 197.

8 Samuel Butler, *Characters and Passages from Notebooks,* ed. A. R. Waller, Cambridge, 1908, p. 402.

9 *Complete English Poems of John Donne,* ed. A. J. Smith, Penguin.

10 'Song: By all Loves soft, yet mighty Pow'rs.'

11 *Collection of Poems Written on Several Occasions,* 1673 (second edn.).

12 *Collected Poems of Sir Thomas Wyatt,* ed. K. Muir, pp. 68–71.

13 Eric Partridge, *Shakespeare's Bawdy,* 1968 (revised edn.), 'will'.

14 Pinto, p. 14, ll. 69–70.

15 J. B. Leishman, *The Art of Marvell's Poetry,* 1966, chapter 3 'Pastoral and Semi-Pastoral'.

16 Pinto, p. 11, ll. 65–72.

17 'Draft of a satire on Man', Pinto, p. 116, ll. 1–4.

18 See D. Farley-Hills, *The Benevolence of Laughter,* 1974, pp. 137–8. Other examples not cited there are Cleveland *Young man to an old woman courting him* and Suckling's *Deformed Mistress.*

19 *Poems etc. on Several Occasions; With Valentinian, A Tragedy. Written by the Right Honourable John late Earl of Rochester,* 1691.

20 *ibid.*

21 Vieth, p. 82, ll. 16–20.

22 *School of Love,* pp. 5off.

23 *Shakespeare's Bawdy,* p. 53.

24 Thomas Nashe, *The Unfortunate Traveller and other Works,* ed. J. B. Steane, Penguin, 1972, p. 336.

25 See C. S. Lewis, *Images of Life,* ed. A. S. Fowler, Cambridge, 1967, pp. 27–8.

26 Andrew Marvell, *The Complete Poems,* ed. E. S. Donno, 1972, pp. 235–6. The phrase 'iron grates' that Donno proposes to substitute seems to me (in spite of Tennyson's approval) meaningless. She does not suggest a possible meaning.

27 Vieth, p. 25, ll. 13–18.

28 *Poems on Several Occasions,* 1691, p. 64.

29 Ezra Pound, *ABC of Reading,* 1961, p. 158.

30 *Poems on Several Occasions,* 1691, p.28.

31 Griffin, *Satires against Men,* pp. 17–20.

32 *Poems on Several Occasions,* 1691, p. 41.

33 E.g.*2 Henry IV,* II, ii, 20–6 (bawl); *All's Well,* II, iii, 30; *Women beware Women,* III, iii, 79–82; Dekker, *Meet me in London,* II, i, 243 (bowl); *White Devil,* I, ii, 64–6 (bowl); Dekker, *Roaring Girl,* III, ii, 168–70; pseudo-Dekker, *O per se O* ed. Pendry, p. 302, 'My bowls did fit her alley'.

34 *Complete Poems,* p. 235.

35 Treglown, *R.E.S.*n.s. xxiv (1973), p. 44.

36 Rymer's edition punctuates: 'You wiser men despise me not; Whose Love-sick Fancy raves, On Shades of Souls, and Heaven knows what; Short Ages live in Graves.' *Poems on Several Occasions,* 1691, p. 26. Although it is meaningless with this punctuation most modern editors follow it.

Chapter IV

1 R. P. Bond, *English Burlesque Poetry 1700–1750,* Cambridge, Mass., 1932, p. 3.

2 *ibid.,* p. 5.

3 *Benevolence of Laughter,* chapter 3.

4 ed. Ker, ii, 105.

5 *ibid.,* ii, 107.

6 E. A. Richards, *Hudibras in the Burlesque Tradition,* N.Y., 1937, p. 24.

7 See A. Adam, *Histoire de la Littérature Française au xviie Siècle,* Paris, 1962, ii, 87.

8 *Op. cit.,* pp. 3–4.

9 *Benevolence of Laughter,* pp. 57–65.

10 G. Kitchin, *A Survey of Burlesque and Parody in English,* Edinburgh 1931.

11 Ed. Bliss, iii, 776.

12 George Kitchin, *op. cit.,* does not discuss Marlowe's poem as burlesque, but it is not difficult to agree with James Smith that it is burlesque, though of a subtle kind.

13 *Wit Restor'd,* 1658, p. 148.

14 *ibid.,* p. 152.

15 *ibid.,* p. 11.

16 Richard Corbett, *Poems,* ed. J. A. W. Bennett and H. R. Trevor-Roper, Oxford, 1955. pp. 44–5, ll. 387–99.

17 (Paul) Scarron, *Le Virgile Travesty en vers burlesques,* Paris, 1648, sig. Kii^{r–v}.

18 (Charles Cotton), *Scarronides: or, Virgile Travestie. A Mock Poem,* London, 1664, pp. 68–70.

19 *The Grounds of Criticism in Poetry, 1705,* ed. N. Hooker, I, 336. Hooker cites parallels to Dennis' thinking in the note on this passage (i, 514.)

20 *Brief Lives,* ed. Lawson Dick, p. xxxiii.

21 *Poems,* p. 51.

22 *Satires and Miscellaneous Poetry,* ed. R. Lamar, Cambridge, 1928, p. 36, ll. 95–114.

23 *Benevolence of Laughter,* chapter 3 *passim.*

24 Quotations are from Wilders' edition of *Hudibras,* Oxford, 1967.

25 *Benevolence of Laughter,* pp. 50–3.

26 Elish Coles, *English Dictionary,* 1676, glosses the entry 'Friga': 'A Saxon Goddess in the shape of an Hermaphrodite'.

27 D. H. Griffin, *Satires against Man,* pp. 32–4.

28 Robert Graves, in *The White Goddess,* argues that satire is the one literary mode that belongs to the death aspect of human experience, 'only if he is writing as satire does he (the poet) play the serpent'. (second edn, 1961, p. 388).

29 R. E. Quaintance, 'French Sources of the Restoration Imperfect Enjoyment Poem', *Phil. Quart.* 42 (1963), pp. 190–99.

30 George Etherege, *Poems,* ed. J. Thorpe, Princeton, 1963, p. 8, ll. 341–2.

31 *Poems on Several Occasions,* 1680, p. 87.

32 *Poems on Several Occasions,* 1680, p. 29.

33 'Life of Rochester' in *Critical Heritage,* p. 54: 'A man could not write with life, unless he were heated by revenge; For to make a *Satyre* without Resentments, uopn the cold Notions of *Phylosophy,* was as if a man in cold blood cut men's throats who never

offended him: And he said, the lies in these Libels came often in as Ornaments that could not be spared without spoiling the beauty of the *Poem*.'

[34] *Characters and Passages from Notebooks,* ed. A. R. Waller, p. 330.

[35] R. C. Elliott, *The Power of Satire,* pp. 14, 75, 76–7.

[36] Milton's defence of his own satire in *Of Reformation* is a case in point (*Prose Works,* ed. D. M. Wolfe, New Haven, 1953, i, 535) 'I have done it (employed satire) neither out of malice, nor any vaine-glory; but of meere necessity, to vindicate the spotlesse *truth* from an ignominious bondage.' Joel Morkan, 'Milton's ideas on Satire' *SP* 69 (1972), p. 477 comments: 'At the core of almost all defenses of satire (in the seventeenth century) lies just such a moral justification'. For Milton's defence of the charitableness of satire see *Animadversions* (*Prose Works,* i, 662–4).

[37] I quote from the version published by Danielsson and Vieth in their facsimile edition of the Gyldenstolpe Manuscript, Stockholm, 1967, p. 134.

[38] *ibid.,* p. 135.

[39] *ibid.,* pp. 141–2.

[40] *ibid.,* p. 143.

[41] *ibid.,* p. 144.

[42] Elliott, *Power of Satire,* p. 30.

[43] See Pinto, *Enthusiast in Wit,* p. 75.

[44] Pinto, p. 137.

[45] V. de Sola Pinto, 'The History of Insipids, Rochester, Freke and Marvell' *M.L.R.* 65 (1970), pp. 11–15.

[46] *Enthusiast in Wit,* pp. 148–9, 113.

[47] *Court Wits of the Restoration,* Princeton, 1948, p. 117.

[48] *Poems of Etherege,* pp. 79–84.

[49] *Attribution in Restoration Poetry,* pp. 346–50, 369–70.

[50] *Satires against Man,* pp. 61f.

[51] *Gyldenstolpe MS,* p. 259.

[52] *ibid.,* p. 130.

[53] *Satires against Man,* pp. 68–9.

[54] *Op. cit.,* p. 71.

[55] Cf. Wolseley's 'Preface to Valentinian', *Critical Heritage,* p. 152: 'Bawdry alone . . . is as poor a pretence to Wit as 'tis to good manners . . . But he (Mulgrave) cannot be suppos'd to charge any of my Lord Rochester's Verses with such barrenness as this. The notorious Evidence of Fact and the contrary Testimony of

a whole Nation wou'd fly too full in his face.'
56 *Critical Heritage,* p. 143.

Chapter V
1 John Marston, *Scourge of Villanie, 1599,* ed. (in facsimile)
   G. B. Harrison, 1925, pp. 17–18.
2 Everard Guilpin, *Skialetheia, 1598,* ed. (in facsimile), G. B.
   Harrison, 1931, Sig. B7^r.
3 Adam, *Histoire,* iii, 74.
4 See J. O. Campbell, *Comicall Satyre and Shakesperae's Troilus and
   Cressida,* San Marino, 1938, for a discussion of Shakespeare's
   debt to the formal satirists.
5 Harold Love, 'Rochester and the Traditions of Satire', *Restoration Literature,* ed. Love, 1972, pp. 145–175.
6 Brian Morris, 'Satire from Donne to Marvell', *Metaphysical
   Poetry,* 1970, p. 211.
7 BM Add MS 5832 f.200^r.
8 *ibid.,* f.202^r.
9 *ibid.,* f.204^r.
10 *ed. cit.,* p. lix.
11 For a full discussion of the structure of this poem see my
   Benevolence of Laughter, chapter 4.
12 *Critical Heritage,* p. 194.
13 *ibid.,* pp. 193–4.
14 *The Dissertator in Burlesque,* 1701, p. 8.
15 Nicolas Boileau-Despréaux, *Satires,* edited C-H. Boudhors,
   Paris, 1966, p. 57 (ll. 35–8).
16 *Satires against Man,* chapter 4, 'The Background to Rochester's
   Satyre', pp. 156–96.
17 *Critical Heritage,* p. 49.
18 Quoted by Adam, *Histoire,* iii, 78.
19 *Op. cit.,* pp. 174–5.
20 Mathurin Régnier, *Oeuvres Complètes,* ed. G. Raibaud, Paris,
   1958, op. 148.
21 *ed. cit.,* p. 36.
22 Adam, *Histoire,* iii, 115–6.
23 *ibid.,* p. 89.
24 Théophile de Viau, *Oeuvres Poétiques,* ed. J. Streicher, Geneva,
   1951, p. 83.

Chapter VI

1 Robert Wolseley, 'Preface to Valentinian', 1685, in *Critical Heritage*, p. 148.

2 Phillip Massinger, 'To his Sonne, upon his Minerva', *Wit Restor'd*, 1658, p. 142.

3 Quoted by R. P. Bond, *English Burlesque Poetry*, Cambridge, Mass., 1932, p. 51.
(The translation is that of the present writer).

4 Gilbert Burnet, 'Some Passages of the Life and Death of . . . Rochester', *Critical Heritage*, p. 53.

5 *ibid.*, p. 53.

6 *ibid.*, p. 60.

7 *ibid.*, p. 65.

8 *ibid.*, p. 56.

9 R. Colie, *Paradoxia Epidemica*, Princeton, 1966, p. 229.

10 *ibid.*, p. 5.

11 H. K. Miller, 'The Paradoxical Encomium', *MP* 53 (1956), pp. 173–5.

12 *Satires against Men*, pp. 273–4.

13 Robert Graves, *The White Goddess*, 1961, pp. 24–5.

14 *Op. cit.*, p. 270.

15 'Life', *Critical Heritage*, p. 60.

16 *ibid.*, pp. 65–6: 'the first three chapters of *Genesis* he thought could not be true, unless they were Parables.'

17 *ibid.*, p. 65: 'He thought the Penmen of the Scriptures had heats and honesty, and so writ.'

18 See Chapter 3, pp. 37-8.

19 For an account of the titles of the various early versions of the poem see D. Vieth, *Attribution in Restoration Poetry*, Yale, 1963, pp. 370–5.

20 See, for instance, the discussion of Montaigne and Charron in George Boas's *The Happy Beast in French Thought of the Seventeenth Century*, Baltimore, 1933.

21 *Critical Heritage*, pp. 244, 213.

22 *Op. cit.*, p. 200.

23 Quoted from Boas, *op. cit.*, p. 27.

24 *ibid.*, p. 89.

25 (Thomas Rymer), 'Preface to the Reader', *Poems etc. on Several Occasions*, 1691.

26 Pinto, p. 87 (with emendation of 'it' to 'that' in line 7).

27 *Op. cit.*, p. 43: 'The satire is both structurally uninteresting and thematically ununified'.

28 *Les Oeuvres de Monsieur Scarron,* Amsterdam, 1712, i, 167–8.

29 Vieth, p. 120 (headnote).

30 H. F. Brooks, 'The 'imitation' in English Poetry, Especially in Formal Satire, before the age of Pope'. *R.E.S.* 25 (1949), pp. 124–40.

31 Howard D. Weinbrot, '*Allusion to Horace: Rochester's Imitative Mode, SP* 69 (July 1972), p. 351.

32 *ibid.,* p. 367.

33 *Ed. cit.,* p. 124 note to ll. 81–4.

34 John Dryden, *Of Dramatic Poesy and Other Critical Essays,* ed. George Watson, i, 171–2. The lines from Horace's tenth satire Watson translates: 'Nor should I dare to tear away the wreath which with great glory clings to his head.'

35 *ibid.,* pp. 173–80.

36 Dryden takes strong exception to these lines in his dedication

of the *Discourse* on satire to Charles Sackville, calling them 'an insolent, sparing and invidious panegyric' (ed. Watson, ii, 75).

37 Four lines (5–8) quoted from Pinto.

38 *Op. cit.,* p. 135.

Index

Absalom and Achitophel (Dryden) 10, 92, 121, 147

Adam, Antoine *Histoire de la Littérature Française au xviie Siècle* 161, 162

Aeneid (Vergil) 98

Aithorne, Ulster Satirist 122

All's Well that Ends Well (Shakespeare) 67

Amores (Ovid) 113

Amphitheatrum sapientiae socraticae joco-seriae 174

Annus Mirabilis (Dryden) 116

Answer to the Satyr Against Mankind (Pococke or Griffith) 179

Anti-Platonic Poetry 6, 15, 19–23, 53–73

Aretino, Pietro 15

Ariosto, Ludovico 97

Arnold, Matthew 8

Astrophil and Stella 74, 198

Athenae Oxoniensis 94, 179

Aubrey, John 12, 101, 148

Augustine, St 161, 162

Barreaux, Jacques Vallée des 153

Barry, Elizabeth (Rochester's Mistress) 55

Batteux, l'Abbé Charles 177 *Parallèle de la Henriade et du Lutrin* 170

Beckett, Samuel 5

Behn, Aphra *The Disappointment* 113–4

Belinda (*Rape of the Lock*) 210

Bembo, Pietro 15

Berni, Francesco 15

Beys, Charles *La Jovissance Imparfaite* 113

Billingsley *Praise of Nothing* (1658) 174

Blount, Charles 4, 37

Boileau, Gilles 153

Boileau, Nicolas 13, 22, 132, 153–161, 165, 167
   Art Poétique 90, 153
   Embarras de Paris (Satire VI) 155
   Lutrin 90, 153
   Repas Ridicule (Satire III) 10, 132, 153, 155–9 Comparison with *Timon* 186–190
   Satire IV 150, 151–2, 161, 167
   Satire VIII 10, 132, 150, 161

Bond, R. P. *English Burlesque Poetry 1700–1750* 89

Bowdler, Thomas 17

Braithwaite, Nicholas 138

British Museum Sloane MS 826 154

British Museum Additional MS 5832 139

Brome, Alexander 63

Brooks, H. F. 197

Broussin (Brothers) 153, 155, 187

Buckhurst *see* Dorset, Lord

Buckingham, 1st Duke of 139

Buckingham, 3rd Duke of 132

Burlesque 90

Burnet, Gilbert 14, 122
   Life of Rochester 30, 37, 79, 117, 152, 171–3, 175–6

Butler, Samuel 9. 13, 14, 91, 101, 105
   on Donne 39–40
   On Satire 118
   Hudibras 89, 90, 91, 92, 101, 102–4

Satyr upon the Weakness and Misery of Man 101-2

Campbell, O. J. 136
Cantenac, *L'Occasion Perdue Recouverte* 113
Carew, Thomas 32
  Ask me no more 64
  Divine Mistress 75
  Murdring Beauty 75
  The Rapture 26, 47, 50
Carlell, Ludovick 19
Carpe Diem 24, 34
Cartwright, William
  The Gnat 74-5
  No Platonique Love 22
  On a Gentlewoman's Silk Hood 74
Casaubon, Isaac (*De Satyrica*) 150
Castiglione (*The Courtier*) 15
Charles I 3, 19, 39, 44, 142
Charles II 2, 38, 122, 131, 188, 203
Charron, Pierre 185
Chaucer, Geoffrey 10, 16, 23, 149, 168, 186, 191, 194
  Nonnes Preests Tale 94
  Portrait of the Squire 38
  Tale of Sir Thopas 94
Cleveland, Duchess of 140
Cleveland, John 6, 8, 14, 32-35, 139, 141, 148, 149, 160
  The Anti-platonic 19-21
  Mixt Assembly 145
  Rebell Scot 142, 144, 147, 148
  Smectymnuus 145-6
  To Julia 34
Cobb, Samuel 150
Codrington, Robert 140
Cole's *Dictionary* (1676) 210
Colie, Rosalie, *Paradoxia Epidemica* 170, 174
Contemptus Mundi 137
Corbett, Richard 96
  Faeryes Farewell 101
  Iter Boreale 96
Cornwallis, *Praise of Nothing* (1616) 174
Cotton, Charles 9, 105

Scarronides 91, 94, 97-100
  Voyage to Ireland 97
Country Wife (Wycherley) 39
Cowley, Abraham 6, 7, 8, 10, 12, 32, 33, 38, 56
  Bathing in the River 24
  The Discovery 17
  Inconstancy 62
  Miscellany Poems 14
  The Mistress 6, 14, 15, 16, 29, 39, 63, 77
  Pindaric Odes 14
  Platonick Love 20
  Puritan and the Papist 147
Croix-Blanche 153, 155
Cromwell, Oliver 12, 203
Cymbeline (Shakespeare) 138

Davenant, Sir William *Gondibert* 116
Decorum 133
Defence of the Epilogue of the Conquest of Granada (Dryden) 199-202
Dennis, John 14 *Grounds of Criticism in Poetry* (1704) 100
De Rerum Natura (Lucretius) 37
Des Barreaux *see* Barreaux
Descartes 185
Despréaux *see* Boileau
Discordia Concors 211
Dispensary (Garth) 90
Dr Faustus (Marlowe) 96
Donne, John 4, 12, 15, 23, 33, 38, 56, 138, 143
  The Apparition 29
  The Damp 47
  Elegy xvii 49
  Elegy xix 24
  The Exstacie 31, 46
  The Good Morrow 68, 88
  The Inconstant 62
  Nocturnall 170
  Paradoxes and Problems 60-61
  Progress of the Soul 49-50
  Relique 30
  Satires 143
  Songs and Sonets 6, 16, 40, 62

Valediction forbidding Mourning 18

Donno, Elizabeth 82

Dorimant 14, 209

Dorset, Lord 12, 155, 203

Douglas, Archibald 148

Drant, Thomas 134, 149

Dryden, John 8, 12, 128–9, 142, 149, 157, 198
  Absolom and Achitophel 10, 92, 121
  Annus Mirabilis 116
  Defence of the Epilogue of Conquest of Granada 198, 199–202
  Essay of Dramatic Poesie 35, 52
  Mac Flecknoe 10, 90, 148
  Original and Progress of Satire 90, 150
  Troilus and Cressida 138

Dunciad (Pope) 92

Durfé *Astrée* 12

Eliot, T. S.
  Waste Land 5
  Hollow Men 181

Elizabethan Formal Satire 13, 132–139

Elliott, R. C. *The Power of Satire* 118

Eochaid, King 122

Essay of Dramatic Poesie (Dryden) 35, 52

Etherege, Sir George 12, 64, 201–2, 202
  Ephelia to Bajazet 123
  Imperfect Enjoyment 113
  Man of Mode 57, 58, 209, 210
  She Would if She Could 57

Faerie Queene (Spenser) 67, 83

Fasti (Ovid) 65

Fielding, Henry 191

Flatman, Thomas *Advice to an Old Man* 59–60

Fletcher, John 12

Fletcher, Richard, Bishop of London 140

Fopling Flutter 209

Freke, John 123

Frigga, fertility Goddess 107, 109

Frye, Northrop 4, 10

Garth, Sir Samuel, *The Dispensary* 90

Gascoigne, George 16

Georgics (Vergil) 169

God, his sense of humour 173

Goethe, Johann Wolfgang von 181

Gondibert (Davenant) 116

Graves, Robert 175

Griffin, D. H., *Satires against Man* (1973) 13, 79, 80, 109, 125, 128, 129, 152, 174–5, 182, 193

Griffith 179

Grounds of Criticism in Poetry (1704) (Dennis) 100

Gryllus (Plutarch) 185

Guilpin, Everard 138, 141, 143
  Skialtheia (1598) 135

Gulliver's Travels 197

Guss, Donald 15

Gyldenstolpe MS 128

Hall, Joseph 138, 143

Henrietta Maria, Queen 19, 44

Henry VIII 197

Herbert Edward
  Platonic Love 18
  Satires 138

Herbert, George 18

Hero and Leander (Marlowe) 94

Heroic couplet 8

Heroides (Ovid) 95, 123

Herrick, Robert 39

Hobbes, Thomas 22, 162, 205
  Leviathan 13, 85, 162, 182, 211

Horace 13, 133, 154,
  Odes 60
  Satires 10, 96, 123, 155, 189, 197–204

Horatian Satire 150, 154, 158

Hudibras (Butler) 89, 90, 91, 92, 101–4

Imitation 10–11, 197–8
Inferno (Dante) 5
Iter Boreale (Corbett) 96

Jacobus, Lee, *John Cleveland* (1975) 141, 146
James I 140
Johnson, Samuel, *Life of Rochester* 39
Jonson, Ben, 6, 12, 20, 31, 39, 133, 134, 150, 200
  Poetaster 134
Joyce, James, *Ulysses* 5
Juvenal 133
Juvenalian Satire 154, 203

Kemp, Hobart, *Collection of Poems* 45
Kitchin, George, *A Survey of Burlesque and Parody in English* 94
King, Henry
  Paradox 60
  Tell me no more 64
King Lear (Shakespeare) 110, 184
Kinsayder 133

La Mothe le Vayer 153
Last Instructions to a Painter (Marvell) 2, 12, 142, 145, 148–9, 160
Lawrence, D. H. 23
Lee, Nathanial 12
Legende de Bourbonne (Scarron) 194–5
Leishman, J. B. 53
Leviathan (Hobbes) 13, 85, 162, 183, 211
Libertine Poetry 6, 16, 23–31
Love, Harold 139
Lovelace, Richard 12–13, 26–7, 39, 53, 148
  Dialogue between Lucasta and Alexis 29
  Loose Saraband 26, 71
  Love made in the first age 27, 66
  Scrutiny 62
  To Lucasta 7, 29, 62, 71

Lucilius 198
Lucretius 13
  De Rerum Natura 37
Lutrin (Boileau) 90
MacFlecknoe (Dryden) 10, 90
Magna Meter 62

Malherbe 13, 154
Mannerism 32, 83
Man of Mode (Etherege) 57, 58, 209, 210
Marino, Gianbattista 13
  Ninfa Avara 53–4
Marlowe, Christopher 77
  Dr Faustus 96
  Hero and Leander 94
Marprelate, Martin 140
Marston, John 181, 141, 143
  Malcontent 141
  Scourge of Villanie 133–4
Marvell, Andrew 8, 12, 36, 53
  On Rochester 12
  As Satirist 141
  Character of Holland 12, 148
  Flecknoe 148
  Last Instructions to a Painter 2, 12, 142, 145–6, 160
  Rehearsall Transpros'd 12
  To His Coy Mistress 67, 81–2
  To Richard Lovelace 148
Marx, Groucho 192
Massinger, Philip 94, 170
Maynard 15
Mennis, Sir John 8, 64, 95
Merry Drollery Complete (1661) 65
Metre 7, 143
Miles, Josephine 11
Miller, H. K. 174
Milton, John 10, 11, 12
  Paradise Lost 10
Misanthrope (Molière) 138
Mixt Assembly (Cleveland) 145
Mock Songs and Joking Poems (1671) 65
Molière, Jean-Baptiste 153
  Misanthrope 138
Montaigne 13, 160, 165, 185
Morris, Brian 139, 141

Mulgrave, Earl of 3, 119, 128, 154
   An Essay on Satire 126–7

Nashe, Thomas, *The Unfortunate
   Traveller* 67
Newcastle, Marquis of 185

Oldham, John 149–150
   compared to Rochester 8
Original and Progress of Satire
   (Dryden) 90, 150
Otway, Thomas 12
Ovid 13, 16
   Amores 113
   Fasti 65
   Heroides 95, 123
   Remedia Amoris 72

Paradox 6, 45, 56, 60, 87–8
Parsons, Robert 13
Partridge, Eric, *Shakespeare's
   Bawdy* 45, 48, 66
Percy Society 139
Persius 133
Peters, John 139
Petrarch 5, 10, 15, 44, 198
Petrarchists 6, 15, 31–4, 45, 56,
   79
Petronius 13
   Satyricon 113
Pinto, V. da Sola 70, 87, 123, 127,
   179
Plain Dealer (Wycherley) 138
Plato 15
Platonic poetry 6, 15, 16–19,
   44–53
Plutarch *Gryllus* 185
Pococke, Richard 179
Poetaster (Jonson) 134
Pope, Alexander 5, 6, 8, 141, 147,
   149, 198, 203, On Rochester
   8, 149
   Dunciad 92
   Essay on Criticism 10
   Essay on Man 204
   Imitations of Horace 197
   Rape of the Lock 6, 67, 75, 90,
   210

Portland MS 29, 128
Pound, Ezra 78
Praise of Nothing (ballad) 174
Précieux poets 19, 57
Presbyterianism 145
Priapus 115
Prosopopeia 63, 127, 142, 154
Puritan and the Papist (Cowley) 145
Purity 23
Puttenham, George 8

Quaintance, R. E. 113
Quarles, Francis *Emblems* 11

Radcliffe, Alexander *The Ramble*
   97
Rape of the Lock (Pope) 6, 67, 75,
   90, 210
Rebell Scot (Cleveland) 142, 144,
   147, 148
Régnier, Mathurin 13, 47, 153
   Satire V 165–6
   Satire VI 162–3
   Satire VIII 155, Z95–6
   Satire XI 155–9, 189–190
   Satire XIV 166–7
Reich, Wilhelm 23
Remedia Amoris (Ovid) 72
Richards, E. A. *Hudibras in the
   Burlesque Tradition* 91
Richmond, H. *School of Love, 1962*
   66
Rochefaucauld 13
Rochester, Lady 29
Rochester, John Wilmot second
   earl of
   anti-platonic verse 53–73
   his aristocracy 2, 173
   burlesque 8
   conventionalitly 3
   debt to French satire 152–3
   deism 171–2
   dialogues 51–6
   easiness 6
   fondness for paradox 6, 86, 117
   174
   honesty 2
   iconoclasm 3, 131

knowledge 12–13
libertine verse 73–88
lyrics 6, 36–88
metaphysical beliefs 171–23
metres 7
mistress 55
morality 172
parodies 63
platonic verse 44–51
not a pornographer 2, 56
rebelliousness 1
respect for form 1, 105
satire 7, 170
scepticism 171, 176–7
sexual attitudes 56
soubriquet 53, 119
style 6
use of hudibrastic verse 4
views of women 55
wife 29
Works
Absent from thee I languish still
   42, 78–9
Advice, the 45
Allusion to Horace 8, 12, 13, 14,
   36, 119, 129, 132, 135, 152,
   173, 197–202, 205
An Age in her embraces past
   (*The Mistress*) 43, 86, 125
Artemisia to Chloe 40, 43, 52,
   55, 72, 93, 106, 124, 132,
   147, 160, 165, 172, 173, 181,
   204–12
*As Chloris full of harmless
   thoughts* 41, 65–9, 73
*By all love's soft, yet mighty
   pow'rs* 42, 72
*Dialogue between Strephon and
   Daphne* 53–5
Discovery, the 45–6
Epistolary Essay from MG to OB
   43, 123, 127–31
Fair Chloris in a pigsty lay 27, 30,
   43, 65–9, 176
Fall, the 27, 30, 41, 47–51, 111,
   181, 185
Fragment of Satire against men 55
Give me leave to rail at you 29

History of Insipids 123
How happy, Chloris 26
I cannot fuck as others do (*I swive
   as well as others do*) 11, 64
Imperfect Enjoyment 9, 29, 41,
   93, 96, 105, 106, 111–16, 167,
   181, 212
Lines to a Postboy 1, 5, 96
*Lines Written in a Lady's Prayer-
   book* 13
Love and Life 13, 42, 80–8
Love a woman, you're an ass 69
Maim'd Debauchee 4, 37, 43, 60,
   63, 93, 115–17
My dear Mistress has a heart 78
My Lord All-Pride 123, 126–7
*On the Supposed Author of a late
   poem* 120–1
On Poet Ninny 121
Paraphrase of Lucretius 37
Paraphrase of Seneca 37, 84, 151,
   177
*Pastoral dialogue between Alexis
   and Strephon* 53–4
Phyllis, be gentler I advise 29
Platonic Lady, the 40, 76–7
Ramble in St James's Park 4, 8,
   71, 93, 96–7, 105–12, 114–5,
   120, 130, 174, 181, 209, 212
Satyr against Mankind 10, 13, 22,
   42, 52, 60, 73, 88, 93, 104,
   117, 132, 147, 150–2, 160–6,
   167–8, 173, 174–5, 178–9,
   185–6, 190–1, 196, 205, 211
Satyr on Charles II 36, 122
Signior Dildo 9, 93, 105, 111–12,
   115
Song of a Young Lady 40, 60, 116
Tell me no more of Constancy 63–4
Timon 13, 38, 132, 136–7, 150,
   152, 153, 155, 160, 168, 173,
   181, 186–91, 212
To a Lady in a letter 70–1
Tunbridge Wells 12, 73, 132, 141,
   160, 168, 173, 181, 188,
   190–5, 212
*'Twas a dispute twixt heaven and
   earth* 17, 30, 41, 74–7

Upon his leaving his mistress 62, 63, 65

Upon Nothing 52, 84–5, 93, 117, 173–8, 205

Valentinian 12

Very Heroicall Epistle 123, 127, 129

What cruel pains Corinna takes 26, 47, 58

While on these lovely looks I gaze 46–7

Woman's Honour 47, 125

Rockall 139

Rosa, Salvatore 13

Rymer, Thomas 86–7

S.S., *Paradoxes and Encomiums* 174

Sackville, Charles *see* Dorset, Lord

Saint-Pavin *Sonnet, Ma Vie est plus réformée* 28

Satire 135–168

Satyricon 113

Saville, Henry 155

Scarron, Paul 90, 94, 97

   Légende de Bourbonne 194–5

   Virgile Travesty 90, 97–8

Scarronides (Cotton) 91, 92, 94–5

Scourge of Villanie (Marston) 133–4

Scroope, Sir Carr 119

   As Amoret with Phyllis sat 119

   Epigram 121

   I cannot love as others do 10, 64

   In defence of Satire 119–20

Sedley, Sir Charles 12, 155, 203

Seneca 4, 13

Shadwell, Thomas 12, 200, 203

   Medal of John Bayes 201

   Timon 136

Shakespeare, William 12, 17, 135

   as satirist 201

   All's Well that Ends well 67

   Cymbeline 138

   King Lear 110, 184

   Sonnets 16, 48

   Taming of the Shrew 124

   Timon of Athens 136–8, 141, 142, 153, 181

Troilus and Cressida 138

Twelfth Night 67

Winter's Tale 67

Shaw, Bernard 22

Sheffield, John *see* Mulgrave, Earl of

She lay all naked in her bed 66

She Would if she Could (Etherege) 57

Sidney, Sir Philip 10

   Astrophil and Stella 74, 198

Sigogne 15

Skialethia (Guilpin) 135, 141, 143

Smectymnuus (Cleveland) 142–4

Smith, James 8, 64, 94, 170

   Innovation of Ulysses and Penelope 94–5

   Verse Letters 95–6

Songs and Sonets (Donne) 6, 16, 39, 60

Sons of Ben 6

Spence, Joseph 8, 149

Spenser, Edmund

   Amoretti 18

   Epithalamion 18

   Faerie Queen 67, 83

Spratt, Thomas 33

Style (in the lyrics) 31–35

Suckling, Sir John 7, 12, 14, 20, -39, 53, 56

   His dream 66

   Out upon it 62

   There never yet was woman made 69

   Upon my Lady Carlisle 32–3, 52

   Why so pale and wan fond lover 69

Swift, Jonathan 72

   Gulliver's Travels 197

Taming of the Shrew (Shakespeare) 124

Tenison, Archbishop 139

Tennyson, Lord Alfred 181

Théophile de Viau 13

   Satire I 163–4

Theriophily 73, 151, 179–80

Thorpe, James 123

Timon of Athens (Shakespeare) 135–7, 141, 142, 155, 188

   (Shadwell) 136

Timon of Phlius 136
Treglown, J. 64
Tristan l'Hermite 25
   Fantasy 25
Troilus and Cressida (Shakespeare)
   136
   (Dryden) 138
Twelfth Night (Shakespeare) 67

Ulster 122

Varronian Satire 90
Vergil 10
   Aeneid 98
   Georgics 169
Vieth, David 37, 41–2, 46, 47, 65,
   78, 87, 123–4, 126, 178, 191,
   198
Villiers, Barbara see Cleveland,
   Duchess of
Villiers, George see Buckingham,
   Dukes of
Virgile Travesty (Scarron) 90, 97–8

Waller, Edmund 12, 14, 157, 203
   The Fall 24, 47–8
   To a fair lady playing with a snake
   24–5
Walsh, William 5
   Preface to Letters and poems 1692
   5–6

Walton, Isaac 18
The Waste Land (T. S. Eliot) 5
Watt (Beckett) 5
Weever, Thomas 64
Weinbrot, Howard 198, 202
White Goddess 110, 174
Wilmot, Elizabeth see Rochester,
   Lady
Wilmot, John see Rochester,
   second Earl of
Wilson, J. H. 12, 123
Winter's Tale (Shakespeare) 67
Wither, George 138
Withington, Eleanor 141
Wit Restor'd, 1658 64, 94, 95
Wolseley, Robert
   Preface to Valentinian 130, 169,
   190–1
Wood, Antony 179
   Athenae Oxoniensis 94, 179
Wyatt, Sir Thomas 10, 15, 23, 45,
   79, 197
Wycherley, William 12, 138, 203
   Country Wife 39
   Plain Dealer 138–9

Yeats, W. B.
   Circus Animals' Desertion 5
   Crazy Jane Talks with the Bishop
   42